TAKING SOCIETY'S MEASURE
A Personal History of Survey Research

TAKING SOCIETY'S MEASURE

A Personal History of Survey Research

HERBERT H. HYMAN

Edited and with an Introduction by
HUBERT J. O'GORMAN

With the Assistance of
ELEANOR SINGER

RUSSELL SAGE FOUNDATION   NEW YORK

The Russell Sage Foundation

Library of Congress Cataloging-in-Publication Data

Hyman, Herbert Hiram, 1918–1985
   Taking Society's Measure: A personal history of survey research / by Herbert H. Hyman ; edited and with an introduction by Hubert J. O'Gorman ; with the assistance of Eleanor Singer.
      p.   cm.
   Includes bibliographical references and index.
   ISBN 0-87154-395-8
   1. Social sciences—Research—United States—Methodology—Case studies. 2. Social surveys—United States—Case studies. 3. Economic surveys—United States—Case studies. 4. Public opinion polls—Case studies. 5. War and society—Research—Methodology—Case studies. 6. Surveys—Case studies. 7. Social scientists—United States—Biography. 8. Hyman, Herbert, 1918–1985 I. O'Gorman, Hubert J. II. Singer, Eleanor. III. Title.
   H62.5.U5H96   1991   90—46449
   300'.72—dc20

10 9 8 7 6 5 4 3 2 1

To Bob O'Gorman
with the gratitude
of Herb Hyman's family

Contents

Preface

Herbert H. Hyman began work on this book in the summer of 1982, with the help of a grant from the Russell Sage Foundation. The manuscript was left unfinished by his untimely death in March 1985, while on a visit to China, where he had presented a paper on the possible applications of survey research to the problems of that society. The paper reflects his enduring faith in the survey method even under trying conditions, a faith engendered during the years he writes about in this book.

Although the manuscript was left unfinished, the chapters included here had undergone several revisions by Hyman and are probably close to the way he intended them. He had planned to add three sections: one, on the precursors of the sample survey; another, on the expansion of surveys from the U.S. to other countries; and a third on the development of various institutions—the American Association for Public Opinion Research, *Public Opinion Quarterly*, data archives—which served to further the establishment of the survey method here and abroad. Except for the first, these developments, like the others treated in the book, would have been told from the perspective of a participant observer, since Hyman played an active role in the evolution of organizations and institutions devoted to the cause of survey research and was an active exporter of the method abroad.[1]

---

[1]For a history of survey research from the perspective of a historian rather than that of a participant, the reader is referred to Jean Converse's excellent *History of Survey Research in the United States.*

The book is divided into two main parts. The four chapters in Part One describe the growth of survey research in the United States from shortly before through the end of World War II—in the Division of Program Surveys of the Department of Agriculture (Chapter 1), the Surveys Division of the Office of War Information (Chapter 2), the Research Branch of the Information and Education Division of the U.S. Army (Chapter 3), and the U.S. Strategic Bombing Surveys of Germany and Japan (Chapter 4).

Part Two resumes the history of the postwar development of survey research by recounting the early history (through about 1962) of the National Opinion Research Center (Chapter 5) and the Bureau of Applied Social Research of Columbia University (Chapter 6).

This history of survey research is essentially a history of certain key organizations, their key personnel, and the important researches they carried out during a crucial developmental period in American survey research, roughly from 1937 through 1962. With one exception (the Research Branch), they are organizations in which Hyman was personally involved and in which he played an important role in developing and codifying the principles of what only later came to be known as survey methodology.

Many people helped bring this project to fruition, and their help is gratefully acknowledged here. Among them are Alida Brill who, as a former project officer at the Russell Sage Foundation, encouraged the proposal and followed the work from the beginning; Charles Glock, Daniel Katz, and the late Paul Sheatsley, who served as Hyman's advisory board and read and criticized many drafts of the various chapters; Charles Wright, who also commented critically on early drafts of each chapter; Clara Shapiro, who assisted and encouraged the research; Irene Spinnler, who typed the manuscript in its many drafts; and Ann Pasanella, whose help in compiling the bibliography was invaluable. We regret that two separate chapters, by Daniel Katz and Charles Wright, which were written for an earlier version of the manuscript, could not be included here.

The book received its final editing from Hyman's close friend and colleague, Hubert J. ("Bob") O'Gorman, who also wrote the Introduction. O'Gorman himself died, much too soon, after preparing Hyman's unfinished manuscript for publication. The book is, thus, a memorial to these two men, who were friends and colleagues and partners in scholarship for much of their lives.

ELEANOR SINGER
October 1990

Introduction

The emergence of sample survey research as a technique of social inquiry was significant in the evolution of social knowledge. Although its immediate origins can be traced back to the late nineteenth century, survey research became increasingly visible as a coherent mode of empirical investigation between the late 1930s and the late 1950s. More particularly, it was during the war and postwar years that sample survey research was first applied on an extensive scale, studied and tested intensively, codified, and then taught as a distinctive research technique. This is the period to which Herbert Hyman devotes most of his attention in *Taking Society's Measure: A Personal History of Survey Research.*

Hyman's account is a remarkable contribution to the history and the sociology of social research. Its historical value grows chiefly out of his skill in constructing an autobiographical approach to institutional history. In the chapters describing his experiences with the U.S. Department of Agriculture, the Office of War Information (OWI), the U.S. Bombing Surveys of Germany and Japan, the National Opinion Research Center (NORC), and the Bureau of Applied Social Research (BASR), and the chapter describing Stouffer's experiences with the Research Branch of the War Department, Hyman discusses at length most of the difficult technical problems, critical events, innovative research, and prominent individuals and organizations that helped to shape the field of survey research during the decades under review. His story begins with his first postdoctoral job in Washington, D.C., late in the spring of 1942, as a young social psychologist assigned to the Program Surveys Division of the Department of Agriculture. Hyman next moved to a similar post with the Surveys Division of the OWI in New York City, and then to a position in London and Germany designing and carrying out the Bombing Surveys. He returned to New York and a ten-year stint with NORC before moving in 1951 to Columbia University's sociology department and BASR, where he remained for eighteen years. Hyman's story ends with his account of the demise of the BASR. Aside from the chapter on Stouffer's work, Hyman largely ignores organizations that did not directly impinge on his career.

In the course of narrating his professional odyssey, Hyman emphasizes several points: Because neither he nor his associates had the training or experience to do what they were asked to do, they had to teach themselves survey research. Moreover, they had to learn this new craft within the severe limits imposed by the practical problems they were given, an applied constraint that left little room for exploring substantive or theoretical issues. Consequently, they had to concentrate on methodological problems for the simple but powerful reason that the core of their ongoing work had to do with ensuring that the survey data, whatever their substantive content, were as reliable and valid as possible.

The important effect of networks of informal personal relations on the development of survey research is also stressed by Hyman. There was no formal device for identifying individuals with the interests, motivation, and capacities required by survey research or for evaluating research performance. The emerging friendship patterns among researchers therefore became the channels for communicating needed information about professional skills, personnel, and job opportunities.

These informal networks were especially important, as Hyman notes, in locating individuals able to recruit, organize, supervise, protect, and represent these new teams of incipient survey researchers. His detailed and vivid portrayals of Rensis Likert, Samuel Stouffer, Clyde Hart, and Paul Lazarsfeld, among others, is particularly informative, partly because Hyman himself became an admired and influential researcher, and partly because each portrait, though varying in detail, reaffirms the close relationship between the specific values and norms associated with solving group problems and the willingness of group members to seek the counsel of those who embody those values and norms. The leaders singled out by Hyman were not always efficient administrators. What made each of them effective was their firm understanding of the basic strategy and everyday tactics of good sample survey research and their demonstrated ability to do such research. No less important was their willingness and ability to make the public case for sample surveys as an effective research tool for dealing with a certain class of recurring empirical problems.

No one met these criteria better than Hyman, one of those pioneering investigators whose talents were so closely associated with the rapid growth of survey research that their professional careers and reputations became virtually indistinguishable from the field itself. Hyman did exemplary survey research and often consolidated what he and his co-workers learned about their craft in publications that sustained several generations of young social researchers. His role in the diffusion of this newly emerging research procedure among academicians was particularly impressive. Perhaps more than any other survey researcher of his day, Hyman helped to persuade those academicians who were ignorant, indifferent, or suspicious of survey research of its legitimacy as a research tool. Because of his wide-ranging substantive interests, Hyman's publications were read by a large academic audience, most of whom did not conduct surveys. He helped to persuade them of the value of survey research in the most effective manner possible: by allowing them to see how it could illuminate their own areas of specialized concern. Hyman also demonstrated with subtlety and skill how the accumulating empirical results of original survey research could be later reanalyzed for scientific and scholarly purposes not initially intended. Although this technique of "secondary analysis" was plainly no substitute for longitudinal studies involving the same sample of respondents, it did bring a much needed time dimension into the use of survey data, and it made those data available to social scientists without the resources to conduct large-scale research projects.

Its title notwithstanding, Hyman's history is not primarily concerned with his own influential contributions to survey research, though they are not ignored. Nor is it principally concerned with the private lives, idiosyncrasies, or personal aspirations and problems of Hyman or of those he encountered in the course of his career, though there are, to be sure, passages that refer to personal matters.

In approaching his subject from a personal point of view, Hyman had two goals. He wanted to write an objective chronicle of relevant events from the subjective perspective of an informed participant. Using himself as a case in point, he thought it important to put into the historical record the candid expression of the professional experiences of someone who understood the specific technical problems faced by particular investigators who had to grapple with sample surveys in the course of carrying out their roles. Hyman saw himself as such a participant, one who fully appreciated how it came to be that a relatively small number of individuals, working together in particular organizations on a cluster of practical problems, consolidated, elaborated, and transmitted to subsequent researchers a new mode of social inquiry. For this purpose, he drew from memory and his private files information that he confirmed, modified, and enlarged through interviews and correspondence with key actors, and with unpublished research reports and private correspondence from other sources. In addition, Hyman took the unusual step of incorporating into his discussion of particular sample surveys some respondents' verbatim replies to specific questions. He uses this interview material both to illustrate technical issues and to convey the personal nature of the experiences that survey research attempts to capture.

Hyman's second goal in writing a personal history was to tell the story of survey research as a social psychologist. What we find repeatedly reflected in this historical account is his conception of social psychology, a description and explanation of the psychological reactions of groups of individuals to their objective social world. This conception stood, in Hyman's view, in sharp contrast to either a sociological analysis of that objective world or a psychological analysis of the subjective world of individual experience. It was this social psychological perspective that Hyman, like so many survey researchers, consistently applied to his analysis of aggregate data, a perspective that, for all its utility, frequently leaves unexplored the rich social structural implications of those same aggregate data. Hyman's history is personal, then, in the sense that he depicts himself and others who did similar work as individuals carrying out their research-related role responsibilities in an objective and changing world that increasingly valued their skills to cope largely with institutionally defined problems. The historical, cultural, and structural contexts within which these role assignments were carried out and the fact that the content of these contexts was markedly altered by the growth of survey research are carefully noted by Hyman.

On the other hand, the contextual analysis of these historical trends never becomes as salient to Hyman as, for example, the discovery and use of the contextual analysis of survey data. If this history of the institutionalization of survey research is not, paradoxically, institutional history, Hyman's personal recollections remind us that institutions are invariably constructed by individuals who jointly adapt their cultural and structural heritage to form coordinated ideas and practices like sample survey research to resolve urgent problems.

They also remind us how useful the personal experiences of one sagacious individual can be in helping us to grasp the collective meaning of a particular historical period. Ironically, even well-designed survey research does not ordinarily yield the valuable personal information and understanding that characterize Hyman's account.

The significance of Hyman's narrative extends well beyond its merits as a firsthand history of sample survey research. To appreciate its additional value we must bear in mind that his depiction of how certain methods of collecting and analyzing data from large aggregates of individuals were devised, employed, codified, and transmitted during a particular historical period implicitly but inescapably bears directly on a fundamental sociological problem: How are the members of any human society—its representatives as well as those they represent—informed of the conditions that affect their common welfare? This question cannot be adequately formulated, let alone addressed, apart from the profound issue of the validity of social knowledge, nor can the rise of sample survey research be properly understood apart from the general problem of the socially induced need for accurate social information. It is, therefore, hardly surprising that the validity of survey data appears as a compelling theme in Hyman's book. Viewed from this perspective, *Taking Society's Measure: A Personal History of Survey Research* is an important contribution to sociology and to the sociology of social research in particular.

In describing the development of the distinctive features of one specific research technique in terms of his personal role responsibilities, duties defined by organizations that were institutionally accountable to the larger society, Hyman reminds us of the generic problems encountered by any sustained effort to acquire and validate social knowledge. More specifically, by locating the growth of survey research within the personal framework of his particular status and role obligations, Hyman not only reminds us that virtually all such obligations involve the quest for valid knowledge, but at the same time tacitly points to the similarities between sample survey research and the cognitive problems of everyday life. We may not need personal descriptions of the eating habits of alien cultures to convince us of the general human need for food. But we may need Hyman's personal history of survey research to convince some of us that the gathering and analysis of social data is as much a part of daily life as eating. Once we recognize this point, it becomes evident that a systematic presentation of the history and practice of survey research can add appreciably to our understanding of the acquisition of social knowledge in areas of social life not ordinarily associated with prob-

lems of sample surveys. But this promising line of inquiry is not apt
to be pursued unless we pay serious attention to some of the similarities between survey research and the everyday acquisition of
knowledge.

For all its technical complexities, sample survey research remains
an extension and elaboration of the procedures through which ordinary people in the course of their everyday lives acquire social knowledge. In coping with the exigencies of social life, we are all amateur
social researchers who daily survey our social terrain. Our own well-
being and the welfare of others depend on the collection, interpretation, transmission, and application of personal and social information
that enable us to live together. To acquire, construct, and employ
this knowledge we necessarily rely, as do professional survey researchers, on interviewing and sampling.

Without interviews, social life, like sample survey research, would
of course be impossible. An interview is, after all, a face-to-face exchange of views between two human beings. Through our cooperative activities, conversations, and mutual observations that make up
much of our daily patterns of role activities, we are, in effect, repeatedly interviewing each other to confirm and modify what we know
about the world around us. We edit, code, and interpret what we
say, hear, observe, and pass on to others, learning as we go along
to assess the accuracy of what is communicated. Sometimes we participate in more formal and more asymmetrical interviews associated,
say, with job applications, school admissions, medical examinations,
tax audits and the like. These occasions aside, we do not normally
think of our daily lives as a sequence of interviews involving the
mutual exchange of necessary information, even though all role
transactions require the elicitation and interpretation of some specific
piece of reliable and valid knowledge. Precisely how much and what
kind of knowledge depends, as it does in survey research, on the
information thought to be needed.

The reciprocal interviewing inherent in the social enactment of everyday roles is necessarily conducted among a relatively restricted
number of individuals who more or less regularly encounter one
another in some particular social context. These role partners constitute a small and biased sample. They are not, as individuals, representative of the larger populations from which they are drawn, populations who inhabit or encircle the role partners' families, friends,
neighborhoods, workplaces, communities, and regions. The nature
of this sampling bias varies with the social characteristics of the participants in different contexts. The bias, however, includes far more

than a skewed distribution of those from different social backgrounds. It includes the additional and significant bias inherent in
the very nature of any social interaction. The visible actions of any
one individual in any one role context are, as we know, but a segment
of contextually induced behavior, a small sample of that individual's
larger daily routine, and an even smaller sample of his or her life
history. While everyday samples of social and individual behavior are
therefore inevitably biased, they constitute nonetheless the principal
basis on which the participants construct imputations and draw inferences concerning themselves and identifiable others. The samples
provide the data base from which they make estimates of the parame-
ters of larger but otherwise remote populations. Without such sampling procedures, social life, like survey research, would not be feasible.

The samples of everyday personal and social experience are largely
determined by the particular set of roles engaged in by various subgroups of the population, roles that constitute their major interpersonal source of social knowledge. These role sets are, in turn, derived
from their particular set of status characteristics, the cultural categories with which they are classified in terms of their residence, age,
gender, and race, or their education, occupation, income, and marital
status. From the individual's point of view, it is this status set, this
structural location, that establishes the primary sampling units
through which social knowledge is personally acquired. From the
perspective of the community or the society, it is the larger social
structure—the daily patterns of countless interactions regulated by
the aggregate of status sets and role sets—that constitutes the general
sampling frame within which all differentiated samples of experience
and social knowledge are extracted, distributed, and applied.

Of course we no more think of our lives as segments of experience
drawn from a sampling frame than we think of ourselves as infer-
ence-drawing interviewers and respondents exchanging social information within biased samples of the population. Nevertheless, we
share with survey researchers the same objective of acquiring the
knowledge needed to do what we have to do, and we rely on the
same social sources and procedures that they refine with the greater
technical care dictated by their tasks. In fact, all modes of empirical
social inquiry share similar objectives, sources, and procedures, a fact
that advocates and critics of particular research techniques repeatedly
ignore. Whether we are informally assessing the latest neighborhood
gossip or mobilizing more formal inquiries under the flag of survey
research, anthropological field work, ethnomethodology, a laboratory experiment, content analysis, or comparative historical studies,

we invariably employ information taken from samples of social experiences both to impute properties to those in the samples and to draw inferences regarding characteristics of larger populations.

Whatever their basic similarities, it was the perceived inadequacies of everyday procedures for acquiring knowledge that led to the development of more specialized modes of social inquiry, each attempting to supply a cognitive need unmet by the others. But instructive similarities between the cognitive tasks of ordinary life and more specialized modes of inquiry like survey research do remain. If the latter are taken to be a special case of the former and incorporated into the sociology of social research, then strictly technical questions associated with special techniques of research need not be limited to their methodological implications. They can be used to explore substantive dimensions of theoretically related problems.

Once we are alerted to the similarities between survey research and the everyday processing of information, once we recognize that the systematic study of particular research techniques can illuminate more general social, social psychological, and sociological problems, Hyman's personal history takes on new meaning. His chapters on federal research agencies, NORC, and BASR can be read, for example, in terms of their bearing on theories of organization, while his analysis of the controversies concerning open and closed questions and quota and probability samples can help to clarify the ways in which personal and organizational loyalties contribute to types of trained incapacity. Or his observations on the discovery of interviewer effects may lead us to recognize that the accumulated findings associated with those effects have direct relevance for questions arising out of studies of perspectival thinking in the sociology of knowledge. But perhaps the most effective ways in which the sociology of survey research can illuminate more general issues are to be found in Hyman's depiction of the legitimation of survey research and his penetrating discussions of the validity of survey data.

Precisely because it concentrates on the period during which survey research emerged as a legitimate method of social research, Hyman's detailed account bears directly on a number of critical questions concerning the still poorly understood process of institutionalization. One such issue concerns what Parsons called the mechanism of institutional integration: To what extent does the institutionalization process depend on the internalization of emerging norms and values by the participating actors? Another issue concerns the relative importance of patterns of value consensus: Is value consensus in fact so central to institutionalization that relatively little theoretical attention need be paid to conflict of values? While Hyman's empirical material clarifies both issues, it is, because of the book's personal character, especially illuminating on the question of institutional integration.

One of the most remarkable features of this book is its compelling documentation of a fundamental change in one man's professional self-identity. When he went to work in the Department of Agriculture in 1942, Hyman could not possibly have planned to become what he became. Trained as an experimental social psychologist, he intended to spend his life after the war teaching psychology and doing experimental research in an academic setting. At the time, survey research was just beginning to emerge as an important research tool, and Hyman and others were struggling to master and apply it. By the end of the decade, things had changed dramatically. Survey research had become a widely recognized and influential mode of social inquiry, and Hyman had become, in his own eyes and the eyes of others, a skilled and respected survey researcher. As he himself tells us, in unassuming but revealing passages, his increasing experience with and competence in his new role were matched by his increasing pleasure and pride in thinking of himself as a survey researcher. By the end of the decade, Hyman knew what there was to know about the practice of survey research as well as anyone in the field, and he had, even before that point, so incorporated its associated norms, beliefs, and values into his own style of thinking that he judged the works of others accordingly, and, as he admits, not always justly.

By the time he went to Columbia in 1951, Hyman's professional self-respect was anchored securely in survey research. While he never stopped thinking of himself as a social psychologist, it was the image of a survey researcher that controlled his professional role orientation. And understandably so. By then he was recognized as a key member of the cognitive reference group that, by example, consultation, teaching, and publication set the standard for competent work in survey research. Insofar as Hyman's experiences were representative of others like himself, and the available evidence suggests that they were, there seems little doubt that the internalization of the core values of survey research, at least by its leading practitioners, was one component in its institutionalization.

On the other hand, these values were by no means the object of widespread consensus. There was, of course, general agreement regarding the existence of serious problems engendered by the economic depression and by World War II, and it was agreed that the federal government had a major responsibility to cope with them.

There was also an increasing understanding that a massive amount of information regarding the conditions of large numbers of people was needed to address many of those problems. But once survey research began to be employed in the collection and analysis of the needed empirical knowledge, it evoked, along with spreading support, hostility and opposition from, among other quarters, Congress, the military, and curiously, the universities. The fact that both advocates and opponents of survey research were often found in the same institutional setting testifies to some of the diverse ways in which the institutionalization of survey research was intimately associated with an intense conflict in values.

In any event, Hyman's history is clearly consistent with the view that a basic conflict of values, as well as a basic value consensus, is probably an inevitable component of institutionalization. In addition, his comparison of wartime research in civilian and military organizations and, in the postwar years, of the quite different developments at NORC and BASR strongly suggests that the intensity and outcome of the conflict depend in no small measure on the structural context within which it occurs.

Another way in which the sociology of survey research can increase our understanding of more general sociological problems is found in Hyman's discussions of the validity of survey data. While these discussions are, of course, an integral part of his larger study of the institutionalization of survey research, they are intrinsically interesting and contain lessons that apply beyond the immediate confines of survey research.

Survey research became a widely accepted mode of social inquiry largely because it met the pressing needs of individuals, groups, and organizations with markedly different and often conflicting social, political, and economic interests. It is true that the financial support for survey research usually comes from those who seek advantages or benefits from its results. But what is so striking as one reads the Hyman book is the astonishingly wide variety of broad and narrow interests that have been effectively served by this one mode of investigation. The lesson seems simple. If one research technique can consistently produce empirical knowledge that serves disparate and even radically different interests, then to impute either that knowledge or the technique to the self-serving interests of those who sponsored the research begs and obscures the underlying sociological question: What are the conditions under which groups and organizations with divergent interests agree on a method for describing accurately some designated state of affairs? Plainly this question applies to all manner of everyday situations outside the immediate concern of survey research.

Another lesson we can extract from Hyman's discussion of the validity of survey data bears directly on this question of the circumstances that led to cognitive agreement among divergent interest groups. The most important of these conditions was, of course, the demonstration that survey data were valid, that they in fact measured what they were intended to measure. Although issues of sampling, questionnaire construction, interviewing, and the statistical analysis of data all played a part, the heart of the validity problem was (and remains) quite simply the credence to be assigned to the replies of survey respondents. If there is substantial reason to challenge the validity of these responses, if there is reason to suspect that those being interviewed or filling out questionnaires are misstating what they themselves believe to be true, the enterprise of survey research collapses.

It is important to point out that this conventional view of the validity of survey data masks a basic ambiguity in the meaning of the term "valid." Not only does valid refer in this context to the honesty of a respondent's replies, but it also refers, quite apart from candor, to the objective truth of the respondent's answer. An answer to a question can be candid and objectively false. There is no reason to doubt the honesty of those officers who made factual errors in their estimates of enlisted men's satisfaction with the Army, or the honesty of whites who made equally mistaken estimates of blacks' satisfaction with American race relations. Similarly, there is no need to call into question the candor of those who bought war bonds on the mistaken assumption that their purchases would shorten the duration of the war. The point in citing these examples of pluralistic ignorance is that survey data can be, at the individual and aggregate levels, subjectively valid by accurately recording respondents' invalid cognitive beliefs. In social research validity is as much a substantive problem as it is a methodological one. Hyman's discussion inadvertently conflates the two.

That having been said, what makes Hyman's material on validity particularly relevant is that, in every case he cites, the researchers had reason to believe that their respondents might not know the information being sought or had an incentive to dissemble. Could or would respondents provide the needed data? Consider some of Hyman's cases. Were the shopkeepers who said they were cooperating with the federal government by displaying patriotic war posters in fact doing so? Were war bond purchasers who told interviewers that they had not redeemed their bonds reporting accurately? And could workers in wartime industries be counted on to recall accurately how often they had been absent from work?

If there was reason to wonder about the validity of replies from American civilian respondents, consider the problem faced by Stouffer and his colleagues in their surveys of the U.S. Army and the even more formidable problems raised by the surveys of German and Japanese civilians. During the war the enlisted men and officers studied by Stouffer were coerced by their superiors into providing the Army Research Branch with information regarding their experiences. Under these conditions, surely it was unreasonable to expect soldiers to cooperate with Army-sponsored research by reporting their true views of military life. And in the case of the U.S. Bombing Surveys, how could anyone reasonably expect German and Japanese civilians to cooperate with researchers who, as representatives of a conquering army, wanted to interview them regarding their wartime experiences, particularly their personal reaction to being bombed? Surely, many otherwise staunch advocates of survey research might have thought that it was futile to seek valid answers from respondents under such conditions.

Nonetheless, in each of these carefully documented cases the problem of validity was resolved—often, as Hyman points out, in ingenious ways. There is no need to repeat his meticulous analysis of this validation process except to add the obvious point. If the validity problem had not been resolved in particular instances involving quite different substantive problems, survey research would not have attracted much attention from many sponsors, let alone those with divergent political and economic interests. In the same way, the problem of validity in everyday life is presumably resolved in particular instances to allow role partners, groups, and organizations with their distinctive values and interests to exchange the knowledge they need. We could learn an important lesson from Hyman's case materials by undertaking similar validation studies in ordinary social life. As matters now stand, we know relatively little about the cultural, structural, and psychological mechanisms that facilitate and interfere with this process. In fact, we probably know far more about errors in sample surveys than we do about mistakes in everyday communication. We may, however, begin to learn more by applying to the latter the sort of inquiries that are routinely applied to the former.

Consider, for example, the issue of social desirability in survey responses. We know that some unknown proportion of respondents are sometimes prone to give answers that are, in their view, desirable. On some specific issues, depending on their social characteristics and those of the interviewer, respondents may provide less than candid answers largely because they want to make a favorable impression or because they wish to avoid saying something that might disrupt the interview relationship. They give what they think are desirable replies. This pattern has long been known in survey research; and while the meaning of social desirability is still unsettled, reasonably effective efforts have been made to cope with some of its distorting effects. But this same problem is pervasive in everyday life. The information we provide to each other in our various roles is, depending on the context, influenced by the value we place on the relationship. As a rule, we want to make a favorable impression. Indeed, most social relationships normatively require role partners to make some effort to sustain their role sets by, among other things, tailoring their communications in such a way that disruption is minimized. Communicating in socially desirable ways is not only an integral part of many roles; it is also, in many cases, the only effective mode of communication. How then do we obtain valid instrumental and affective information from each other? And how, in light of the biased samples on which all social relationships are based, do we manage to draw valid inferences about those we do not know personally?

These are not idle questions. Until they are answered, we shall not understand how human beings accurately inform themselves regarding the cultural and social conditions of their lives, how they manage to create and share true social propositions that are no less a collective achievement than their false, and more celebrated, counterparts. We now understand some of the conditions under which respondents in sample surveys speak their minds candidly or not, and we can often distinguish between their true and false conceptions of the social world. This same line of inquiry can be applied profitably to the acquisition and dissemination of social knowledge in everyday life. But to do so, sociologists, and like-minded social scientists, will have to move beyond the point where they are satisfied to repeat ritualistically what they already know: that knowledge is socially constructed, that knowledge is the object of social interests, that some kinds of knowledge are culturally constrained, and that subjective definitions of social situations often have real consequences. Although the merit of these familiar ideas depends on their standing as factually true propositions, the very ideas paradoxically tend to deflect sociologists' attention away from questions concerning the objective validity of knowledge among those they study. These questions need to be restored to their rightful place in sociological consciousness. No society can afford to ignore them, as the history of survey research testifies. And, as Hyman's personal account eloquently suggests, these are central questions in our everyday lives.

HUBERT J. O'GORMAN
April 1990

PART ONE

The War Years

· 1 ·

The Division of Program Surveys: U.S. Department of Agriculture

In June 1942, when I joined the Division of Program Surveys of the U.S. Department of Agriculture, the agency—directed and inspired by Rensis Likert—was just beginning to develop and conduct sample surveys of opinions and attitudes of Americans on a variety of wartime problems. The agency was the forerunner of the Survey Research Center of the University of Michigan, founded in 1946 when Likert and some of the original staff relocated in an academic setting.

Prewar Origins

The Division had been established in 1939, following a reorganization of the Department of Agriculture to carry forward research begun in 1936 on farmers' reactions to New Deal programs to reduce their problems during the Depression. Gradually the research expanded to include the reactions of the urban population to the department's programs to remedy their problems. Henry Wallace, then secretary of agriculture, tells us, for example, that when the policy of direct distribution of food to people on relief was changed to distribution through grocery stores to holders of food stamps, the department needed to know the response of its urban clients. "It was possible to get the opinions of relief families only from the families themselves,"

3

since the poor were not organized and had no spokesman. So the Division's predecessor within the department began "to conduct a continuous analysis of understanding and opinion among the citizens affected by these programs" (1940, pp. 222–223). Likert, at age 36, became the first director of the Division.

Sustained opinion research by our government thus has its origin in the Department of Agriculture between 1936 and 1939. However, continuing sample surveys by the department did not begin until 1942. The "continuous analysis" of opinion which Wallace mentions was based initially on spot reports of six full-time roving observers. The standardized instruments, rigorous sampling, and quantitative analysis—sine qua non of any sample survey—were completely lacking. A field staff of six cannot provide, in the short time needed to be meaningful and useful, the coverage and size of sample that impart generality and confidence to any survey.

As late as 1941, the method had changed very little. The full-time field staff had increased to nine members, still too few to conduct large-scale widespread surveys. By then, there were five analysts on the staff, but still no sampling statistician. None of the five had a doctorate or the practical experience that would have served them well in helping to create and operate sample surveys.

Wartime Changes in Method

The distinctive sample survey born in 1942 in the Division of Program Surveys was created by Likert and a new staff and nurtured by the social conditions of the period. The need for information to guide the agricultural programs of the Depression had led to the establishment of the Division; the need for information to guide the wartime programs of various government agencies—notably the Office of War Information (OWI), the Office of Price Administration (OPA), and the Treasury—led to lucrative survey contracts with Likert and a rapid expansion of the Division. By the fall of 1942 there were over 100 social scientists on the staff, many with doctorates. Although most of them lacked experience in survey research, some were knowledgeable about attitude research, which had been long established in social psychology. Some were sophisticated statisticians. Most were quantitative and empirical in orientation. Their backgrounds prepared them well for their novel assignment.[1]

That so many qualified social scientists entered government service requires no special explanation: They felt strongly identified with the war effort and believed they could make a greater contribution in government than in the university. The thought of doing practical, socially useful research attracted them; they were activists as well as academics. Most of the social psychologists, for example, were members of the recently founded Society for the Psychological Study of Social Issues. Why so many joined the Division rather than other wartime agencies seeking their services is problematic, but Likert's vision and persuasiveness certainly were important factors. The first recruits lured by Likert in turn made the Division all the more attractive, and the recruitment snowballed through a network of friends and former colleagues. Mine is a case in point. In the spring of 1942, with my dissertation just completed and the Ph.D. virtually assured by June, I went job hunting in Washington. There were openings at the Federal Broadcast Intelligence Service, the Department of Justice, the Office of War Information, and the War Department, all of which had recently established social research units where I had a friend or former teacher. However, after visiting Likert at the suggestion of Gardner Murphy, who had taught both of us, I was sold on the Division and happily accepted the offer of a position.

Likert's "vision," communicated to the staff with sincerity and enthusiasm verging on religious fervor, was of a survey method distinct from and superior to both the commercial polling and academic attitude research of the period. That method would help solve the social problems of peacetime as well as wartime, and the theoretical problems of social science, and would be developed by our joint efforts. Our great mission inspired us and intensified the passions already aroused by the war. So we worked hard and creatively although, as will be seen, Likert's persuasiveness and our passions sometimes dulled our critical judgment.

The survey method that developed was derived in part from the earlier tradition of the Division. The depth, comprehensiveness, subtlety and shading, and authenticity essential to describe and understand a respondent's views would be achieved by a long series of open-ended questions accompanied by nondirective probes which led to the elaboration and clarification of the initial answers. In that way, much of the rich and natural conversational quality of the interviews with farmers conducted by the earlier field observers would be retained. However, the earlier procedures—in which the observers asked whatever questions they wished, took no notes, jotted down the results later from memory, and then summarized their findings in qualitative reports from the field—would be replaced by a standardized instrument, verbatim manual recording of the interview, and carefully supervised coding of the answers and quantitative analysis of the data in the office.

The earlier method of the Division, which had lacked even the semblance of sampling, was replaced by rigorous procedures evolving gradually to full-scale probability sampling. In choosing J. Stevens Stock as his first sampler, Likert again showed his good judgment and flair in recruitment. Stock and Lester Frankel, in working for the Works Projects Administration (WPA) during the Depression, had developed the first national probability sample to measure unemployment, leading to the later regular measurements of unemployment (Frankel and Stock 1942), and they taught in the graduate school of the Department of Agriculture the first regular course in sampling methods offered in the United States. Under Stock's direction, the Division in 1943 developed the master sample of agriculture, which divided the rural area of the country into a grid of small sampling units from which samples could be drawn repeatedly and efficiently. Stock's history suggests his skills in translating sampling theory into feasible, relatively economical and proper practices for sampling dispersed populations.

Although the use of sampling was a radical change from the previous practice of the Division, it was in line with the traditions of the larger department, which had pioneered in the teaching of sampling methods. The department had close relations with agricultural colleges and experiment stations, where many of the important contributions to sampling theory and practice had developed. William G. Cochran and others then at the Statistical Laboratory in Ames, Iowa, became regular consultants to the Division and aided in the development of its sampling procedures.

The Open-Ended Question Controversy

By contrasting the survey method of the Division in 1942 with the worst polling practice of the period, Likert had a dramatic selling point in the competition with other survey agencies for contracts and also heightened staff morale. Such psychic and real income, however, could be maximized only by ignoring the better practices of some agencies and stereotyping all the competitors. Although none followed Likert in his move toward probability sampling, there was considerable variety in their approach to measurement. To be sure, some used only a few "closed" questions, too few to describe the multiple aspects of thought and attitude on a complex issue and their determinants. By forcing the respondents to give a definite answer in terms of a limited set of fixed alternatives, some agencies distorted their true opinions. Some agencies used no open-ended questions to elicit the reasons for the opinions. Since the analysis of some merely presented the discrete distributions on each question for the aggregate sample and for a few subgroups in the population, their findings lacked any explanation.

Other agencies, although in the minority, did use better procedures. They asked open-ended questions—perhaps too few—after an initial closed question to obtain the reasons for an opinion. Such a practice had a long history in market research. Lazarsfeld's "The Art of Asking Why" appeared in 1935 in the *National Marketing Review*. A battery of related closed questions—perhaps not lengthy enough— was sometimes used to describe a complete multifaceted issue, the items chosen on the basis of some conceptual principles and/or pretesting.[2] The answer boxes these agencies attached to closed questions, or the alternatives stated in the question itself, permitted respondents to express finer shadings of opinion than simply "approve" or "disapprove" and to indicate their uncertainty, qualified opinion, or lack of opinion. A few agencies instructed their interviewers to record spontaneous comments which enlarged upon the initial answer to a closed question. As Lazarsfeld noted in another paper, "Actually there is hardly a poll where there is not some freedom left for the respondent to express himself in his own way" (1944, p. 40). That the Division of Program Surveys staff functioned in ignorance of the better polling practices is easy to understand. Almost all were innocents out of academia, untainted by past association with pollsters. Encouraged by Likert and sustained by each other, they maintained their comforting, albeit false, image of commercial research practices of the period. Likert's behavior is much harder to understand, since, although from academia originally, he had a long association with market research and polling.

Despite the merits of questionnaires that combine a variety of closed and open questions and the advantages they offer in speed and economy, Likert advocated that the questionnaire be totally open-ended, with the exception of the background items (or facesheet, as it was called in the Division) and occasional simple factual questions. The faithful staff accepted his position. One of the wittiest analysts formulated the perfect probe to begin the interview: "What you are about to say interests me very much." We were amused but ignored the implication that open-ended questions could be too open.

Interviewing was a costly procedure. Although the series of open-ended questions was standardized, the obligatory probes to clarify, enrich, and yet not bias the answers could not be standardized and provided in advance. A repertoire of stock, neutral probes and techniques was taught during training—"Tell me more about it," saying

"Uh-huh," pausing, and so on—but the interviewer still had to improvise to meet all sorts of special circumstances. In 1942, perhaps because of the Division's earlier tradition, it was assumed that such discretion and skill in interviewing required a professionally qualified, carefully supervised, full-time field staff whose relatively high salaries had to be paid even when there was no interviewing to be done. (By contrast, other agencies used lower-paid part-time interviewers, although a small network of supervisors in strategic locations might be full-time employees.) So the Division's small corps of roving observers had to be greatly enlarged. Interviewers of the caliber of anthropologists John Bennett and Herbert Passin and directors of the caliber of Charles Cannell, who served through most of the war years and continued in that capacity for many years at the Survey Research Center, had to be recruited.

Coding the volume of verbatim interview material produced by this method was obviously difficult, slow, and costly, and, for reasons less obvious, created contention. Day after day, question after question, the coders had to exercise good and subtle judgment in making the ratings, scorings, and classifications which quantified the lengthy, sometimes obtuse, free answers of the respondents. In order to measure precisely the abstract variables that interested him, the analyst sometimes built codes that strained the tolerance of the coders who had to find in the concrete answers evidence of the magnitude of the variables. Pursuing his purpose single-mindedly, the analyst sometimes would ignore material the coders thought too priceless to be neglected, further straining their tolerance. Despite the difficult task, uniformity in the judgments of different coders had to be achieved. This entailed a laborious procedure titled "round robining": The coders would try out the codes and arrive at a common understanding through discussion and consultation, if necessary modifying the initial codes. Sometimes, hassling would have been a better term than robining. Given the requirements of the task, the coders had to be perceptive and intelligent, but able to tolerate tedium and frustration. They were paid a clerk's wages and awarded the undignified civil service title of "quantification clerk." Their discontent burst forth periodically, mobilized by the more militant coders, and rebellion often was incipient. These burdens, which would have been reduced by judicious use of closed questions, were accepted by the analytic staff.

In the early phase of his career, Likert expressed no vociferous objection to closed questions or part-time interviewers, whose pay during the Depression reached a low of two cents an interview. In the early 1930s, he had worked closely with the Psychological Corporation, one of the earlier agencies to conduct nationwide market and opinion surveys. Those surveys used mainly closed questions.[3] Moreover, Sidney Roslow, his assistant in those surveys and later a well-known media and market researcher, was brought to the Division by Likert and given a high status. But by 1942, a radical and mysterious conversion had occurred, and Likert displayed an almost puritanical intolerance toward anything resembling commercial polling.[4] As one informant and colleague in that period described Likert, "He made it clear to me, in many emotionally toned comments, that he just could not stand doing things in the same way as 'the pollsters' were doing" (Don Cahalan, personal communication).

Likert's position in 1942 becomes even more perplexing when we recall his earlier academic career. His fame in the history of attitude measurement rests securely on the invention of a scaling method which forced the respondent to answer a long battery of closed questions by checking one of five alternative answers ranging from "strongly approve" to "strongly disapprove" (Likert 1932). In a postwar paper he explained why he abandoned that procedure:

> Most attitude scale research was based on work with students. They, at times, objected to being restricted to the question alternatives as stated and insisted that none of the alternatives gave them an opportunity to express their attitudes correctly. These objections were usually ignored and the students were told to answer the questions as directed. This procedure worked reasonably well with students, but when it was tried on the adult population entirely different results were obtained. When respondents, in their own homes, were told that the fine points in *their* thinking did not matter, that they had to restrict their thinking on the problem to the dimensions seen by the experimenter and that alternatives were limited to those that *he* stated, rapport went out the door and often the interviewer was close behind. . . . This experience led to the use of the open question. [1947, pp. 199–200][5]

That this experience led Likert to change in some degree is understandable, but the radicalism of the change still eludes explanation. Although thirty-four closed questions—the number in his original scales—in a repetitive format with rigid and arbitrarily chosen answer boxes could not be used in surveys of the general population,[6] a shorter, more varied battery of closed questions with answer boxes formulated on the basis of pretesting in a less constraining way has proved workable. Surely, rapport would not have been shattered if the instrument had included some open-ended questions that gave the respondent freedom of expression.

While any explanation of Likert's extremism in 1942 is bound to be conjecture, we should consider the situation he then confronted. Open-ended interviewing was the long-standing practice of the Department of Agriculture. Tradition and the need for its continued budgetary support urged him toward that special method. The great expansion of the Division, however, had been the result of contracts to conduct surveys for other government agencies, notably the Office of War Information (OWI), and the competition for such funds was intense. Indeed, OWI had its own survey unit to conduct research unless there was a compelling reason to let the contract to Likert: that is, the unique and superior research provided by Program Surveys. The thoroughly open-ended interview, unblemished by closed questions or other polling practices, was just what Likert needed to stamp the Division's surveys with a distinctive hallmark of quality.[7]

That an aura of distinctiveness was essential and that duplication of services could not be tolerated is suggested by OWI's rechristening of the two survey units. Its own Surveys Division was labeled the Division of Polling or Extensive Surveys, and the Division of Program Surveys, its proper name within the Department of Agriculture, was given a dual identity as a part of OWI under the label Division of Surveys or Intensive Surveys. (A memorandum of July 8, 1942, outlined and clarified the complex organization within OWI.) Likert's surveys truly had to be distinctive and intensive, all the more since the OWI unit was available to conduct surveys under contract for other government agencies such as OPA and Treasury, who were also major sources of funding for Likert. These circumstances shaped the method into its extreme form in 1942.

But Likert was not simply scrambling for business in a tight market. He was a true believer in his method. He had a genuine and seemingly unbounded faith in its power to solve wartime and peacetime social problems, and his surveys adhered to the highest standards. The spirit and talents of an entrepreneur and the values and skills of a scientist somehow came together harmoniously and attractively in Likert. And no one should see his entrepreneurial features as blemishes on an otherwise admirable portrait. In those early days when survey research was still a struggling enterprise, Likert and other entrepreneurs were crucial to its development. His enthusiasm over new ideas and ventures, which at times made him act impulsively and even excessively, his appeal "instilled the spirit of adventurous excitement," as Dorwin Cartwright, his longtime associate, noted in the tribute paid Likert after his death in 1981. This quality, and his "vision, persuasive ability and personal magnetism," made him an irresistible leader. So what otherwise might have been a calm scientific discussion resolved on its merits in 1942 took on the tone of a small holy war for the supremacy of the open-ended method.[8]

That the image is not far-fetched is suggested by the work of the methodology section of the Division, staffed by Douglas Ellson, David Krech, and me under Richard Crutchfield's direction. Our full-time assignment was the improvement of method, and no constraints were ever imposed on our work. Many problems were studied. Yet, as best I can recall, it never occurred to us to conduct a rigorous and fair test of the central methodological problem, the merits of the thoroughly open-ended interview. Our section conceptualized complex problems in the most subtle ways. Yet we never suggested that the superiority of the Division's surveys—which we felt keenly—depended on many variables implicated in the procedures other than the open-ended questions. The quality of the research design and of the analysts, their scholarly inclination toward elaborate explanation rather than simple description, the honesty and skill of the interviewers, the auxiliary material the interviewers provided, such as ratings and "thumbnail sketches" of the respondents and background reports on the community contexts, and the probability sampling were only some of the possible sources of the superiority. Such variables would have to have been controlled in isolating the intrinsic effects of the open-ended questions on the overall quality of the Division's surveys.

Another important uncontrolled variable was the stated sponsorship of the surveys. The Division interviewers were government employees and established that identity to the respondents with the aid of an impressive credential. By contrast, field work for the OWI unit was conducted by the National Opinion Research Center, then at the University of Denver, through a contractual arrangement. Their interviewers were identified to the respondents as private employees of NORC. Since there was a spy scare and the public had been warned against loose talk to suspicious strangers, the use of official government interviewers might have raised the completion rates of the Division's surveys. To be sure, the fancy ID card did not guarantee cooperation. One of our interviewers was mistaken for a German spy in Tishomingo County, Mississippi, and driven away at the point of a shotgun. Other less dangerous skirmishes occurred, but the sponsorship seemed generally helpful in reducing refusals.

It is also plausible that government sponsorship might have affected the validity of answers to certain questions: The direction of the effect, however, is not easily predicted. Dissatisfaction with various government programs, for example, might have been less readily voiced to official employees out of politeness, or more readily voiced because respondents assumed that the criticism would reach those who could improve the program. Special groups alienated from the war effort might have toned down their true feelings for fear they would be reported by interviewers in the employ of the government. After more than forty years, I can still hear the black respondent who expressed her resentment of the government's treatment of blacks to me during a pretest in Pennsylvania, and who ended the interview with the fearful remark, "I'll see if they come and take me away." Ellson, years later, recalled a similar experience: "In Milwaukee . . . I interviewed two Polish workers in the middle of loud family arguments in which the contingent from the old country kept whispering, then yelling, 'Don't tell him anything, he's from the government' " (personal communication, February 3, 1983).

I cannot recall, despite its obvious importance, our testing the effect of sponsorship on the success of the Division's surveys. Ironically, the OWI unit conducted a large and well-designed experiment in which government versus private sponsorship was alternated over a sample of about 1,100 respondents and found that refusals were reduced by half with government-identified interviewers, from 13 to 7 percent.[9]

These examples suggest that our emotional attachment to the open-ended method at times dulled our critical judgment, but the belief that we were developing a superior method and conducting surveys useful to the war effort intensified our efforts. Simultaneously we were serving a worthy scientific cause and the larger cause. Indeed, the surveys were of high quality and the findings were useful.

Practical and Scientific Implications of the Surveys

When our surveys had a quick and dramatic impact in high places, morale zoomed upward and we worked all the harder. Our previous scholarly research, even when important, often went unnoticed and its impact at best was felt slowly and in a narrow academic circle. What an exhilarating change to see the impact the surveys sometimes had! Douglas Ellson, after forty years of productive scholarship, could still write about those old times:

> Never before or since have the results of my research been reported by the President two weeks after the work was finished. . . . One

interview I will never forget was with a little wrinkled old black lady at the corner of a gray wooden shack in the middle of Mississippi, who said, "The government don't want my opinion—they're sending me to the 'sylum' tomorrow." But I did, and her opinion was represented about a month later in President Roosevelt's fireside chat on . . . rationing policy. On the strength of our analysis of that sample of opinion, country people, or perhaps all Americans, were given an extra 10 pounds of sugar for canning in the fall. [Personal communication, February 3, 1983]

Work in the Division, of course, did not always produce such rewards. Sometimes useful findings were ignored and frustration rather than elation, or even more extreme reactions, occurred. Several surveys, including one in the Sojourner Truth Housing Project in Detroit, had documented the black population's grievances and the tensions among the surrounding whites which might have been alleviated by government action early in the war. After the Detroit Riot of June 21, 1943, one of the analysts felt so morally outraged that he leaked the classified reports to the *Detroit Press* to make the argument that ample forewarnings had been willfully ignored. However, for most of us much of the time, the balance was tilted toward the gratifying sense that our work was useful. Such useful applied research was accomplished without the feeling that scientific standards had been sacrificed. The methods were rigorous and sharply contrasted in our minds with the practices of commercial pollsters.

When surveys intended for purely practical purposes also yielded substantive findings of scientific significance, that was an extra dividend and the pleasures of work were enhanced. This often happened for reasons that might escape the modern reader. In the 1930s, what was supposed to be a generalizable social psychology was, in fact, as critics put it, only the social psychology of the "college sophomore." Practical procedures for scientific sampling of human populations had not been established, and even if scholars had been knowledgeable they would not have had the resources to conduct wide-ranging sample surveys. Private foundations were few and government foundations nonexistent. So social scientists usually distributed questionnaires in their college classes, occasionally in their hometowns, or to the members of accessible organized groups, and perforce rested their conclusions on shaky foundations.

Given the state of social psychology then, findings on particular attitudes or behaviors obtained routinely in the course of the sample surveys were bound to strengthen its empirical foundation and thus contribute to the science. Some of these surveys using large and good samples of the general population, although conducted for practical purposes, had special and obvious value for social science. For example, the surveys on attitudes toward Germans, Japanese, and Italians, toward blacks and Jews, or on attitudes *of* blacks dealt with classic problems of prejudice and intergroup relations. Angus Campbell's paper (1947) on anti-Semitism and its determinants, based on a 1942 nationwide survey, illustrates the benefits to social psychology. Ironically, in the midst of the war against the Nazis, a considerable minority expressed anti-Semitism, and a very small percentage went so far as to urge "aggressive measures against Jews" (p. 518). But the number and variety of surveys in this area indicate that many valuable findings of the Division never were exploited for scholarship.

Many other surveys were on topics of no obvious scientific relevance, yet they often had hidden value for social science. For example, the Division conducted a series of surveys on motives for buying and redeeming war bonds and on sales strategies and appeals. Although of great practical use, findings about bond sales seemed to have little scientific value. Beneath the surface, however, there were also findings on classic problems of communication and persuasion, on the potency of personal influence versus mass media influence, on the strength of altruistic versus selfish motives. Cartwright's paper (1949) on the sale of war bonds illustrates the way this series of surveys benefited social psychology specifically.[10]

At a much higher level of abstraction, many of the surveys could be recognized as having a common theme of great scientific importance, although one neglected by American social scientists. The reactions of the civilian population to the experiences and institutions of war were being systematically, repeatedly, and comprehensively studied in the course of the surveys. Just as Samuel Stouffer and his staff synthesized their many surveys of soldiers in *The American Soldier,* one can imagine Likert and the staff synthesizing their findings and creating *The American Civilian.* Unfortunately, this opportunity was neglected by the director and staff of the OWI survey unit as well as by the Division. Although never realized, the potential of the surveys to illuminate such an important social and scientific problem did motivate the staff.

Of course, some surveys were of little or no value to social science and even seemed of trivial and transient practical value. "Second Hand Tractor Problems in the Middle West," "Factors Motivating Production and Marketing of Hogs," and "Baltimore Reactions to the Proposed 'Share the Meat' Campaign" excited few of us. There were periods of boredom and periods of intense pressure. There were frustrations in dealing with a few colleagues and administrators, and sometimes in obtaining clearances from the Bureau of the Budget, the watchdog agency empowered to cancel surveys that were duplicative or an excessive burden on respondents. Most of us, however, were realistic enough to know that work is not always pleasurable and some of us—however surprising it may seem—could become fascinated by a tiny technical intricacy or eccentric substantive problem. We were fascinated with a new technology, the IBM machine, which had been no part of our prewar research equipment. To the generations now accustomed to the high-speed computer, a card-counting sorter may seem a relic of the Dark Ages. To us, used to hand-tabulated data and a hand-cranked desk calculator, it was an expensive, wonderful tool and toy.

The novel milieu in which we worked was especially stimulating. Our former academic milieu was parochial, individualistic, and hierarchically organized by the principle of professorial ranks. We did research alone or with a local collaborator from the same discipline and trained in the same intellectual tradition, or with a mentor far superior in rank. Social science institutes with large research teams working on projects were a postwar innovation in most American universities.[11] In the Division we worked in groups characterized by intimacy, with others trained in different traditions recruited from different universities and representing different generations. The lowly and the mighty in the academic pyramid worked together on a more equal footing. True, we all had received new ranks in the civil service system ranging from P-1 to P-7, and there were section chiefs and subordinates in the formal structure. But informally the lines of stratification were loose, and all of us were comrades-at-arms fighting for a common cause.

My experience is illustrative. One of my co-workers was Daniel Katz, trained at Syracuse in the social psychology of Floyd Allport, fourteen years older, already well established in academia, and a P-5 in another section of the Division. Despite the fact that I was a youngster with a brand-new Ph.D., trained at Columbia by Gardner Murphy and Otto Klineberg in a different social-psychological tradition, and only a P-2, we collaborated for a period of about five years and began a close friendship lasting more than forty years. My closest co-workers, understandably, were my colleagues in the methodology section. Douglas Ellson was from Yale, David Krech and Richard Crutchfield had been trained at Berkeley, and their social psychology was Gestaltist and phenomenological in tone while mine was developmental and anthropological.

When we worked together in the Division, Krech was tough, smart, impassioned, and, from temperament and trauma, the most tendentious colleague I was to meet over the next forty years of professional wanderings. Despite our close friendship (lasting through all his years), I could make no advance in method without being engaged by him in fierce intellectual combat. One day in 1942, over some methodological problem so trivial that it is long forgotten, he raised a question. Since I had already suffered many days of unrelenting battle, my reaction was so extreme that I chased him down the long halls of the South Agriculture building in a screaming rage. Periodically, he stopped and asked in good humor if I really wanted to fight. As usual, our mediator and chief, Crutchfield, intervened and back we went to work. In such fiery fashion, our little section made its exciting, if not easy, advances toward a better survey method.

Progress elsewhere in the Division was made in more serene fashion, often with the pleasure we shared in informal groups that crossed the section lines. Angus Campbell, Jules Henry, and I were the regular, appreciative audience for Burt Fisher, his boisterous comedy and Falstaffian air in sharp contrast to Campbell's dour exterior and formidable stature. Fisher's wit frequently conveyed a serious point which corrected excesses in method. The Fisher principle—"Be meticulous without being ridiculous"—was one of his correctives. When Fisher was not performing, Henry would regale us with anecdotes from his life among the headhunters of Amazonia.

Apart from the fun, so diverse a quartet could provide serious stimulation. Henry was a cultural anthropologist, trained at Columbia by Franz Boas; the three of us were social psychologists from very different backgrounds. Fisher had been trained at Kansas in a special Lewinian and Gestalt tradition. Campbell had been trained at Oregon and Stanford initially as an experimental psychologist but then greatly influenced toward social psychology by Kurt Lewin and toward anthropology and studies of culture and personality by Herskovits and by field work on the black population of St. Thomas. As already noted, my social psychology reflected training in the psychology and anthropology departments at Columbia.

The friendly relations among staff were matched by Likert's interpersonal relations, making our environment all the more pleasant. Although he held a lofty rank and was directing a large staff, he was approachable, unpretentious, nonauthoritarian, and warm and kind. Although he displayed the entrepreneurial skills to outsmart competitors and the intellectual flair to develop new methods and applications of survey research, his enthusiasm and innocent air shattered any austere, Olympian image of him the staff might otherwise have had. Under this director, the large and diverse staff that had come together through the fortunes of war was making rapid progress in creating and applying a unique survey method. Then, in November 1942, progress was suddenly halted. Ironically, the very thing that had brought about the meteoric rise of Likert's enterprise led to its decline.

The Crisis over Method

Likert's enlarged enterprise, as already noted, depended in great measure on the contracts with OWI to conduct unique, presumably essential surveys in its capacity as the Division of Intensive Surveys of that agency. Since its own Division of Extensive Surveys or Division of Polling was also conducting surveys, OWI's administrators understandably had already begun in early 1942 to ponder the need to maintain such a possibly duplicative and expensive arrangement. Were Likert's large-scale surveys, conducted by a completely open-ended method that was slow and costly, really essential? They retained Paul Lazarsfeld as a consultant to review, with "earnest effort toward impartiality," what he later titled "The Controversy over Detailed Interviews" (1944, p. 39).

In light of our previous discussion of good polling practices, we can anticipate Lazarsfeld's verdict. He stressed that the open-ended interview (OI) "is necessarily an expensive and slow procedure" and that most (not all) of its benefits could be achieved by a method that is "more objective, more manageable on a mass basis" (p. 50) by using "an interlocking system of poll questions" (p. 52). For most purposes, "the OI, although much preferable to isolated straight poll questions, is not as good as a well-structured set of straight poll questions" (p. 53). He also stressed that these "techniques do not make the OI superfluous but give it a new and, as we feel, more valuable place in the whole scheme of public opinion research" (pp. 50–51). "The OI is indispensable at the beginning of any study where it clarifies the structure of a problem in all its details," providing the guidance in designing the interlocking battery of poll questions, and "it is also invaluable at the end of a study," to clarify, guide, and enrich the analysis. "Good research consists in weaving back and forth between OIs and the more cut-and-dried procedures" (p. 59).

Lazarsfeld therefore recommended that OWI continue both survey operations, not in their former way but in a more efficient, economical, and integrated way. Program Surveys would conduct small-scale surveys at the beginning and the end, and the extensive unit would conduct large-scale polls in between. The final outcome in November 1942, however, was that OWI canceled its contracts with Likert, and about half the staff had to be terminated. To understand why Lazarsfeld's sensible, seemingly appealing plan was not accepted we must recall Likert's character and the atmosphere of the Division, and also learn about Elmo Wilson, the director of the OWI polling unit.

By accepting the plan, Likert would have saved a substantial part of his enterprise. He saw the plan, however, as downgrading his cherished and superior method and elevating polling, which he regarded as inferior and no substitute for open-ended interviewing.

In theory, there was another solution to the crisis Likert faced. He might have offered to implement the entire plan himself by doing both the polling and intensive surveys for OWI, or by incorporating both open and closed questions into the questionnaire used in each survey, but such a solution also would have violated his principles. Ironically, the staff's allegiance to open-ended interviewing and hostility to polling—so helpful for the growth of the Division—had also become a hindrance to such compromises.

Wilson was neither a crude pollster nor a weak competitor. Originally on the journalism faculty at the University of Minnesota, he was drawn into survey research by Elmo Roper, no ordinary pollster either. Wilson then became the director of field work for the surveys described in *The People's Choice* (Lazarsfeld, Berelson, and Gaudet 1944). That classic panel study, conducted during the 1940 presidential campaign, was no superficial poll. Wilson brought the experience and sophisticated view of survey research gained from the study and associations with Roper and Lazarsfeld to the work of the OWI unit, as well as the long research experience of Hazel Gaudet, whom he appointed his first assistant director. Wilson, like Likert, was an entrepreneur interested in promoting his enterprise, and he had the energy, charm, and persuasive ability to succeed. Unlike Likert, he was not doctrinaire about method and was eager to develop a sophisticated form of polling compatible with the Lazarsfeld proposal if released from the confined status of the Division of Polling. Indeed he was willing, though not eager, to conduct *both* the intensive and extensive surveys envisioned in Lazarsfeld's proposal; and Keith Kane, the head of the Bureau of Intelligence of OWI and ultimately in charge of all its surveys, strongly preferred such an arrangement, since it would be economical and bring the intensive surveys under his direct control.

Program Surveys After the Crisis

As a result, Likert's staff had to be reduced substantially in November 1942. But the Division was able to retain many of its senior members—Angus Campbell, Charles Cannell, and Dorwin Cartwright, for example—and to add others in a short time—George Katona and Leslie Kish, for example. Although the OWI contracts were a serious loss, the Division still received basic funds from the Agriculture Department and was able to get contracts from other agencies, notably the Treasury Department. Those clients were attracted because the Division did conduct excellent surveys, although expensive and slow because of the insistence on totally open-ended interviewing. The clients, however, were getting a lot for their money: probability sampling as well as high-quality research design and analysis. In the competition for OWI contracts, Wilson's in-house unit had a built-in advantage. In the competition for other clients, the Division had no such handicap and won enough contracts to sustain itself, albeit not on its former grand scale. Thus the Division continued to make major contributions to the growth of the field, by producing survey findings of practical and scientific value and by improving methodology. One might even argue that the contribution was increased by the crisis the Division had faced and weathered.

The emphasis on open-ended questions, pushed to the extreme in the earlier days, declined as time passed. Under the pressure of costs and as a result of the dialectic process that Lazarsfeld had initiated, closed questions began to be used selectively in conjunction with open questions, and part-time interviewers were hired. A method that was more viable and less costly thus developed without sacrificing the Division's guiding principle that open-ended questions served various essential functions in survey research. In the spirit of that principle, the Division continued to develop the methodology of open-ended interviewing, and in toned-down form it was more acceptable to others and had greater influence on the field.

Toward the end of the war, the Division's surveys became more narrowly focused on the problems of farmers and the marketing of farm products, given its major and stable source of funds from the Department of Agriculture. Nothing could be a more significant sign of the times than the abolition of the Division of Program Surveys by a memorandum of August 1, 1946, and its replacement by the Division of Special Surveys, which became incorporated into the Marketing Research Division of the Agricultural Marketing Service in 1953. By 1946, Likert must have seen the handwriting on the wall and anticipated his fate. He had raised the Division from respectable but humble origins on the farm to its glorious wartime status. He would not end up back on the farm.

Using his entrepreneurial talent and his scientific credentials, spurred by what Cartwright called his "spirit of adventurous excitement," Likert searched for and found a university where he and a nucleus of senior staff from the Division relocated in a setting more congenial to their broad interests and the growth of survey research. At the University of Michigan in 1946, they established the Survey Research Center, initially a small enterprise. Then, with the sense of a great mission and the research skills they had developed in the Division, and with just the right balance of prudent management from Campbell and risk-taking from Likert, they ultimately created the great enterprise known today for its contributions to survey method and the training of students, for its many scholarly publications, and for the numerous surveys that serve in the solution of social and scientific problems.

Notes

1. Psychologists predominated and by mid-1942 included Jerome Bruner, Angus Campbell, Charles Cannell, Dorwin Cartwright, Dwight Chapman, Kenneth B. Clark, Richard Crutchfield, Douglas Ellson, Burton Fisher, Ernest Hilgard, Rosalind Gould, Daniel Katz, David Krech, Robert MacLeod, Eleanor Maccoby, Sidney Roslow, Jane Shepherd, Charles Herbert Stember, and Ruth Tolman, joined later by the psychologist-economist George Katona. Sociologists included Nicholas Demerath, Nelson Foote, John Riley, and Julian Woodward. Anthropologists included John W. Bennett, Jules Henry, and Herbert Passin. The sampling statistician was J. Stevens Stock, followed by Leslie Kish.

2. In "The Quintamensional Plan of Question Design" (1947), Gallup describes "a system of question design which has evolved out of many years of research by the American Institute of Public Opinion and which, it is believed, answers many of the frequently voiced criticisms of public opinion measurement. . . . Because the system provided an opportunity to probe five different aspects of opinion it has been called the 'quintamensional' approach." Two of the aspects involve the use of an "open or free answer" question and a "reason why" question. Although the system evolved over many years, it is possible that it was not finally in operation until after 1942. Nevertheless, it suggests that pollers were aware of the need to use a battery of related questions.

3. In a methodological paper (1943) describing how a questionnaire containing mainly closed questions was developed, the director of the Psychological Corporation, Henry Link, reports that it "began, as has for years been our practice, with an informal interview" (p. 270). Thus Likert certainly was well acquainted with this method of reducing arbitrariness in the design of closed questions.

4. Roslow and others at the corporation had conducted a series of method-ological studies on question wording, including tests of open-ended questions, which were published before World War II. Thus, Likert surely knew that other agencies used open-ended questions; he knew, too, both their value and their limitations. For some of the papers, see Roslow and Blankenship 1939; Roslow, Wulfeck, and Corby 1940. For Likert and Roslow's collaboration in market and media research, see, for example, "Eddie Cantor and the Chase and Sanborn Radio Program" (1934–35).

5. Likert's 1947 paper is probably his most thorough and persuasive argu-ment for a totally open-ended method, and the quotation from it does not convey all the reasons he advanced for the change. Yet the paper does not seem to provide sufficient grounds for the extreme position he had taken in 1942.

6. Long attitude scales were used successfully during World War II in surveys among soldiers, but this does not contradict Likert's argument. Soldiers, like students, were a captive group, and the authority of the Army—like that of the teacher, only more so—could assure cooper-ation.

7. Although probability sampling distinguished the work of the Division, it did not serve to establish its superiority to clients. In 1942, a battle was raging over the merits of quota versus probability sampling. The issues were so technical and the evidence of how well those methods worked in practice was so meager that the battle lasted until well into the postwar period.

8. Jean Converse's conclusion that "the open-ended debate was shaped by institutional needs and capacities and ideologies about research" is in line with my explanation. For her fine review of the sources and consequences of the controversy over questionnaire design, see "Strong Arguments and Weak Evidence: The Open/Closed Questioning Contro-versy of the 1940s" (1984). Lazarsfeld's important role in the controversy will be discussed later. He titled a paper reviewing the issues "The Controversy over Detailed Interviews: An Offer of Negotiation" (1944), and introduced it with the statement: "If in methodological discussions, competent workers assume vehemently opposite positions, it is gener-ally a good time for someone to enter the scene and suggest that the parties are both right and wrong." Although the private report on his role as mediator was submitted in 1942, his published account did not appear until later.

9. To my knowledge, the study was never published. However, I still have a copy of the detailed, typed report: "Interviewing Under Government Auspices versus Private Auspices: A Methodological Experiment," ad-dressed to Keith Kane, director of the Bureau of Intelligence, OWI, November 9, 1942. No statistically significant differences in response

were found on a wide range of questions, but the direction of the differences was suggestive, and a few of the tests revealed dramatic differences. Criticism of the government was dampened in the responses to government interviewers, and the black respondents were much more likely to report confidence in the superiority of our military forces over the German military forces when they spoke to government interviewers.

10. As the title indicates, only selected findings from the series of surveys were presented. A brief summary of findings from the last survey in the series appeared in a later paper and showed the power of the instrument and analytical model in predicting bond redemptions in the first postwar year, 1946. See Cartwright 1950, especially pp. 55–62. However, as late as 1953, reference was still being made to an unpublished manuscript then titled "The Selling of Government Bonds to the Public," covering those wartime surveys more comprehensively. That it never got published illustrates the strange and sad fact that much of the Division's wartime research never was codified and communicated to a wide scientific public.

11. The few exceptions do not undermine the generalization. The Bureau of Applied Social Research, named the Office of Radio Research when it first became established at Columbia University in 1940, was a small and, as its name suggests, specialized research organization, its growth stimulated by the war. Similarly, the Office of Public Opinion Research, established at the University of Denver in 1941, was small in size, its growth spurred by the wartime contracts.

· 2 ·

The Surveys Division:
Office of
War Information

I t was late 1942 when the crisis at Program Surveys led a group of us to join the Office of War Information (OWI). The Surveys Division of OWI began conducting research in November 1941 and continued until July 1944, when it was liquidated after the Congress terminated its appropriation.[1] Despite its short life, the Division played an important part in the development of survey research. It was crucial to the survival and growth of the National Opinion Research Center—then only an infant organization facing a precarious future. The complexity and variety of its wartime studies and the pace of the work improved the staff's skills immeasurably, which in turn enriched the American survey organizations they joined in the postwar period.

The Division at the Transition

In November 1942, prior to our arrival from Program Surveys, the Division's professional staff under the immediate direction of Hazel Gaudet (Erskine) consisted of six analysts, all women recruited mainly from the Office of Radio Research, none with a Ph.D. A small clerical staff, a few machine operators for data processing, and a small coding staff constituted the full-time organization. Elmo Wilson, originally a journalist and then involved in the survey in Erie County,

Ohio, reported in *The People's Choice* (1944), had been appointed director at age 36. Wilson had strengthened his small organization with a team of consultants: Raymond Franzen, a statistician and sampling expert; Paul Lazarsfeld, director of the Office of Radio Research and of the Erie County study; Elmo Roper, who had been a co-sponsor of the Erie County study; and Frank Stanton, who had been an associate director of the Office of Radio Research before ascending to the presidency of the Columbia Broadcasting System.[2]

There was, however, no sampling section and no field director or field staff. Wilson, wisely as I sensed later, had contracted with the National Opinion Research Center to conduct the field work. Recruitment, training, and supervision of interviewers was the immediate responsibility of a NORC field director housed in an office near ours in the same building, thus in close contact with the OWI study directors and responsive to their suggestions and even to methodological experiments and interviewing innovations proposed by them. Paul Sheatsley, originally a journalist and then an interviewer and a field director for one of the Gallup organizations, held the NORC position from early 1942 through the war. All interviewers, though part-time employees, were hired and trained personally in accordance with the policy NORC had promulgated at its founding. In effect, Wilson had all the advantages of his own exclusive field staff but none of the burdens, and NORC profited from the experience and flow of funds at a critical point in its development. For its nationwide surveys and some local studies, OWI simply adopted the sampling designs and procedures already in place at NORC, again being spared the burdens but suffering the limitations of quota sampling. It was the prevailing practice of the period, but NORC and the Division were selective, critical, and experimental in the way it was applied.[3]

Initially, the Surveys Division seemed to me too small and the staff inferior. Although my first impressions may have reflected the snobbery of a young Ph.D. and perhaps an unconscious streak of male chauvinism, my recent experiences at Program Surveys provide a better explanation—not that I wish to deny the sins of my youth. Program Surveys had more than a hundred members; many of the large professional staff had Ph.D.s, and some already had established academic reputations. The formal structure provided an elaborate apparatus and extensive resources for conducting surveys and improving methods. In addition to the planning, sampling, field, coding, machine, analysis (with a staff of fourteen), and report sections, there was my section with four members freed to devote themselves full time to methodology. Against this dazzling, star-studded background, the Surveys Division was bound to seem small, almost insignificant.

Survey research was in its infancy in 1942, still in an inchoate stage of development, which helps explain my first impressions. The facts I shall cite are presented not to justify my distorted view but as vivid reminders of the early history of the field. Wilson's contribution to the classic panel survey in Erie County, involving six reinterviews of a sample during an election campaign, is noted in the opening pages of the first edition of *The People's Choice*. He "resided in Sandusky for six months and was in charge of all the work in the field. His resourcefulness in meeting innumerable technical difficulties and the many ideas he contributed to the study as it progressed foreshadowed the important role he was to play later in governmental public opinion research" (p. v). How would I or any other outsider have known of that in 1942? The survey had been conducted only two years earlier, during the 1940 presidential election, and was not published until 1944. Similarly, it took us until 1944 to learn that Helen Schneider (Dinerman), of the OWI staff, had made a contribution to the panel study, that she "was in charge of the statistical analysis and guided us indefatigably through material which required seven Hollerith punch cards per respondent" (p. v). Nor could any outsider have known in 1942 that Hazel Gaudet's contribution to the panel study was important enough for her to become a co-author in 1944 of *The People's Choice*.[4]

Certainly, no one knew in 1942 that the agency responsible for the panel study was the Bureau of Applied Social Research, since it came into existence only in 1944, when the Office of Radio Research was renamed. The Office had become attached to the Department of Sociology at Columbia in 1940. However, it was still so marginal to the university in the spring of 1942 that I had never visited its quarters three miles off campus or met its director, Paul Lazarsfeld, despite the fact that I was completing my Ph.D. in social psychology at Columbia at that time. In 1942, NORC had just begun to function and its prominence as the first nationwide nonprofit private polling organization had not yet been established.

As these examples suggest, survey research was still so new in 1942 that achievement and reputation for pioneering figures and agencies still lay in the future, and competence was not easy to recognize ahead of time. Thus, some of us saw the Ph.D. or academic distinction as the only clear signs of competence in survey research. Although advanced training in the social sciences was valuable background, as noted earlier, formal training in survey methods had not yet been incorporated into the curriculum in that period.

Likert, a social psychologist and anticommercial, sought and attracted social psychologists from academia, mainly men since women had not yet been welcomed in those halls. Lazarsfeld, unconventional to start with, was forced by necessity to be hospitable to all sources of funds and personnel that could help his struggling center. Thus he welcomed people without regard for their commercial or academic origins, their credentials, or their sex, and for historical reasons was especially friendly to and supportive of underdogs. His center, first established on the fringe of the academy and no part of that establishment, was not trammeled by tradition and regulation. Thus the original OWI staff, recruited through Wilson's association with Lazarsfeld, consisted predominantly of women without academic credentials. Their achievements were substantial, but not yet visible.

The Nature of the Work

The termination of OWI's contract with Program Surveys had liberated the Surveys Division from its former confined status and simple mode of operation as the Polling Division. With the increased funds at his disposal and the freedom to undertake more complex and intensive surveys for OWI and other agencies, Wilson in November 1942 brought Ernest Hilgard, Daniel Katz, John Riley, and me, with our experience from Program Surveys, onto his staff of analysts, along with some of the full-time intensive interviewers to conduct pretesting and scouting or background field work. Crutchfield joined us a few months later. With his own staff strengthened and the NORC staff continuing under contract, Wilson eagerly moved into a larger realm of work.

He was, of course, still shackled by all the bureaucratic controls over governmental survey research. However, by bringing Julian Woodward from Program Surveys to act as liaison in Washington with other agencies and the Bureau of the Budget, Wilson had more than a fighting chance to win those battles. Woodward, a trained sociologist with a special interest in applied research, was judicious, responsible, straight-shooting, skilled in reporting results in terms relevant to the client, and unflagging in devotion to good and useful works. He needed all those talents. His description of just one memorable battle is worth quoting.

> On a recent study made by OWI for a sister agency each of the following persons had to approve before the study could go into the field:
>   The division chief in the client agency who wanted the study; he was the primary research client.

The public opinion research expert in the client agency, who acted as a sort of research broker in the proceedings.

The chief of the Division of Statistical Standards of the client agency who clears all that agency's questionnaires.

The assistant administrator for the agency; he had to decide whether it was good agency policy to make the study with its funds.

The budget officer for the client agency; he had to approve the transfer of funds.

A representative of the Estimates Division of the Bureau of the Budget; he had also to approve the transfer of funds to OWI.

A representative of the Division of Statistical Standards in the Bureau of the Budget; he supplied the vital Budget Bureau number without which no government schedule can be administered to more than ten people.

The Director of the Domestic Branch of OWI; he had to decide whether it was good policy for OWI to do the requested research for the other agency.

The Assistant Director of the Domestic Branch; the study went over his desk to the Director.

The Chief of the Bureau in OWI in which the research was actually done; the study went over her desk to the Assistant Director.

The Chief of the Division in OWI actually doing the research.

The Chief of a Division in a third government agency who was brought in by the Bureau of the Budget because his agency was believed to have an interest in the subject matter of the study. To get all these people to put their stamp of approval on the research project, and any one of them could force modifications in it or halt it, took about a month of conferences and telephone calls. Not all clearance problems are as bad as this one, but at least two weeks is an average time to get all the necessary signatures. [1944, p. 672]

Studies Related to Information Campaigns

The Division's prime obligation from its founding was to conduct research to help guide the informational activities of the domestic branch of OWI. Many necessary measures for the war effort had to rely on voluntary labor. There was no draft of manpower, no draft of capital, no governmental compulsion to contribute to salvage campaigns or to buy bonds. Even rationing and price control were set up with a minimum of enforcement machinery. In short, full participation on the home front was largely a voluntary matter for our citizens. One consequence of this was the need to inform people of specific war measures and to urge them to take part. This became the main function of the Domestic Branch of OWI.

Correspondingly, the main function of the Division was to produce findings of practical value in improving the effectiveness of the various information programs. Sometimes this led to complex, deep, and broad surveys into the underlying attitudes, beliefs, emotional resistances, and conditions affecting the support of specific war measures—for example, into whether optimism and complacency about the progress of the war reduced people's salvaging of tin cans and waste fats. Sometimes this led to even broader inquiries into the fundamental causes of lack of identification with the larger war effort; at times to narrow but complex quasi-experimental surveys evaluating the effects of specific programs on special target audiences.

Duty, however, often compelled us to conduct simple surveys that, nevertheless, served the agency's operations. These were of three major types, each subject to considerable variation and some elaboration: (1) copy testing of OWI materials, first on small samples for comprehensibility, appeal, and other reactions prior to general public release and later by surveys of the reactions of the public to the quantity and quality of the materials; (2) audits or counts of the campaign materials on display—for example, posters in stores and public vehicles—to determine whether the distribution system had been deficient or the proprietors noncooperative; (3) trend surveys, more complex but routine repeated studies of public knowledge and understanding, of attitude toward and participation in various activities to guide the planning of campaigns and to provide gross evaluations of the effects of the disseminated materials. Even the simplest surveys of these types were tolerated by the staff for several reasons. The OWI unit, like the other survey units, was identified with the war effort. No matter that the work was dull some of the time, it was a service to the cause. And at other times, surveys with especially interesting methodological or substantive features counterbalanced the tedium. Moreover, even surveys that seemed trivial in content and rudimentary in method often turned out to be interesting. We learned not to prejudge and disdain those assignments and found the experience profitable. Two of the auditing surveys I directed provide illustrations.

The first survey ("A Study of Boy Scout Distribution of OWI Posters in Twelve Cities," Memorandum no. 74, March 15, 1944) dealt with a continuing OWI campaign involving a chain of voluntary efforts. Periodic bulk mailings of posters were sent to Boy Scout headquarters in various cities. Then, through the voluntary participation of the leaders and the troops, they were distributed to storekeepers, who voluntarily displayed them in the windows, the resulting exposure of the mass audience to the message triggering some psychological process, which ultimately was to lead to voluntary popular participation in some essential war activity. The unit might have presupposed that the distribution system was working. I might have been given the task of designing a complex survey to evaluate the effects on the public and of conceptualizing and measuring the social and psychological factors impeding or facilitating popular participation in various activities.

Fortunately for OWI, I was given the duller task of conducting an audit to check on the distribution of the posters, it being so much at the mercy of a chain of volunteers. A sample of the cities and areas within them included in the distribution system was drawn. In the first part of the survey, the interviewers simply checked windows and counted the number of stores displaying "Be a Marine," "Careless Talk," and "Runaway Prices," the three posters scheduled for distribution in the previous month. The tragicomic finding was that only 6 percent of the 8,564 stores checked had any of the posters on display. Such audits taught me the cautionary principles often neglected in evaluation research: that there may be a great difference between a program on paper and a program in reality, that its actual nature must be checked, and that lack of effects often may be explained simply by low output rather than by subtle factors within the audience.[5]

The design of this survey included not only the audit but also intensive interviews with local officials of the Boy Scouts and retail store executives on problems of distribution and a quasi-experimental brief survey of subsamples of storekeepers displaying or not displaying the posters (about a thousand cases) to determine factors influencing their cooperation. Admittedly, that made the assignment more exciting, and the findings indeed were interesting and useful in revealing a web of factors snarling the distribution. We learned about the limits of voluntarism even when heightened by involvement in war.

We learned sympathy for the volunteer troop leaders. As one Scout official said: "They're asked to do so many things. You can't push these volunteer Scout masters. They're asked to collect salvage, clear fire hydrants of snow, serve on the 4th war loan campaign, etc." (p. 10). We also learned sympathy for the volunteer storekeepers. As one official noted: "Many of the stores are small, and there are so many posters that they just don't have room for all of them. Most of them have their own signs in the window, too" (p. 15). And another underscored the point: "I think the height of folly was the way the 'Four Freedoms' posters were handled. . . . All four came at once. Yes, they were beautiful posters and a swell lithographing job. But who on earth is going to put up all four posters at once, except maybe a public utilities company that doesn't know what else to put in their window" (p. 17).

One intensive interview in Chicago made us lose sympathy for some storekeepers and feel sympathy for the Scouts. "A lot of the storekeepers and other businessmen around here aren't tolerant. It's a crying shame, but they are so prejudiced against Negroes that now when I send my colored Scouts in—who are as polite boys as you can imagine—they refuse to have anything to do with the posters—they think there's something screwy with colored boys doing the distributing" (p. 15). One Scout told his leader, "I joined the troop to become a Scout, and all I've been doing is everything but clean the streets. All I've been doing is working," which poignantly described another problem of the voluntary distribution system (p. 9).

The second auditing survey ("Display of OWI Poster The Cost of Living,' " Memorandum no. 78, May 26, 1944) checked the display of posters in grocery stores receiving them by direct mail, a different and dependable distribution method up to that point in the chain, but thereafter dependent on the voluntary cooperation of the grocers. The design of this survey was simpler than the Boy Scout study; yet the work turned out to be not only interesting but of scientific value.

A random sample of some 1,200 grocery stores was drawn from the mailing lists stratified by region and city size, and the field staff first checked whether the poster "The Cost of Living" was displayed either in the window or inside the store between 10 and 15 days after the mailing date. In 83 percent of the stores that existed at the specified addresses the poster did not appear to be on display, and a brief interview was conducted. To avoid confusion, a reduced picture of the poster was shown, and the grocers were asked if they had received it. Those who reported receiving it were then asked if it was on display. Those who answered no were asked for their reasons. Among those who answered yes, the interviewer asked politely to see it and then terminated the interview no matter what he observed. This double check added a few more stores where the poster had been missed on first observation, but the final tally was that only 19 percent of the grocers at the specified addresses were displaying the poster, reinforcing the lessons learned from the earlier audit. One lesson was explicit in the report: "The low rate of display points to the difficulty of getting active voluntary cooperation in such an activity" (p. 2). The methodological lessons for evaluation research, though implicit, again were clear. Simple auditing surveys are essential checks on the actual output of information programs, and low output rather than factors within the audience may explain lack of effects.[6]

The simple, seemingly dull survey among the grocers also contained valuable findings on a general methodological problem. It provided a large-scale test at the individual (not aggregate) level of the validity of respondents' answers. Along with tests from two other OWI surveys, it was the basis for a paper written at the end of the war (Hyman 1944–45), one of the few publications on the problem of validity.

Recall that 72 percent of the 790 grocers who did not appear to be displaying the poster reported that they had not received it, although "it is exceedingly unlikely that the storekeepers really did fail to get the poster. The stores were at the addresses specified on the list, and in each sample district there were some grocers who had received it. The answers may have some psychological reality in the sense that there is a tendency to forget or ignore second-class mail. Nevertheless, a high percentage of the answers almost certainly do not speak the objective reality" (Hyman 1944–45, p. 557). Another check on validity was provided by asking the 221 grocers who reported receiving the poster, "Did you put it up?" The interviewer's second observational check indicated substantial distortion of the facts—42 percent said yes, but the poster was not on display; another 4 percent said yes and the poster was observed; and the remaining 54 percent reported that the poster was not on display (p. 558). Such scholarly by-products from routine auditing added to the gratification from work.

Just as simple audits sometimes produced valuable methodological by-products, surveys involving copy testing sometimes produced findings of substantive or theoretical importance. One series of surveys attempted to clarify a basic problem that nagged OWI and other agencies throughout the war. Would a policy of "realism," presenting the harsh facts of war in posters and other campaign materials, increase public participation in various activities or would it produce such fright, revulsion, and so on, that the campaigns would be ineffective or counterproductive? Would the continuing release of war news in the media finally "surfeit" the public, deter further exposure, and thereby reduce knowledge and involvement? Those wartime surveys, of course, addressed the same problem, the effects of threatening information, which social scientists have studied in the years since then with milder stimuli. We were able to study the problem repeatedly, and in the extreme form of the horrors of war, although we never exploited the opportunity in scientific publications.

One copy test in late 1943 provided dramatic evidence on the effects of truly threatening information ("War Workers' Reactions to Realism in Posters," Special Memorandum no. 89, October 5, 1943). A picture showing dead American paratroopers in Sicily, tentatively planned by the Treasury Department for use as a war bond poster, was shown to 116 workers, one third of them women, in five plants with war contracts in five different industries. All the plants had payroll deduction plans for the purchase of bonds. In addition, intensive interviews were conducted with the managers who selected posters for each plant. When asked, "How does the picture make you feel?" many workers reacted with strong emotions: "Turns me inside out"; "That's terrible, but it carries a serious thought"; "Awful, wouldn't like to look at it all the time." Yet, when asked, "If this picture were made bigger, do you think it would make a good poster for the plant here?" 75 percent answered yes, stressing the shock value of the picture: "Something people should know—a little gruesome, but would wake people up a bit." The 22 percent who answered no gave such comments as, "It's too cruel—people can't stand it." Then, when asked, "Do you think this picture would make workers take the war more seriously or not?" 84 percent said yes, and most of the 8 percent who said no explained that "the picture would not make people take the war more seriously because they already are taking it seriously."

In contrast with these findings, three of the five key persons interviewed, construed both as informed judges of the reactions of the workers to posters and authorities who had the power to reject posters, rejected it, but only one rejected it on the ground of gruesome content. The other two critics gave reasons peculiar to their special conditions. One, with difficult labor relations, said: "Labor may interpret such a picture as an attempt of management to sidestep basic issues—to shame labor into doing something by using such pictures of the war." Thus, the view of management did not undermine the consistent findings among workers that "realism" of an extreme and shocking character would be acceptable to most of them and be likely to have positive rather than negative effects. However, since this program, like others, was dependent on voluntary cooperation, the report recommended that posters of "a wide range of types ought to be circulated. Let management make a selection in light of its own problems."

Surfeit with war news in the media was studied repeatedly as the war progressed. National surveys in October 1942, in February, June, and November 1943, and in April 1944 asked questions about the War Department's release of news about shipping losses and casualties, about the government appeals (for example, to join the services, buy bonds, salvage materials), and about war content in news and dramatic programs. Again, it is easy to recognize that these findings are relevant to theories of the function of mass media, specifically whether they are used by the audience to escape from unpleasant reality. The ironic and compelling conclusion, demonstrated repeatedly, was that under the oppressive conditions of war and the barrage of information about it, a large majority of the public showed no signs of surfeit. The need to escape from reality may have been great, but was overridden by the need to know. Many civilians desired involvement with the war, not detachment from it.

One local study bearing on this question, "Surfeit with War on the Radio" (Memorandum no. 47, January 13, 1943), deserves review because of the appropriateness and complexity of the research design and the corresponding clarity of the findings. By doing the survey in Philadelphia in December 1942, a serious ambiguity in the national studies was resolved. After all, no one knew the precise amount of war information being presented to the nationwide audience, the objective source of the potential problem.[7] There was a great deal, but perhaps not enough to surfeit the public. Fortunately a monitoring study of the total amount and kinds of war messages broadcast over the four Philadelphia stations was in progress in December 1942, and the survey, therefore, was done in that time and place. The monitoring showed "that about one-fifth of all radio time there was given to war-related material."

A poll using mainly closed questions, as well as a probe and a checklist question, was conducted among a sample of about 500 residents. Intensive interviews involving persistent probing of 45 residents provided supplementary and more penetrating tests of surfeit. Clearly, by December 1942 the Surveys Division could no longer be labeled or castigated as the Polling Division and was seeking an efficient and optimal combination of polls and intensive surveys.

The consistent evidence from the poll was that only a minority was surfeited. On the direct, general question as to whether there was too much or not enough about the war in radio programs and announcements these days, 15 percent said "too much," which was counterbalanced by the 12 percent who said "not enough" (62 percent said "about the right amount"). However, when pressed with a checklist of six specific types of broadcasts, an additional 20 percent reported that there was too much of one or another particular type of war broadcast, although they had not objected to the overall level on the earlier general question. In totality, the poll yielded a maximum estimate of 35 percent of the public showing some kind and degree of surfeit. In the intensive interviews, "surfeit is more frequent . . . perhaps because more probing is bound to yield greater returns on the question of being 'fed up.' " Those interviews revealed 18 percent surfeited generally and another 27 percent objecting to a particular type of war broadcast, for a maximum estimate of 45 percent showing some kind and degree of surfeit. The most accurate figure probably was between the bounds established by the two methods of inquiry. Thus a substantial proportion, but still a minority, of Philadelphians was surfeited. The majority was not. Indeed, a considerable number wanted *more* war broadcasts.

What accounted for the differential reactions to the very same stimuli? The intensive interviews yielded qualitative evidence. The analysis of the poll provided quantitative evidence and quickly eliminated the possibility that the minority was not genuinely surfeited. The design of the poll had taken into account the idea that

> people who would complain about the amount of war broadcasting are people who are consistent grouches and would say there is too much of anything that might be suggested to them. To check on that point, a seemingly irrelevant question was asked, "How about the amount of popular music on the radio? so far as your listening is concerned, is there too much—or not enough?" The answers on this catch question show that the . . . surfeit group is slightly more inclined than others to say there is *not enough* popular music on the radio. Their reaction to this different kind of offering indicates that they do not snatch at every opportunity to complain of "too much." [p. 15]

The design had included questions on other media, and the analysis indicated that the surfeit with war content was generalized to newspapers and movies as well as radio. Whatever the medium, the content was simply too nerve-wracking for some, and the intensive interviews provided vivid portraits of such individuals. "A young housewife who listens to the radio about four hours a day says she listened more last year because there was more music. 'No one likes the war. You want to know what's happening, yet it's heartbreaking to listen,' she says, even before she is asked the question about too much or not enough war broadcasting" (p. 7). An older woman describes her reaction to war movies and its source: "Mrs. Miniver was a good picture but it scares you and makes you feel bad. I can't stand seeing the Gestapo in the movies; the way they treat people is awful. They should show more of the funny things—not so much of the sad things. I like the news pictures but not the stories with the fights in them. I think maybe my son is in one of them sometimes and that makes me feel sad" (p. 14).

Individual differences in sensitivity to the horrors of war helped to explain why some members of the audience became surfeited, but it does not follow that the nonsurfeited majority were all tough and callous people. There were sensitive individuals who, unlike their surfeited counterparts, were fortified by a strong identification with the war. Many war workers were shocked by the poster of dead paratroopers, but nevertheless wanted it to be displayed. So, too, many members of the radio audience in Philadelphia were shocked by particular types of war broadcasts, but they felt highly involved, wanted to know what was happening, and had confidence in our allies, in our officials, and in the way the war was going. Their answers to questions on such basic attitudes, drawn from scales developed empirically by the Division to track such variables over time, correlated with their answers on surfeit.[8]

One information campaign which the Division studied repeatedly illustrates the way the surveys sometimes were imbedded in complex experimental designs and produced valuable methodological by-products as well as practical results testing and guiding the campaigns. The "Security of War Information" campaign warned people against the dangers of loose talk, of innocently telling others bits of apparently harmless information about troop movements, ship sailings, war production, and so on, that might be harmful to the war effort when pieced together by enemy intelligence agents. The message was conveyed through posters, broadcasts, newspaper articles, and pamphlets produced by OWI for an interagency committee representing the Army, Navy, FBI, Office of Civilian Defense, and War Production Board. That campaign produced such memorable slogans as "Zip your lip," "A slip of the lip sinks ships," "A careless word may lose a life," "Somebody talked"—in one instance on a poster of a dead marine. Understandably, the gravity of the problem made the surveys interesting for the staff, and the complexity and methodological by-products intensified our interest.

The effectiveness of the pamphlet "A Personal Message" was tested by surveys arranged in an experimental design conducted in two small comparable cities about fifty miles apart in upper New York State ("The Security Pamphlet 'A Personal Message': A Test of Its Effectiveness and Distribution," Memorandum no. 61, July 17, 1943). The pamphlet cautioned against the dangers of talking about what one has personally seen or heard, but stressed the subtle distinction that it is safe to talk about what was in the papers or on the radio. The pamphlet had been distributed in Hornell, the experimental city, but not in Corning, the control city. (Both cities had been exposed to other material used in the larger campaign.) A few weeks after the distribution, surveys were conducted on samples of about 600 adults per city. However, the samples were screened and restricted to those with relatives in the armed services, such individuals being likely to learn military information from letters and visits and constituting the target group at whom the pamphlet was aimed.

One unusual feature of the design must be noted. In the control city, Corning, every sixth respondent was given the pamphlet, asked to read it, and interviewed the following day. This group was artificially exposed to the pamphlet and might be regarded as serving only to copy test the contents. Or one might conceive of the control city as containing within itself a complete, true experiment, those artificially exposed serving as an experimental group to be compared with the equivalent control group in the same city who had been denied exposure to the pamphlet. However, the artificially exposed in Corning may also be compared with the naturally exposed group in the experimental city, Hornell, about one in six also, who in the ordinary course of the distribution came across the pamphlet and read it of their own volition. Comparisons among the four groups created by the unusual design—the naturally exposed, artificially exposed, those in the experimental city who had remained nonexposed although the pamphlet had been circulating, and the nonexposed in the control city—yielded highly informative findings on the effectiveness of the pamphlet.

The questionnaire used both closed and open-ended questions and covered exposure to the campaign in other media, attitudes about security, problems, and knowledge of the kind of information that was safe or dangerous to pass along. The ability to make subtle distinctions was tested by a battery of vignettes, stories describing items of military information varying in significance labeled as reported by the media or only by another person. Of the many findings, I present only a few to illustrate the scientific by-products of this complex survey.

On a series of tests in the experimental city, Hornell, those who had been naturally exposed to the pamphlet were consistently and considerably more knowledgeable about security problems than their neighbors who had not seen the pamphlet. Thus, the pamphlet seemed to be effective. However, a critic might well reject the conclusion on good grounds. If those who were more concerned about security problems and knowledgeable to start with selectively exposed themselves to the pamphlet, it would explain away the apparent effectiveness of the pamphlet. And under voluntary conditions, such selectivity has become an accepted fact in communication research.

Various auxiliary findings, nevertheless, supported the conclusion of effectiveness. Remember that the entire sample was selective, screened down to those with relatives in the armed forces. Therefore, the nonexposed in Hornell, like the naturally exposed, would be interested in security of information for the welfare of their relatives. Moreover, both groups were found to be equal in education, a major determinant of reading generally and shown in the analysis to be a major correlate of knowledge about security problems. In addition, the distribution of the pamphlet in Hornell, as in many other studies of OWI campaigns, was found to be seriously inadequate—the likely explanation, rather than selectivity, of why so few people had been naturally exposed.[9] Finally, the analysis documented that the experimental and control groups in Hornell had been equally exposed to the security campaign in other media, suggesting that those who had read the pamphlet were not especially predisposed toward such information.

If, despite all this evidence to the contrary, a critic had stood his ground, he surely could not have withstood the evidence obtained from the unusual design in Corning by artificially exposing a randomly sampled subgroup to the pamphlet. That group was found to be much more knowledgeable than their nonexposed neighbors in Corning and as knowledgeable as those naturally exposed in Hornell. Since there was no difference between those exposed at random and those who had voluntarily exposed themselves, it is hard to assert that the latter group was selectively predisposed toward knowledge.[10]

One methodological by-product of this survey shows the attention that the NORC and OWI staff gave to subtle features of the interviewing situation, and the way that practical wartime surveys ultimately benefited scholarship. Two questions had been asked to measure respondents' realization that they and their neighbors might be carriers of strategic information, and therefore extra caution ought to be exercised. It was hoped that the pamphlet would increase such beliefs as well as knowledge of other aspects of the security problem. The staff felt that the two questions as written were useful and good measures, but that their validity might be impaired when asked by nonlocal or stranger-interviewers rather than local interviewers familiar to the other residents of such small cities.

Although systematic evidence on the effect of the interviewer's residence was not then available, it seemed likely in normal times that the effect would be negligible or that a stranger would have the advantage. Because he is talking to an outsider—a temporary visitor—the respondent feels that his answers will not be broadcast all over town and that he will not have an embarrassing encounter with the interviewer in the future. Thus he can be candid. But 1943 was far from normal times. There was a spy scare. Any stranger might be a suspicious character, perhaps an intelligence agent masquerading as an interviewer and seeking out respondents who admit knowing military secrets.

The comparison of the answers given to a crew of five local, widely acquainted interviewers and to a crew of five nonlocal interviewers was the evidence needed but lacking in the literature. Exposure to the pamphlet was controlled in the comparisons since it presumably increased awareness of being privy to valuable information. The interviewer's strangeness did not affect answers to the other innocuous questions, but it did reduce admissions on the two questions by a moderate amount. Although this methodological finding had an immediate value in the analysis of the survey, its scholarly value remained dormant for eleven years. Then, the publication of the NORC peacetime studies on interviewer effects included a brief review of the 1943 findings (Hyman et al. 1954, pp. 168–169). Unfortunately, the OWI staff, as previously noted, did not disseminate the scientific by-products of the wartime surveys. The unpublished experiment cited in chapter 1 on effects of identifying interviewers as employees of government rather than of NORC and a third study to be cited indicate the staff's persistent attention to methodological problems but their chronic failure to disseminate the scientific by-products through scholarly publications.

Studies in Race Relations

Before November 1942, the Division operated under triple constraints: the use of methods fitted to its title as the Polling Division, the very small staff, and the special research agenda suitable for the domestic branch of OWI—not counting the bureaucratic hurdles that always had to be surmounted. Yet—at least part of the time—the staff must have defined the term "polling" loosely, practiced it creatively, and worked overtime. And the powers above, wisely, must have set a broad agenda. That judgment is dictated by reading some of the early studies and can be illustrated by the work in one area.

As early as January 1942, the Division began measuring the beliefs and attitudes about the war of the black population and their participation in the war effort through such activities as civilian defense and the purchase of war stamps and bonds. Blacks had new and legitimate grievances—about discrimination in the armed forces and in war industries, about the inadequacy of civilian defense measures

in their neighborhoods—on top of their prior, long-standing grievances about inequality, and such grievances became all the more
salient during a war fought for freedom. In an address in 1942, Adam
Clayton Powell asserted that "the Negro people are not wholly sold
on this war, even since Pearl Harbor" (Lincoln University Conference
on the Status of the Negro in a Fighting Democracy, May 8, 1942).
The truth of the assertion was already being checked by analyses the
Division had made of two omnibus nationwide surveys—the first
conducted between December 26, 1941, and January 7, 1942, and the
second between January 29 and February 12, 1942—which covered a
range of beliefs and attitudes about the war and types of participation
mainly with closed or polling questions ("Negro Attitudes Toward
Certain War-Connected Problems: A Comparison of Negro and
White Reactions on Economic and Educational Levels," Report no.
8, March 9, 1942).

To reduce misinterpretation of the findings, the answers of whites
and blacks on every item were compared with controls on education
and economic level. Thus, for example, differences in the purchase
of war stamps and bonds were shown to be essentially class, not
racial, differences. However, other sources of error might have
clouded the findings. The black samples were small (286 and 443),
the method of sampling loosely supervised, and one special feature
of the interviewing situation might have produced substantial measurement error. Two large-scale, identical surveys, therefore, were
conducted—one with a thousand blacks in New York City between
April and May 1942 and the other with a thousand blacks in Memphis, Tennessee, between May and June 1942 ("The Negro Looks at
the War," Report no. 21 n.d.; "Memphis Negroes and the War,"
Report no. 26, June 23, 1942). Clearly, the two studies were intended
to reveal differences between the South and the North, but the introduction has the disclaimer: "In referring to 'regional differences' between Memphis and New York, there is no intent to imply that either
city is representative of its own region" (Report no. 26, p. ii).

The notable methodological feature of the surveys were the experiments on interviewer effects. Half of the respondents were questioned "by Negro interviewers, half by White . . . both White and
Colored interviewers were assigned to the same sections of the city;
the former instructed to interview on the odd-numbered side of a
street, and the latter on the even-numbered side" (Report no. 26,
p. i). Especially noteworthy is the attention the analysts gave to qualitative as well as quantitative evidence on interviewer effects. "Each
Memphis interview required almost twice as much time because interviewers had constantly to reassure respondents that their names

were not being recorded and that *no one in Memphis would see the results of the survey.* It is possible, therefore, that differences between New York and Memphis responses reflect not only regional differences in attitudes toward the problems discussed but also regional differences in attitudes toward the questioning situation in general" (Report no. 26, pp. i–ii).[11] The original report summarized the quantitative findings.

> Negroes in Memphis gave such dissimilar answers to White and Colored interviewers on questions vital to an analysis of their war morale that it is virtually impossible to consider the two sets of answers in the same frame of reference. Although it would be impossible to say with certainty that the responses to White questioners were completely false or inhibited, and those to Negroes reflections of true attitudes, it is probably safe to assume a greater degree of reliability in the answers given by Negroes to members of their own race. Certainly so many instances of apparent toadying to white prejudice occurred as to make dependence on the Negro-White [interviewer] findings hazardous in the extreme. [p. iii]

This summary focused on the quality of the survey data, but we should not ignore what is implied about the quality of life for blacks in Memphis in 1942. So, too, the detailed findings on each question obtained by black versus white interviewers in New York and Memphis provided not only methodological information on interviewer effects, but also substantive information on attitudes of blacks toward the war and implicit knowledge of the ways blacks and whites interacted in the North and the South in 1942. Only a few of the findings from the twenty-one questions examined are needed to illustrate the rich information in the two surveys. On the question of whether the Army was "fair or unfair to Negroes," in Memphis, 69 percent said "fair" to white interviewers but only 40 percent to black interviewers. The respective figures in New York were 35 and 31 percent. Even on apparently innocuous factual questions, there were interviewer effects in Memphis. "Some Negroes reported that their White employers had forbidden them to read the Negro press. Thus it is understandable that to White interviewers, 51% said they read no Negro newspapers; in the Negro-Negro [interviewer] sample 35% said they read none" (p. 25).

This valuable large-scale experiment in two cities, like the other experiments on interviewer effect, remained buried for twelve years, until the NORC studies of interviewer effect were published. Then the detailed results on the twenty-one questions were presented and summarized. In Memphis, "Negroes were more reluctant to express to the white interviewers their resentments over discrimination by employers or labor unions, in the army, and in public places, to express any sort of belief in the good intentions or even possibility of victory of Japan or Germany, to reveal to white interviewers sympathy for the CIO. . . . Even on some of the factual questions such as auto ownership . . . apparently some Negroes reported differently to white interviewers than to Negro interviewers." (Ownership was less frequently reported to white interviewers.) When the two cities were compared, there were "eighteen questions on which the standardized differences are higher in Memphis than in New York and only two for which the differences were lower" (Hyman et al. 1954, pp. 159, 170). In New York, nevertheless, on eleven questions interviewer effects were significant.

In July and again in November 1942, the Division continued to monitor the morale of blacks by occasional polling questions asked in national surveys as to whether "Negroes" were being treated fairly and whether "most Negroes" were satisfied or not. I shall not review these incidental findings except to note that even so few such questions when asked in a nationwide survey of both whites and blacks revealed an important aspect of the problem of race relations and remind us of a neglected and fruitful survey design. The ignorance and insensitivity of whites in general and of particular white subgroups (for example, southern whites, uneducated whites) about the feelings of blacks was documented. Thus, although the large majority of blacks answered that "most Negroes were dissatisfied," only a minority of all whites gave that answer. Recognition of the dissatisfaction blacks felt was least characteristic of southern and less-educated whites ("Public Sentiment Toward Negroes," Special Memorandum no. 6, November 25, 1942). For brevity, I shall omit further reference to such continuing surveys and turn to one last and novel type of research on race relations by the Division.

In the summer of 1943, tensions between blacks and whites in Detroit had reached an explosive point for a variety of reasons. Opportunities in war industry had brought an influx of southern whites carrying their traditional views of race relations and an influx of southern blacks living in overcrowded ghettoes under slum conditions. Small fundamentalist groups among the whites preached bigotry and white supremacy, as did large organizations under such gifted demagogues as Father Coughlin, Pastor J. Frank Norris, and Gerald L. K. Smith. The war had created new grievances on top of old ones among blacks and also heightened their sense of injustice, and militant black organizations had further intensified those feelings.

Sunday night, June 20, an incident occurred in the crowd of pedestrians on the Belle Isle Bridge. The false rumors spreading through the city—whites had thrown a black baby off the bridge, blacks had thrown a white baby off the bridge, blacks had attacked a white woman—triggered a race riot. Early Monday morning, groups of whites in downtown Detroit assaulted and beat individual blacks, the ratio in these clashes often running 100 or more whites to one black. Black crowds destroyed and looted all the small white shops in and around the largest black ghetto. At 11 P.M. on Monday, the President sent troops into Detroit at the request of the governor, and order began to be restored under martial law. By Wednesday, when the count was complete, 25 blacks had been killed, 17 of them by the police, and 9 whites, none of them by the police. Those facts led Justice Thurgood Marshall, then counsel for the NAACP, to state that the "record . . . reads like the story of the Nazi Gestapo."

During Wednesday and Thursday, June 23–24, the Division's team of nine black and white interviewers completed 200 informal, intensive interviews with blacks and whites, including participants, eyewitnesses, and about thirty local leaders and expert informants. On June 30 the Division issued a classified, qualitative report analyzing the causes of the riot, factors in riot management that calmed or aggravated it, and the likelihood of recurrences in Detroit and similar occurrences in other cities, and making recommendations for information and action. The report was quickly distributed within OWI and to other government agencies. ("Opinions in Detroit Thirty-Six Hours After the Race Riots," Special Memorandum no. 64, June, 30, 1943).

The study was not called a survey. All the normal safeguards of sampling, standardized questions, coding and counting, and quantitative analysis were willingly sacrificed to capture the evidence while it was still vivid in the minds of observers and participants, to obtain the intelligence as quickly as possible that might reduce the danger in Detroit and avert it elsewhere. It was an example, twenty years ahead of the practice, of what came to be called "firehouse research."[12] Indeed, Detroit was on fire, and the Division was part of the fire brigade. However, the inherent limitations of our firehouse research were minimized by including detailed protocols from many interviews in the report, and the report could be buttressed by large-scale quantitative evidence from the recent surveys on race relations.

Six weeks after the Detroit riot, again on a summer Sunday night, August 1, a riot erupted in Harlem which lasted through Monday night when the 6,000 police on duty and the 8,000 National Guards-men in reserve were able to restore order. By Tuesday morning, the count revealed 5 blacks dead, 543 injured, and property damage estimated at $5 million. Again the Division quickly mobilized a small team for firehouse research. Kenneth Clark, the black social psychologist, and Hylan Lewis, the black sociologist, were secured from the Research Division of OWI, and I functioned as the white member of the team. On Wednesday and Thursday, they conducted informal interviews with blacks and listened in on conversations in poolrooms, bars, stores, and so on, while I interviewed and observed white storekeepers, white policemen, and other whites around Harlem. Although no standardized list of questions was used, we had agreed to cover a common core of items in whatever fashion seemed best suited to the situation. By August 6, we had rendered a brief qualitative report which presumably was sent to the responsible official in the White House.

Recruitment, Morale, and Conduct of Workers in War Industry

One last program of research will illustrate the quality of the work produced by the Division, distinctive features of the Division's surveys, and some methodological and substantive contributions that have remained buried in these unpublished studies. This wartime program was the forerunner of a major survey program on peacetime industry, begun after the war at the Survey Research Center under Katz's direction.

Recruitment   With millions of physically fit men drawn into military service in World War II, the critical needs of war industry could be met only by recruiting those who were physically fit for work but who had never been in or had left the labor force, notably housewives, or those men and women who were currently working in nonessential occupations. The so-called manpower problem was largely a womanpower problem, it being estimated in May 1943 that 1,900,000 women had to be recruited. And since there was no draft of labor during the war, the recruitment depended on voluntary action to be encouraged by an information program describing the urgent need, and by reducing the sources of resistance that might be present. The Division's surveys guided the information program and analyzed the resistances and their sources.

Initially, short batteries of closed questions and probes were used in nationwide surveys of women to establish whether their shortage in war work reflected simply ignorance of the acute need and the opportunities awaiting them. If so, the remedy would seem to be a simple information program. Indeed, surveys in November 1942 and May and October 1943 provided some evidence to support such a formulation. For example, in November 1942, although the majority of women believed that there was a "need for married women without children to work in war industries," only 15 percent believed the need was severe enough for "married women with children" to do such work.

However, there was also evidence suggesting the problem would not be solved by simple information. In November 1942, among unemployed women (who were the great majority of the nationwide sample), three quarters answered that they could "help most to win the war by continuing to do what you're doing now." In October 1943, 73 percent of unemployed women answered that they would not "be willing to take a full-time war job," most giving as their main reason that they were needed at home. Even among those who expressed willingness, the most common reason why they had not yet taken full-time work was that they were needed at home. A substantial number said they were physically not able to do such work, but few mentioned opposition from their husbands or rejection or indifference from employers.

Given such promising, but tentative, findings, the Division conducted a survey in three cities in May and June 1943 to explore thoroughly resistances to taking war work and their sources. The methodology of this survey has special interest for survey researchers. However, its comprehensive substantive findings and suggestive findings of the nationwide surveys—none of which was published—should interest sociologists, economists, historians, and specialists in women's studies for the light they shed on the entry of women into the labor force.[13] There is no doubt that the rate of working for married women rose dramatically during the war and continued thereafter.[14] However, the prevailing images—that when the war created new opportunities for women and legitimated their new role as patriotic workers, the multitude of mothers and other married women felt liberated and rushed to take the jobs—is contradicted by the survey. That fabulous wartime character Rosie the Riveter did appear, but Susie the Homemaker remained on the scene, and for good reasons documented by the survey. The folklore oversimplifies the facts.

The unusual design of the study deserves a brief summary. Limiting it to three cities in New England located near each other made the elaborate survey feasible, ensured close supervision and coordination of the field work, and permitted large numbers to be interviewed in each place whose attitudes and actions could then be examined in the context of the local conditions. After all, many workers—especially married women with families—are affected by the local labor market, not by a distant labor market or a nationwide labor market. The three cities were chosen on the basis of official figures to represent contrasted conditions: Pittsfield, with the least shortage of workers; Hartford, with the worst shortage; and New Bedford, in between but also far short of workers for war industry.

In each city a probability sample of households was drawn and about 800 adults, both men and women whether employed or not, were interviewed with a lengthy questionnaire containing many open-ended probes following up on closed questions. Those working in nonessential occupations were also a target group for recruitment into war industry and important to study. Those already in war work were interviewed with a somewhat different questionnaire, which permitted the study of their morale, important to war production, as well as factors that differentiated those resistant and responsive to recruitment. By interviewing at night and on weekends, those working on various shifts could be reached. Intensive interviews with key informants yielded a background report on the plant and community conditions in each city which then served as the context to explain patterns among respondents.

Only a few of the substantive findings will be presented. The substantial majority of those not in "essential" war jobs in the three cities were housewives distributed over a wide age range, but almost a third did not have children under age 14. By contrast, the tiny minority of unemployed men were over age 65, not good prospects for recruitment. Knowledge of the great need for war workers lagged far behind the facts. In the tightest city, Hartford, 29 percent of the sample answered yes—"war industries around here need workers so much that they have to take married women with children." In New Bedford, where the need was severe but not so great as in Hartford, 39 percent said yes. When the respondents were given a list of fourteen occupations, seven of which were nonessential to the war effort, they consistently overrated their importance—31 percent, for example, labeling "barbers" essential to the war effort. These and some other findings suggested that recruitment might be facilitated to some extent by information. However, the survey soon revealed more intractable sources of the problem.

Among those not in war work, about 85 percent in each city either had never thought of taking a war job or had thought about it but not actually applied. The main reason women gave was that they could not leave their children. When the substantial number who mentioned other home responsibilities is added, the two reasons relating to the role of homemaker accounted for the inaction of the majority. Since about half of these women did have small children, expanded daycare facilities, inadequate at the time, might seem to have been a solution, and federal funds were available under the Lanham Act to underwrite such facilities. However, the background interviews were invaluable in showing how thorny the problem really was. For example, in New Bedford religious opposition to daycare under secular control had prevented the use of federal funds. The nursery fees, even when subsidized, for a woman with several children did not make it worthwhile to work for the low starting wages that prevailed in local war industry. The rigid pattern of social distance between ethnic groups in the city—English, French, Portuguese, Bravos (a group of mixed ethnicity originally from the Canary Islands), and American blacks—made mothers resistant to having children cared for in a multiethnic nursery.

The nature of the local war work deterred about a third of those who might potentially have been recruited. The noise, the heat, the smell, the heavy labor, the health and safety hazards—real features of the factory work but often magnified by rumors and in sharp contrast to the pleasant and "classy" aura of white collar work at the insurance companies of Hartford—were legitimate and formidable obstacles to even a patriotic housewife.

A special battery of questions revealed major obstacles to the recruitment of employed women and men from nonessential occupations into war work. Only a small minority felt that their own businesses could function in their absence or be restored after the war, or that they could get back their former jobs. The history of severe unemployment in the textile industry of New Bedford made that population particularly sensitive to the postwar insecurity a war worker might have to face, and the security of employment in the insurance companies in Hartford made those workers resistant to recruitment.

These and other firmly grounded resistances suggested that further efforts at recruitment would produce only a small yield in the three cities. Ironically, the survey among those who had already entered war work revealed high morale, the main gratifications being financial and patriotic. Over 80 percent said that they were glad they had made the shift. This happy situation was known to their acquaintances not in war work. When asked, "Would you say that people you know who have taken war jobs are glad they made the change?" about two thirds answered yes. If, despite their perception of the happiness war work brought to others, they nevertheless were not interested, that surely emphasizes the strength of their resistances—based, as the other evidence shows, on their family ties and special situations.

The scientific by-products of this survey—its unusual design and its substantive findings—were almost completely neglected in scholarly publications. One brief methodological paper illustrated the use of intensive interviewing of informants in each sample point in this and other Division surveys to create contexts for interpreting the attitudes of respondents (Hyman 1945). The morale of war workers, peripheral in this survey, became central in other Division surveys in the program. The strangely mixed origin of one of those surveys has larger implications for this history, and I turn to it.

Morale   Early in the war, OWI had begun to study the morale of workers as a major factor reducing or increasing production in war industries. One problem was to recruit workers into such rapidly expanding industries; another was to motivate them. As early as May 1942, Program Surveys, under contract with OWI (or its predecessor, the Office of Facts and Figures), had conducted informal interviewing or "scouting" to explore worker morale in the shipbuilding industry, essential to "build a bridge of ships to span the oceans" in order to supply our allies and our own forces ("Some Labor-Management Problems Within the Shipbuilding Industry," Special Report no. 11, May 29, 1942, Division of Surveys, Office of Facts and Figures).

That different shipyards varied greatly in the speed with which they did the very same task with the same materials—producing the "Liberty Ship," a mass-produced, 10,000-ton freighter—pointed to the morale of workers as an explanation. One shipyard in Portland, Maine, took three times as long as another yard in the same city, both confronting the same hazards of weather and drawing on the same local labor supply, and four times as long as another East Coast shipyard. Other factors—the type of plant, the procurement of raw materials, the know-how of management—also were important, but the morale of the workers surely seemed a significant cause, if not the major cause, of the differences in productivity. That hypothesis was strengthened by the variation between yards in quit-rates and man-hours lost. Only a little scouting was needed to reveal the shabby conditions under which the workers lived. In Portland, 3,000 workers were living in trailer camps and summer cottages—poor shelter against the severe Maine winter, and about a third of the workers were commuting more than sixty miles. But the differences quickly observed in the morale of workers living under the same desperate community conditions suggested that in-plant factors and the reaction to circumstances, rather than the sheer objective circumstances themselves, were important.

A more systematic study of the morale of shipyard workers, its determinants and consequences for productivity, seemed in order. Program Surveys, under its contract with OWI, designed an intensive survey, conducting open-ended interviews in their homes with a probability sample of 553 male workers drawn from the rolls of five shipyards (excluding clerical, supervisory, and custodial employees) at the end of October 1942. In addition, the interviewers completed background reports on each community and shipyard based on observations, documents, and intensive interviews with key informants representing the management, community officials, and labor. The five shipyards were chosen for their contrasts in productivity, geographical location, and community conditions, but two adjacent to each other in Portland were included to create an almost ideal field experiment. Community conditions, weather (critical in the outdoor work involved in shipbuilding), local labor supply, size of work force, working hours, and the demands of the task were thus held constant, and the effect of other in-plant factors could be isolated. Indeed, the two yards had even come under the same ownership just prior to the study, which also became a constant in the design, although they remained under separate management staffs.

The field work was completed on November 7, 1942, just when the contract with Program Surveys was being terminated. In midstream, responsibility was transferred to Wilson's Surveys Division, where Katz and I took over the analysis, wrote several preliminary reports, and a final report issued two months later ("Worker Morale in Five Shipyards," Surveys Division, Memorandum no. 44, January 18, 1943). Since the major substantive findings of the survey have been published (Katz and Hyman 1947), I shall only mention that in-plant factors were the primary determinants of worker morale, that the influence of a specific factor—for example, health and safety conditions—depended on the context of other factors, that morale was related to inclination to quit and to productivity, and that productivity in turn—given the identification of the workers with the war effort—had a feedback effect on morale.

The strange history, as well as the findings, of the survey should be pondered. That the study was transplanted from Program Surveys, which was responsible for the design and the field work, to the Surveys Division, which was responsible for the analysis and reports, and was successfully completed without delay shows that there was no chasm between the two agencies that could not be bridged. To be sure, Katz and I also had been transplanted from Program Surveys and, although we had no part in the earlier planning, could serve as the human bridge to transport the study from one agency to the other. But equally important was Wilson's attitude as the new host receiving the study. He was receptive to and supportive of the methods employed. And this was no isolated instance in which the special circumstances compelled his hospitality. The Philadelphia survey of surfeit, described earlier, the study of resistances to war work, and another survey in the program on war industry now to be reviewed—these and others show the frequent use of probability sampling, open-ended intensive interviewing of respondents and/or informants, and complex research designs in the Division's surveys.

Conduct of Workers   One problem for war industries was to recruit workers, a second was to maintain their morale, and a third, related to their morale, was to keep them working—to reduce outright quitting and absence from work. By 1943, absence from war work had become transformed by partisans into an "ism," prejudged as extreme in magnitude, willful in character, and a new evil to be punished. The elementary question of its real magnitude, let alone questions about the causes and remedies of "absenteeism," was rarely asked by politicians or aroused members of the public.

Fortunately, the OWI and other agencies asked the Division to conduct a survey on the causes and methods of treating absenteeism, which Katz and I designed, supervised, and analyzed in early 1943. Eighteen plants were selected to represent good and bad community conditions for workers in six different war industries. As in the shipbuilding study, two aircraft companies in the same community were included, thus controlling living conditions and the workers' task and providing an experimental test of the effect of other in-plant factors on absenteeism. A probability sample of 100 workers was drawn in each plant. Workers were interviewed in their homes, the lengthy questionnaire containing closed questions and open-ended probes covering personal, family, and occupational background; satisfaction with various working conditions; and satisfaction with living conditions. An objective measure of each worker's absences during the previous three months was obtained from plant records and used in the analysis to evaluate the effects of such hypothesized causes of absenteeism as the worker's morale and personal situation at home, in the plant, and in the community. Although the sample of plants had not been selected with reference to their absenteeism rates, the rate over the 1,800 workers—6–7 percent—coincided with the official March 1943 figure of 6.6 percent computed by the Department of

Labor on the basis of 3,000 war plants employing more than 3 million workers. That figure, incidentally, was modest in magnitude, not excessive for industry in general in winter months when illness is likely, and put the "problem" in its proper perspective.

Comparable background reports on community and plant conditions that might have "global" effects on the absenteeism of the sample of workers in each of the eighteen plants were prepared by all the field supervisors on the basis of observation, documentary information, and intensive interviewing of key informants: plant doctors, personnel officers, community leaders, and so on. A major item covered was the type of plant program, if any, to reduce absenteeism, these programs being classified as preventive, educational, or punitive. These factors were used in the analysis either as independent variables that might directly affect the plant absenteeism rates or as contexts that might modify the effect of individual variables on absenteeism.

In the large-scale survey of the 1,800 workers, the causes and remedies for absenteeism thus were determined inferentially, quantitatively, by statistical analysis of the relation between the absenteeism records of the workers and the large array of independent variables that might have direct effects—discretely or in combination—or contextual effects. However, a small-scale, intensive survey of 160 workers recently absent in two of the plants was also used to explore directly the causes of absenteeism and to suggest possible remedies.

The lengthy questionnaire for this study was open-ended except for the elaborate battery on personal characteristics, and the intent was disguised. The respondents were told that the survey dealt with workers' attitudes toward living and working conditions and were not identified as known absentees. After a series of rapport-building general questions and after a question on the absenteeism of other workers, the respondent was asked casually, "Do you happen to have taken any time off recently?" If the answer was yes, a complete case study of the last absence was obtained: the primary and subsidiary reasons, the circumstances, the feelings about the absence, and so on.

In the large-scale survey, a similar question was casually introduced after a question on the absenteeism of other workers: "How about yourself—have you stayed away from the job any time in the last couple of months?" Those who answered yes were probed as to the reasons. Here, too, the respondents were not aware that the survey was focused on absenteeism. (Indeed, many had not been absent at all in recent months, and any such introduction would have been inappropriate.) Since the worker's record of recent absences was known in both the large- and small-scale surveys, the absenteeism study, like the war bond redemption survey and the grocery storekeeper audit, provided rare evidence on the validity of respondents' answers, and those three sources were used in the methodological paper cited earlier (Hyman 1944–45).

The absenteeism study, however, had a distinctive and valuable feature. The large-scale and small-scale surveys provided a comparative test of the validity of reports obtained by the two contrasted procedures: completely open-ended intensive interviewing versus interviewing with a well-designed battery of closed questions and probes. That, it should be stressed, is quite different from a test of the merits of a single question, closed or open-ended. As the discussion in the previous chapter showed, this published by-product of the study was unique at the time.[15] Moreover, the test of the two methods fortunately was conducted under well-controlled, close to completely comparable conditions. In the intensive survey, only 6 workers, or 4 percent, failed to report their recent absences. In the same two plants, among the 200 workers interviewed with closed questions, 134 had been absent at some time within the last three months, 45 of whom said they had not been absent. Even when expressed as a percentage of the entire 200, the invalidity characterized 22.5 percent—a much higher figure.[16]

The two surveys constituting the absenteeism study produced too many findings to be easily summarized, and since a long scholarly paper contains many of the findings (Katz and Hyman 1947) I shall mention only highlights. The main cause of absence (substantiated by hard evidence) was illness or accident. Low morale produced by dissatisfaction with in-plant conditions did contribute to absenteeism. Poor community conditions and dissatisfaction with them had some, but little, effect unless aggravated by in-plant dissatisfaction. How can the effects of morale be reconciled with the fact that illness was the primary cause of absence? "When morale was low it needed only a minor ailment for the man to stay away. Where morale was high, the man would not let his minor illness take him away" (Katz and Hyman 1947, p. 24). Since illness was the main cause, plants with preventive health programs had the lowest absenteeism rates.

The intensive survey revealed beliefs and feelings about absenteeism. Only a small minority expressed strong concern about their own absence, or believed that their fellow workers and management were concerned. An occasional absence, especially for illness or accident, seemed to them natural and no ground for guilt. Moreover, they believed that absence from the plant was rarer than in fact it was, and thus did not see it as hurting the war effort. Punitive programs in fact did not solve the problem of illness. And given the belief system, punishment was seen as unjustified, often aroused moral indignation, and thus was worse than ineffective. It became counter-productive, as shown by the response to a lurid symbolic punishment invented in one plant:

> It tried the method of "Hitler Checks" enclosed along with the regular pay checks for workers who had missed a certain number of days. About 1,500 such checks were distributed on pay-day and the reaction was prompt and vigorous. A few workers were so enraged that they actually walked out on the company right then and there. Other work-ers kept the wires to the personnel office busy all afternoon and eve-ning pouring out their personal indignation. Still others came to the office with evidence showing they had been in the hospital or had other justifiable reasons for being absent. The company dropped the plan like a hot potato. [p. 29]

Contextual effects were demonstrated repeatedly. A particular vari-able influenced absenteeism only in certain plants where other factors were present as a context. I cite one such finding. Long travel time to work increased absenteeism in only four of the eighteen plants, and these were situations where women worked and husbands and wives were both working. The problems for working women and working couples who had to fulfill other duties before and after work obviously were aggravated by long travel time and, of necessity, they were frequently forced into absences.

The Milieu

The Pace of Work

In reviewing the surveys carried out by the Division, I have touched on some of our working conditions, on the division of labor, and on the formal and informal relations within the Division. These matters deserve more systematic review since they influenced our motiva-tion, training, the quality of the surveys, and the technical innova-tions and scholarly by-products created.

The riot studies were the extreme, but not unique, examples of the fast pace of work in the Division. The sense of urgency was pervasive and the need for speed insistent. In describing "the climate" in which we worked, Julian Woodward, our liaison in Washington, mentioned the "basic difficulty" that

. . . in wartime, policy planning tends to be on a short-time basis. The situation is changing so rapidly that administrators can seldom be concerned with problems that will exist next month or next year; instead they have to spend much of their time dealing with today's and next week's impending decisions, upon which opinion research can only with difficulty be brought to bear. [1944, p. 671]

What he only implied was that a survey dealing with last month's problem also was useless if the report was delivered after the problem had dissipated or the policy had been decided. To be sure, he overstated the point, perhaps because he was most exposed to Washington pressures. Some of the wartime problems were indeed prolonged, requiring continuing long-range programs and policies. The surveys correspondingly did not always have to be quick or the reports instant. Race relations is an excellent illustration. The riots required immediate action and firehouse research, but the war morale and participation of the black population was a matter for continuing concern and a long-range program of surveys.

When speed was essential, there were sometimes undesirable consequences. The sample size, the length of the instrument, and the depth of the analysis might have to be curtailed; care might have to be sacrificed. Yet substantial and sophisticated studies were conducted and carefully analyzed despite the tight time schedules. In the experimentally designed security pamphlet study, the 1,100 interviews in Hornell and Corning were completed on June 15, 1943. The final report, based on the comparisons of the multiple groups in the design and despite the methodological detour into interviewer effects, was ready for distribution on July 17, 1943. In the Memphis study, interviewing of the 998 blacks began on May 28, 1942, and was completed by June 7. The report, containing the methodological comparisons by race of interviewer controlling education of respondent and including the parallel findings from the earlier survey in New York City, was ready for circulation on June 23, 1942.

It could be done, and the explanation is basically simple, though it may elude survey researchers reared in a later, more leisurely era. Under pressure and with strong motivation, the wartime staffs learned to be efficient and skillful, thoughtful without becoming obsessive, speedy but not sloppy. It was wonderful training. There were periods of fatigue and frustration when a deadline prevented the pursuit of an interesting analysis, but there were compensations. The deadlines spared us the pains of interminable conceptualizing and analysis, common afflictions in the later era, and there was an exhilarating sense of accomplishment. The need for speed not only

improved the skills of the staff but also led to innovations in procedure. An innovation to speed up the utilization of findings, for example, can be described by a brief illustration from one of the surveys.

In late 1943, interviews with 5,000 people in a nationwide sample
were completed using a long questionnaire with many open-ended
questions. The innovation, not hard to conceive but not easy to exe-
cute quickly, was to draw a random 30 percent subsample of all
the questionnaires and to code, tabulate, and analyze it first. That
expedited the series of preliminary reports on different aspects of the
problem issued beginning June 21. Thus, action did not have to be
delayed seven weeks until the final report and the statistical appendix
based on the full sample were issued in August ("Public Appreciation
of the Problem of Inflation," Memorandums no. 62 and no. 62A,
August 12 and 19, 1943).

The need for almost instant national findings on great events with
wide repercussions—a battle, a presidential decision—led to another
innovation. That need could not be met by the firehouse research
possible for a localized event such as a riot. Special field teams could
not be mobilized everywhere, all at once. Some method had to be in
place in advance of the need, ready to operate at the signal "go."
An innovation developed and operated by NORC—the telegraphic
survey—solved the problem. Trusted interviewers in all the sample
points had committed themselves to handle small assignments immediately upon receiving telegrams; and since quota sampling was
used, they had in hand preestablished quotas of respondents of various types. The telegram spelled out the questions, usually two to
six, and the precoded answer categories for closed questions. The
interviewer transcribed these onto a cleverly devised skeleton form
which permitted recording each respondent's set of answers (including free answers) and background characteristics, and adding up the
distributions on each poll question. Those were wired back, and
the recording forms were returned immediately by airmail. Aggregate
results and geographical breakdowns on the closed questions were
available within 36–48 hours, and more detailed analyses, based on
the free answers and cross-tabulations, could be produced within a
few days. The findings, though limited, satisfied an urgent need,
which arose often enough that thirty-three such surveys were conducted.

Small Staff and Little Division of Labor

The Division had a small professional staff (a dozen analysts, including those who had come from Program Surveys) organized simply.

The only specialized unit was the field department: the full-time intensive interviewers brought from Program Surveys and Sheatsley and the NORC part-time interviewers who, in effect, served as an integral part of the organization. The analysts or study directors were responsible for everything else from the start to the finish of the survey: preparing the overall research design; choosing the special populations appropriate to the problem under investigation; designing the sampling (except for national and some surveys of the general population of cities, where, as noted, the sampling designs already established by NORC were used); designing the questionnaires and other instruments; building the codes; analyzing the findings; and writing the reports and whatever methodological studies were built into the surveys, since there was no separate methodology section with that specialized function.

Even the simple division of labor between field work and all other work was not rigid. Study directors often did pretesting themselves in the early stages of questionnaire design and prepared instructions for the field work in specialized studies. Study directors occasionally supervised field work for considerable periods. For example, on the study of resistance to working in war industries, I supervised the field team in New Bedford, one of the three cities in the sample, and did the intensive interviewing of informants for the background report on the community and plant conditions. On the study of absenteeism in war industries, Sheatsley joined me in recruiting, training, and supervising the field team in Cleveland during several weeks of winter weather that tried the souls of the interviewers and tested our endurance. And I drew the samples of workers from the rolls of the two plants in the study and collected the background information.

When the need dictated, sometimes we even became field workers. As noted, I had an eye-opening assignment as one of the three interviewer-observers in the Harlem Riot study. In another study to provide quick information on the causes of war bond redemptions for the Treasury Department, to supplement national survey data collected in November 1943, the analysts served as the field team in Wilmington, Delaware. Between December 15 and 17, we interviewed a sample of 243 people drawn from an official list of bond redeemers within the previous two weeks with a short questionnaire on their circumstances, their other savings, the extent and method (for example, payroll deductions) of bond buying, previous redemptions, and the reasons for redemption and produced a brief report five days later ("War Bond Redemptions," Special Memorandum no. 97, December 22, 1943).

Note that this was a probability not a quota sample, and though restricted to one location, the November survey data provided national norms and a point of comparison on some variables in the analysis. Even so small, short, and practical a study yielded a methodological by-product, one of the three tests later used in my paper on the validity of answers (Hyman 1944–45).

The shortage of staff and simple division of labor thus forced many varied duties on the study directors and enriched their training. Firsthand experience in the field was especially valuable training. Study directors, the generals, had seen what the frontline troops really faced on the fields of battle and were less likely to make impossible demands that forced interviewers into errors—or to desertion from duty. To be sure, the Division lost the benefits of an elaborate division of labor and specialization of function among the analysts. Then the distinctive talents of different analysts might have been exploited to the full, and each might have become truly expert and efficient in one special task done repeatedly on many studies. However, since the group was small and informally organized, their pooled abilities were brought to bear on studies. Moreover, through close involvement, the leaders also brought their own substantial and special abilities to bear upon the studies and heightened the efficiency and morale of the staff.

Leadership

Since Elmo Wilson's formal training was in journalism, his professional concern and ability to communicate findings clearly, quickly, and effectively improved the final product the staff produced. As director, he did not oversee work from a lordly height. He developed a general format to make all reports more interesting and understandable and to highlight the important findings and often edited and revised specific reports himself. A research bulletin issued every two weeks described briefly the surveys recently completed and those nearing completion. Preliminary reports, trend reports, special reports, supplementary reports separating difficult statistical material from simpler text so as not to deter some readers, qualitative material illuminating the text, and other journalistic devices all made the surveys more useful.

What Wilson lacked in the way of formal social science training was compensated for by Daniel Katz, who became deputy director and research director. Katz had been the first Ph.D. trained by Floyd Allport, who wrote the first modern text on social psychology (1924) and established at Syracuse University the first doctoral program in the United States in that field. Allport and his students began the systematic investigation and measurement of attitudes and behavior in field settings. Given this background, it is understandable that Katz would take an interest in the emerging field of public opinion research. While teaching at Princeton throughout the 1930s, he made the most of the opportunity presented by a chain of local events which figure large in the history of the field. The town of Princeton became the headquarters of the fledgling Gallup poll in 1935, and the *Public Opinion Quarterly* was founded at the School of Public Affairs at Princeton in 1937, Katz joining its editorial board in 1939. In 1936, Hadley Cantril, a social psychologist, came to Princeton. As a student of Gordon Allport, Floyd's younger brother, and also an authority on attitude research, Cantril, like Katz, had special interest in the emerging field of public opinion research.

Cantril and Gallup developed a close association, which enabled Cantril to begin a program of survey research using as his major vehicle the facilities and data of the Gallup poll. That program became formally organized under the Princeton Office of Public Opinion Research, which Cantril established in 1940 with support from the Rockefeller Foundation, and many of the studies were summarized in *Gauging Public Opinion* (Cantril et al. 1944).

Katz played a major part in implementing the program. Katz also conducted one of the earliest field experiments on interviewer effects, documenting that working class interviewers obtained more radical answers than middle class interviewers from low-income respondents and applied sampling procedures differently (1942). Those findings also were summarized in *Gauging Public Opinion*. Katz, sometimes alone and at other times in collaboration with Cantril, wrote papers on the early election polls, sparing no criticism when it was warranted (Katz and Cantril 1937; Katz 1941, 1944). Thus Katz brought to the Division not only his recent experience at Program Surveys, but also his earlier knowledge of sources of survey error, of the limitations of rudimentary polling, of elaborate methods of analysis, and of a body of theory and findings on attitudes and opinions.

Wilson, like Likert, was a gifted and attractive leader, but the source of their attraction was very different. Likert's magnetism derived from the utopian vision he presented, from the sense he imparted of our great mission in developing a unique and superior survey method. Wilson was a realistic, prudent planner and promoter of survey research who set high, but not unreasonable, goals for the Division. That made him a less exciting but more comforting leader than Likert, since we never confronted surveys beyond our resources or abilities.

Wilson's attractive personality was joined with admirable qualities of character. He was always considerate of the staff and trustworthy in his dealings. Since Katz brought to his role as research director these same virtues plus his rare skill and rich experience, the staff had ideal collective leadership and functioned effectively.

The Death of the Division

As the many examples presented in this chapter indicate, during the years 1942–44 the Division conducted useful surveys carefully, quickly, and economically. So when the Congress eliminated the negligible budget item for our continued operation from the much larger budget for OWI for the fiscal year 1944–45 and the Division met sudden death on July 23, 1944, it came as a great shock to the staff. Program Surveys had suffered a heavy blow in 1942 when OWI terminated its contract, but it had survived. Our fate was worse. We had been liquidated by what seemed a special act of Congress. On that memorable day, after a record-breaking liquid lunch, we packed our slide rules—essential in the precomputer era—and our other belongings and departed, trying to see into our uncertain futures and to understand our strange fate.

Our death had been demanded by the House of Representatives. The saving was so microscopic—less than half of 1 percent of the total OWI budget—that the action seemed to indicate Congress's absolute condemnation of survey methods and public opinion research. There is some evidence to support that interpretation (Converse 1984, p. 274; Gosnell and David 1949, pp. 567–569).

The Division might have been scattered to the winds; individual staff members, embittered by what seemed unjust treatment, might have turned to careers other than survey research; the innovative methods and applications of survey research in process of development might have been aborted. Fortunately, almost immediately, like the phoenix rising from the ashes, Wilson was appointed the director of a new Surveys Section in the overseas branch of OWI attached to the Psychological Warfare Division of Supreme Headquarters Allied Expeditionary Force, with headquarters in London. The senior staff came from the Division—Carol Bookman (Kazin), Hazel Gaudet (Erskine), Hans Gottlieb, and John Riley—and was strengthened by two social psychologists, Jerome Bruner (previously with Program Surveys) and Heinz Ansbacher. The difficult and novel assignment Wilson's unit faced was to survey the state of mind of the people in areas already conquered by our troops, and somehow to estimate the state of the enemy's morale in areas not yet occupied.

Katz, Crutchfield, and I did not join Wilson's overseas unit. A few months after the death of the Division, we were invited by Likert to join him overseas for the U.S. Strategic Bombing Survey of Germany. The pace and variety and complexity of our work in the Surveys Division was essential preparation for the new, exceedingly difficult set of surveys we planned, directed, and analyzed: an investigation of the war's impact on German (and later Japanese) civilians. Our earlier surveys, indeed surveys by all governmental research units, were, with one exception, limited to American civilians. The exception was the Research Branch of the War Department, whose surveys were limited to American soldiers. There were, however, striking similarities between our surveys of enemy civilians and the Research Branch's studies of American soldiers. Before examining the Bombing Surveys, we need, therefore, to discuss the surveys done by Stouffer and his colleagues for the War Department.

Notes

1. In the course of frequent reorganization of the wartime agencies, the Division had various names and was located in several larger organizations. First, in October 1941, it was the Polling Division within the Bureau of Intelligence of the Office of Facts and Figures. The OFF and its bureau were absorbed by the Office of War Information in June 1942, and the Division was named for a brief period either the Division of Extensive Surveys or Polling. After November 1942, and the cancellation of the contract with Program Surveys, the Division's official title was and remained the Surveys Division until its demise. When the Bureau of Intelligence was abolished and replaced by the Bureau of Special Services in 1943, the Surveys Division became a part of that new bureau but retained its name and basic functions.

2. This is one of many instances of the way in which small intimate networks formed in the early days of survey research became reinstated again and again, the members helping each other over long periods of time. Although such old-boy networks smack of favoritism and may protect insiders at the expense of outsiders, various desirable effects on the development of survey research should not be ignored. Career advancement of the members meant that valuable experience was not lost to the field, that some reached positions in which they could foster and fund survey research. For example, on his merits but no doubt

helped by his network, Wilson's first position after the war was as director of research for CBS, after which he founded International Research Associates, one of the first agencies to conduct cross-national surveys, with the aid of Roper. My own career provides another illustration. At OWI the close bond I formed with Paul Sheatsley and Clyde Hart, for whose section of the Office of Price Administration I directed various OWI surveys, led me to join them at NORC after the war.

3. Many of the studies summarized later in this chapter show that probability sampling was used frequently in the nonnationwide surveys. Various internal memoranda, not reviewed here, document careful and prolonged examination of possible biases in the nationwide quota samples, the major finding being that better-educated individuals were persistently overrepresented. Various standing committees at OWI and NORC (Sheatsley, Katz, and Hyman; Crutchfield, Katz, and Hyman; Crutchfield, Salstrom, and Hyman) then proposed procedures to improve the sampling, which were tested experimentally. The major change proposed was the assignment of various small areas or segments to restrict the interviewer's choice, a procedure that came to be called in later years "modified probability sampling." In the spring of 1944, this modification was used on a nationwide survey and evaluated by comparisons with previous national surveys using the traditional quota control method and by interviewers' reports on the field problems. The findings were reported by Sheatsley in a memorandum, "Area Control Experiment Tried on Survey T-32" (April 21, 1944). This is only one example of the careful, and critical, cooperative study of sampling methods.

4. However, a careful reader of the literature would have recognized Gaudet's contributions to the field by 1942. She had written with Cantril and Herta Herzog *The Invasion from Mars* (1940), a study by the Office of Radio Research of the panic following Orson Welles's 1938 broadcast of "The War of the Worlds"; papers on radio research (1939, Cantril and Gaudet 1939); and a brief paper with Wilson on mortality in the panel sample (1940). For Gaudet's contributions in later years to the field and to the public good, see the series of obituaries in *Public Opinion Quarterly* (1975).

5. These principles helped me years later when I became deeply involved in teaching and conducting evaluation research at Columbia and the Bureau of Applied Social Research. For a more elaborate review of the need to describe the actual magnitude, and the variability, multiplicity, occasional chaos of large-scale, long-term, and decentralized programs in order to conduct unambiguous and useful evaluation studies, see Hyman and Wright 1967, pp. 744–751.

6. The point is even stronger in light of another finding. Out of 1,187 stores in the original sample, 196 were not in existence at the designated address and the posters sent to those out-of-date addresses obviously were of no use in the campaign. Thus the output of posters that might

ultimately reach the public was diminished immediately by 16 percent, before taking into account the huge diminution of output because of noncooperation of the grocers.

7. In radio and newspaper campaigns as in other sectors, OWI was dependent mainly on voluntary cooperation, on the contributions that the networks and businesses made, and a rough tally of their dollar contribution of space and time was available, but this was far from a precise measure of the amount and kind of war material reaching the public. In 1943–44, the contribution of businesses was estimated at approximately $300 million, whereas the budget allocated by Congress to OWI for domestic informational activities was $2.5 million.

8. Similar statistical findings were obtained in an earlier survey on fatigue with war broadcasts. And in a nationwide survey in April 1944, those who favored a policy of "realism" (showing pictures of dying and suffering soldiers in newspapers and magazines, and reporting stories of Japanese harsh treatment of American prisoners) scored higher on items from the "identification with the war" scale (belief that people in the community have not made enough sacrifices; people are not taking the war seriously enough, participating in war bond and blood donor programs, and so on). See "What the Civilian Thinks" (Memorandum no. 82, July 18, 1944, p. 15). This same report documents a growing trend in the desire for more war news on four surveys spaced between February 1943 and April 1944, the opposite of what one would expect if becoming surfeited had been in process (p. 11).

9. Background study found that about 600 copies of the pamphlet had been sent to the city of about 16,000 population, with an estimated 2,000 families having men in the armed services. Instructions on the distribution of the pamphlets were not specific and depended, as in other campaigns, on volunteers. In Dunkirk, New York, which had been considered as a sample point for the survey, the pamphlets by error were distributed to people without relatives in the armed forces, and that city was eliminated from further consideration.

10. With minor variation, Sheatsley and I applied the basic experimental design in two national surveys that NORC conducted in 1946, and the findings in those instances served for one of the early scholarly papers providing large-scale evidence of selective exposure (Hyman and Sheatsley 1947, pp. 417–418).

11. In evaluating the substantive findings on differences in the morale of Memphis and New York blacks, and the methodological findings on the effect of the interviewer's race within and between cities, the analysts also were careful to control the respondent's education, which might have accounted for some of the city differences in attitude or sensitivity to the race of the interviewer.

12. One might also see the riot studies as the prototype for the "disaster research" developed in the 1950s. It seems more than coincidental that

after NORC's involvement in the wartime riot studies, it established in the 1950s a mobile team that did almost instant studies of communities that had been struck by disasters such as earthquakes, tornadoes, or mine explosions. For an introduction to such studies by NORC and other agencies, see [the *Journal of Social Issues* 1954, 10, no. 3; 26–41.]

13. Some of the findings from the simple, nationwide surveys of women are reported in "Do War Plants Need Married Women?—Consider the Problem" (Special Memorandum no. 54, June 3, 1943) and in "Willingness of Women to Take War Jobs" (Special Memorandum no. 93, November 22, 1943).

14. For a critical review of the evidence and documentation of the trend, see Lebergott 1964, pp. 58–73.

15. That by-product has retained its rarity and value for over forty years. After a careful review of the literature, Schuman and Presser still wrote in 1981: "In sum, the previous evidence on the open-closed controversy after almost 50 years of survey research is meager, usually quite specialized in form or setting, and almost always lacking in validity data" p. 110).

16. Some of the difference may have been caused by the greater demands on memory, since the record of absence in the large-scale survey referred back three months, whereas the intensive survey included only those most recently absent in the plant. That factor was not completely comparable, but the lapse of time in both surveys was small, and the difference trivial. There is, however, one imponderable lack of comparability in the two procedures. In the intensive survey, the interviewers knew that all respondents had been absent and their interviewing may have been more effectively guided, whereas the interviewers in the large-scale survey did not know whether the respondents had in fact been absent or not.

· 3 ·

Stouffer's Surveys:
Research Branch
of the War Department

Beginning in the fall of 1941 and throughout the war, the Research Branch of the War Department's Information and Education Division, under the direction of Samuel A. Stouffer,[1] conducted over 200 different surveys. In the course of these surveys more than half a million soldiers spread across the world were questioned on their knowledge, beliefs, and attitudes about the war and their conduct and adjustment to military service. The substantive findings from this massive, systematic, and unique program of survey research were important enough to earn the Research Branch a place in this history. In addition, it also contributed to methodological advancement of the field and trained survey researchers who then established and expanded postwar facilities in many places.

Civilian Surveys Versus Army Surveys

The Research Branch surveys, like the civilian surveys, involved sampling and focused on the adjustment of Americans to the war, but they differed in one crucial respect. They were examples of what we shall term an inquest, an inquiry enforced by authority, whereas the civilian surveys relied on the voluntary cooperation of respondents. That crucial feature of the military surveys, mentioned in passing in the introduction to Stouffer's *The American Soldier* (1949), deserves special attention.

Within each unit included in a survey, the field team ordinarily drew "every Nth man, usually by checking off names on a roster. . . . Men drawn from the roster were ordered to appear at a designated mess hall or other building at a given hour . . . the study explained and assurances of complete . . . anonymity given" (vol. 1, p. 21). Under such authoritarian conditions, refusals—often an imponderable and major source of bias in civilian surveys—vanish as a problem. Civilians not at home when the interviewer calls create another source of bias and lead to the expense and delay of repeated callbacks. Soldiers not present for the survey would be few in number, their characteristics and reasons for absence readily determined.

Putting the theory of probability sampling into practice in American surveys of the civilian population involves an intricate and costly multistage process, subject to errors at all stages along the way. The Research Branch, by contrast, translated the theory into practice by a simple two-stage procedure subject to little error. "Using latest available classified information as to the strength of the army and the location of particular units, a sampling specialist would select organizations" (p. 21). Then, as noted, individuals were drawn from the rosters.[2]

In order to complete field work within a reasonable time and budget, small samples—rarely larger than 3,000 and generally much smaller—have been the rule in civilian surveys. Correspondingly, the sampling variance of the aggregate estimates is fairly large, though within tolerable limits, and refined analysis involving small subgroups is limited. Since the Research Branch collected data wholesale by self-administered questionnaires to soldiers assembled in groups, a large sample could be surveyed quickly, at little cost, and with a small staff. "Usually a team of one officer and one enlisted man would visit a camp. While the officer was making arrangements for the survey with the local command, the enlisted man was training a few local enlisted men . . . to assist in the work" (p. 21). A long instrument could be imposed on the captive respondents, different forms of an instrument distributed efficiently, and repeated surveys accomplished at little extra cost.

Stouffer and the staff had to seize the rare opportunities the organizational setting and recordkeeping the Army provided and design the surveys to best advantage. They had to gain and maintain the support of the authorities—and therein lies a fascinating story. Once they succeeded they could produce surveys easily with samples of, say, 12,200, 16,000, or 18,100. The famous "point system" for demobilization was derived from survey findings on five cross-sections stationed in the U.S., European, Pacific, and India-Burma theaters, all the data collected in two weeks. Thus they produced a body of survey research with a distinctive stamp, with such hallmarks of science as measurements based on multiple indicators and scaling methods, findings derived by multivariate analysis involving a large constellation of factors and refined subgroups, and findings checked by replicated tests. An extreme example of this research is a summary of findings on the correlates of favorable adjustment to the Army based on 8,554 pairs of percentages (vol. 1, pp. 228–229).

The research of the Experimental Section on the effects of orientation and training films (see vol. 3) involved matched and randomly allocated groups of soldiers, some exposed to the films and others serving as unexposed control groups. This long series of large-scale studies (a thousand or more soldiers often serving as subjects), adhering to the classic design of laboratory experiments, could be achieved only because the authoritarian structure of the Army provided controls on a grander scale than any experimentalist could have achieved in civilian society.

Collecting data in such wholesale fashion necessitated literacy, but "ordinarily only 2 or 3 men out of 100 could not read the questionnaire." In unusual situations involving a large number of uneducated soldiers, the recordkeeping of the Army again aided the research. In addition to the rosters, Form 20 classification cards in the personnel office "contained AGCT score and educational level, and all men with very low AGCT or little schooling could be segregated in advance for personal interviewing" (vol. 1, p. 21n.).

Stouffer's respondents did not have to volunteer; they were dragooned. But, knowing the GI's proverbial talent, one might expect subtle, insidious forms of noncooperation. Bias in sampling might have been eliminated only by aggravating response bias. That fear was allayed. In the authoritarian setting of the Army, the surveys, given complete anonymity, provided a unique opportunity to talk back, to express grievances. (It should be noted that when the group was "composed of enlisted men, the class leader" or proctor was also "an enlisted man and no officers were present during the session. No names or serial numbers are placed on the questionnaires.") That is exactly what the generals must have expected and may account for their initial, categorical opposition to the use of survey research. In May 1941, some six months before the Research Branch was established, the secretary of war issued the following directive:

Our Army must be a cohesive unit, with a definite purpose shared by all. Such an army can be built only by the responsible effort of all of its members, commissioned and enlisted. Anonymous opinion or criticism, good or bad, is destructive in its effect on a military organization where accepted responsibility on the part of every individual is fundamental. It is therefore directed that because of their anonymous nature, polls will not be permitted among the personnel of the Army of the United States. [vol. 1, p. 12]

Indeed, the soldiers spoke their mind, once the surveys began.

In the course of studying half a million soldiers, upwards of 10,000 "classroom" interviewing sessions were held, and there was no session at which untoward incidents occurred. Respondents cooperated with what seemed like complete sincerity. The painstaking detail with which many of the men wrote out free comments, in addition to checking answers to check-list questions, was objective evidence that these studies were taken seriously. Not that there was an absence of cynicism. Sometimes men who were hostile to the Army would write a note like this: "I don't believe the Army will do a damn thing about this situation, but I'm giving it to 'em straight just the same." In Alaska 87 percent of the men said they thought such studies would be of help in winning the war if the Army paid attention to them, while only 4 percent said they thought such studies were not a good idea. The reader of these volumes will see for himself that the men did not hesitate to voice their disapproval and also that they were discriminating, approving some things, disapproving others. [vol. 1, pp. 22–23]

From the many findings presented, a few examples will substantiate the assertions. These are from a survey in November 1945 of enlisted men and company grade officers, representative of those stationed in the United States. By that time a majority had served overseas and were at a late stage of their military careers. They certainly were not sparing of criticism and not paying lip service to the official ideology. The survey also shows the way measurement error was examined with parallel forms of an instrument allocated to random subsamples of about 1,000 enlisted men and 300 officers (vol. 1, pp. 422–423):

Promotions in the Army are based on *who* you know,
and not *what* you know.

	Agree
Officers	60%
Enlisted men	80

Promotion in the Army is based on *what* you know
and not *who* you know.

	Agree
Officers	31%
Enlisted men	24

Two other pairs of questions show more sharply the differing views
of officers and enlisted men, not that officers were uncritical of the
promoting system. The relation between class or privilege and ideology is, of course, a basic problem in sociology and social psychology
and illustrates the scientific yield from applied survey research.

When the Army *says* it will do something the men want,
most of the time it ends up by *not* really doing it.

	Agree
Officers	41%
Enlisted men	76

When the Army *says* it will do something the men want,
most of the time it ends up by really doing it.

	Agree
Officers	60%
Enlisted men	26

The honest cooperation of the respondents was not the problem;
the cooperation of the authorities was.

The Mysterious Beginning
of Army Survey Research

The American Soldier begins like a mystery story: "The full story of
how the War Department changed from a position of flat opposition
to such research to one in which it would use such research not only
for internal planning but as justification to the American people for
such a vital program as its demobilization system should some day
make instructive reading" (p. 12). The mystery deepens when one

realizes the extent of the survey research. This was no flimsy, short-lived, narrowly contained operation that a hostile authority could afford to ignore. The mystery becomes all the more intriguing when we note that the Navy during World War II never adopted a similar program for its military personnel. The strategy that broke the barriers to Army research in World War II may be applicable elsewhere and in the future.[3]

Major General Frederick Osborn, the commander of the Information and Education Division, provides a clue in his foreword to *The American Soldier.* But perhaps out of modesty he does not elaborate on the full role of innovative leaders.

> The organization of the Army was such that at the word of command groups of men could be drawn out for study with a minimum of effort, provided only that the Army authorities were willing that such studies should be made.
>
> The Army was willing that such studies be made. What was too novel, too contrary to tradition to have gained general acceptance in our universities or in industry, was accepted by the Army at the very time of its greatest pressures for training and combat. The conservatism natural to professional men everywhere, and often particularly ascribed to the professional soldier, was broken down by the imaginative grasp of the abler leaders. . . . The list of such officers would be long and difficult to compile in its entirety. At the top would be the Chief of Staff, General George C. Marshall, whose rare qualities of intelligence and character provided understanding and much needed support. [vol. 1, p. vii]

When Stouffer describes the character and background of General Osborn, we get another important clue. He might have mentioned Osborn's formidable stature, almost as tall and impressive as General de Gaulle.

> He was a businessman who was also the author of two volumes on social science. From boyhood he had been a personal friend of Franklin D. Roosevelt, the President of the United States, and of Henry L. Stimson, the Secretary of War. He won the immediate confidence of the Chief of Staff, George C. Marshall, who was to give to research throughout the war informed and unswerving support. This support was to be needed, too. In spite of General Osborn's personal prestige, his persuasive skill which had served him so well in business, and his deep sincerity, there were times when even these assets might have availed little against occasional opposition at intermediate echelons had not General Marshall unequivocally supported the strange new program. The commissioning of General Osborn provided the opportu-

nity . . . to get an Army agency to undertake a task hitherto explicitly forbidden by the Secretary of War. [vol. 1, p. 13]

The consent of the theater commanders was required for the expansion of the research to overseas. "A cable from General Eisenhower in London, inspired by a conversation with Elmo Roper," began what later became a full-scale overseas research program. That is all we learn from Stouffer about that strategic conversation. Fortunately, the mystery of what happened finally was clarified by Roper's own account in 1957.

I first met General Eisenhower in London when he was preparing for the African invasion. This was in early August of 1942, and I had flown to Europe at the request of General William Donovan, who was head of the OSS.[4]

By that time the Special Services branch of the Army under Major General Frederick Osborn had been set up and well staffed; but its research branch was, in a sense, "all dressed up with no place to go" because it was having great difficulty getting any generals to make use of what seemed to them a brand-new and untried tool—the discovery of significant facts about the state of morale in the Army. Samuel A. Stouffer, who was head of the research branch, was particularly anxious to have General Eisenhower use the services of this branch, not only because of the importance of his assignment but because his use of it would tend to cause other generals in other theaters to look on this particular tool more receptively.

I called on General Eisenhower at his headquarters for the purpose of outlining what seemed to me to be the compelling reasons for doing public-opinion research among the soldiers stationed in England and to match that with research which the British would undertake as to the attitudes of British civilians towards the "foreign" soldiers stationed in their midst. There were, of course, by this time some signs of misunderstanding between American military personnel and British civilians.

I had expected to give about fifteen minutes of exposition, which would be followed by an indeterminate period of what I had expected to be critical questioning. Knowing that time was a very critical factor with General Eisenhower, particularly then, I had prepared my case carefully. At the end of eight minutes of uninterrupted listening, General Eisenhower leaned forward and asked me just what steps he should take if he decided to seek the help of the research branch. I told him that Sam Stouffer's people were ready and waiting and that all that would be required was a cable from him to start two competent men on their way to England at once and then the assignment of one of his staff to the job of working with them. He immediately called in an officer, dictated such a cable, leaned back in his chair, and said,

"Now never mind giving me any more reasons why I should use this. I'm already convinced it can be very valuable. Let's spend the rest of our time in your giving me pointers as to its proper use and how it can be made more valuable." [pp. 233–234]

For those who wonder what manner of man, in eight minutes, could convince General Eisenhower of the value of survey research for the Army, this fragment may only deepen the mystery. It may surprise some that a commercial pollster was trusted by academics and generals alike, was an excellent spokesman for noncommercial surveys, and was for sure a gifted salesman. Yet all this was within Roper's capacities.

Wise and fortunate selection of military personnel below the topmost level was equally important in the expansion of the enterprise. "As first head of the Branch, General Osborn appointed a young West Point officer, Major (eventually Brigadier General) Edward L. Munson, Jr., whose knowledge of Army ways and whose vigorous and resourceful tactics in using Army machinery to accomplish ends for which the machinery was never devised, were indispensable to the establishment of this research within a military framework" (vol. 1, p. 13).

Other chiefs of the Research Branch included Lt. Colonel Charles Dollard, subsequently president of the Carnegie Foundation; Lt. Colonel Leland C. DeVinney, later a senior officer of the Rockefeller Foundation; Lt. Colonel Lyle M. Spencer, later the patron and founder of the Spencer Foundation; Lt. Colonel W. Parker Mauldin, later vice president of the Population Council. The positions of power in scientific foundations to which these officers ascended in the postwar period suggest both their scholarly gifts and their leadership abilities. The ascent in later life of Leonard S. Cottrell, Jr., civilian head of the Survey Section under Stouffer, to vice president of the Russell Sage Foundation, and William McPeak, the civilian in charge of the field work, to a vice presidency of the Ford Foundation, illustrates the same point. The stature—then and later—of the officers involved are clues to the acceptance of the surveys during the war and the generous support of survey research after the war.

The initial support of the generals was obtained, but it would not have been maintained for long if the surveys had not proven useful to them. Such evidence should not be sought only in *The American Soldier*, which was written after the war and is a biased sample of the many surveys that were conducted. It is a deliberate selection of studies having some enduring social or scientific significance, and it omitted many studies that were useful to a particular commander at a particular time. As the introduction notes:

Many, if not most, of the engineering jobs done by the Research Branch in the war appear small, indeed, in the perspective of global war. To analyze the factors which led men in the South Pacific not to use Atabrine as regularly as the Army thought they should; to investigate attitudes and practices associated with trench foot; to find which of two kinds of huts men preferred in Alaska; to compare preferences for different kinds of winter clothing among frontline troops in Belgium, Luxemburg, and Germany; to learn what radio programs men preferred or what they liked most to read in *Yank* magazine; to assess needs for different kinds of athletic equipment; to analyze the laundry situation in Panama or attitudes toward the Chinese among troops in India-Burma—inquiries to such ends were almost routine and were made in ever-increasing volume as the war progressed. In the files of the War Department are more than 300 manuscript reports prepared on a great variety of subjects. [vol. 1, p. 6]

Such useful findings began to be disseminated widely and, in turn, the status of the Research Branch was enhanced when General Marshall issued an order that a monthly periodical be prepared for distribution to officers throughout the Army.

This publication, prepared in the Research Branch, was continued until the end of the war. Making extensive use of graphic presentation, *What the Soldier Thinks* sought to summarize in simple and readable style some of the current research findings as to attitudes of soldiers in various parts of the world on a wide variety of problems. Emphasis was given to problems which were susceptible to treatment at the local command level. While care was taken to make sure that the data were as accurate as possible, the publication was not intended to be merely factual. Both in the selection of problems for presentation and in the manner of organizing the charts and text, the practical value to the reader was kept in mind. . . . [vol. 1, p. 10]

Indeed, the practical concerns of the audience were kept in mind. The lead article featured in faded No. 9 (1944) is titled "How's Your Chow?" For nine overseas installations all of which received much the same supplies, the chart shows that the percentage of men rating food preparation as "poor" ranged from 54 to 20 percent. Hardly a finding of scientific significance, but one useful to the Army in pointing the finger at the offending mess officers and at a source of low morale.

An article in the January 1944 number titled "Our Men Like the British" clearly was a comfort to the local commanders and useful to them. Without the statistical findings, unpleasant episodes—one at a dance hall in Warrington in December 1943 and another in Liverpool in November 1943, for example—might have been given inflated importance. The findings of this survey, based on a representative sample of enlisted men stationed in Britain in November 1943, are also of more than passing interest to social psychologists, since the chart shows that liking is greatest among those men longest in Britain.

In the first issue, December 1943, an article titled "Leisure-Time Activities in New Guinea" is based on a survey of enlisted men in all types of installations in New Guinea: In rating the activities they would like most to have, movies three times a week was the most desired, followed closely by good assortments of records and then magazines, with books trailing far behind. Even such ordinary findings, when obtained from so distinctive an audience in so isolated a setting, are of more than passing interest to modern students of the mass media, whose interests will be heightened by other findings on the perennial themes of escapism and violence in the media. Slapstick comedies, westerns and war movies were desired by less than 10 percent of the sample compared with the favorite fare, musical comedy and light romance, preferred by about 60 percent of the sample. When asked about their off-duty activities "yesterday," going to the movies was much more frequent than reading books or listening to the radio. But letter writing far surpassed these activities; "three-quarters of the men on this battle-torn island report that they wrote one or more letters . . . most of them more than one," yesterday, a finding bearing on the role and function of interpersonal versus mass communication.

Useful surveys, done quickly and competently all over the battle-torn globe and then communicated clearly, maintained the support of the commanders.

The Research Staff

To understand how these surveys maintained support, we must take note of the quality of the research staff. Those who later made their mark as scholars included John Clausen, Robert Dubin, Jack Elinson, Carl Hovland, Abram J. Jaffe, Irving Janis, Marion H. Lumsdaine, Nathan Maccoby, Arnold Rose, Frederick D. Sheffield, Brewster Smith, Shirley Star, Edward A. Suchman, and Robin Williams. They were strengthened by such formidable consultants as Hadley Cantril, John Dollard, Louis Guttman, Philip Hauser, Paul Lazarsfeld, Rensis Likert, Quinn McNemar, Robert Merton, Frederick Mosteller, Frank Stanton, and Donald Young.

An essential clue in solving one mystery seems to lead to another mystery. Why would men of scholarly and scientific bent devote themselves to questions so pedestrian and practical as "How's Your Chow?" One explanation is that some—for example, Janis, Maccoby, Rose, Smith—were in the Army and had no choice in the work they did. Of the personnel listed in *The American Soldier*, 65, excluding consultants, were civilians and 54 were in the Army. Thus, the services of almost half the professional staff, including many people of the caliber mentioned, were obtained free of charge. That was one more advantage Stouffer had over the directors of other wartime survey units. For those civilians on the staff who began their careers and/or spent their lives in commercial, opinion, or government research agencies—for example, Robert N. Ford, Dean I. Manheimer, and Seymour Wolfbein—applied research was not inconsistent with their interests, and their special skills strengthened the staff.

> The Research Branch drew many of its personnel from commercial research agencies with practical experience and had close and cordial relationships with leading practitioners in the nation. That background of experience in preparing studies quickly to evaluate specific problems, in drawing representative samples, in constructing questionnaires and pretesting them, and in writing succinct reports which a busy administrator would read and understand, was indispensable to the operation of the Research Branch as a service organization to the Army. [vol. 1, p. 38]

Again, the convergence of academic and commercial forces in the growth of survey research is conveyed.

What about the civilians with scholarly backgrounds and inclinations? Most were equally dedicated to pure science and to the war effort and were glad to have a role in that effort which took account of their skills. The fervor of the staffs at the Agriculture Department and the Office of War Information, described earlier, also characterized Stouffer's staff. Thus even if some of them felt that they had temporarily abandoned science to enlist in wartime service, they made the sacrifice gladly.[5]

While the orthodox belief was that applied research cannot contribute to basic knowledge, that Stouffer's studies were simply social engineering and not social science, the staff regarded their wartime research as also serving social science. As we already noted, the sampling was bigger, and better, and broader than that employed by academics in the prewar era who, perforce, generally based their findings on haphazard samples of college students or groups conveniently at hand. Findings were checked by replication. Statistical treatment of the data was sophisticated and superior to the procedures employed by many academics. New methods for scaling attitudes (subsequently described in volume 4 of *The American Soldier*) were invented and applied to the data. Measurement error arising from question wording was tested routinely, yielding measurements that were more rigorous and refined than normally used in that era. Other sources of measurement error were checked. Williams reminds us that "very complex pretesting was being used; for example, we compared responses to interviews versus group-administered questionnaires, cross-classified by whether the interviewers or group leaders were civilian-officer-enlisted personnel and black or white" (1983, p. 5). The predictive power of various instruments was tested on a large scale. The effects of communication (subsequently described in volume 3) were determined by a series of rigorously designed experiments, conducted on a larger scale and with more heterogeneous subjects than commonly used in the laboratory studies of the period. The staff could point with pride to these hallmarks of science that stamped their applied research, whatever its content.[6]

In totality, the several hundred surveys yielded systematic and comprehensive evidence on the beliefs, attitudes, emotions, and conduct of men drawn into military institutions, enduring the ordeal of war, and about to return to civilian life. These findings in *The American Soldier* are prefaced by the remark, "If by some miracle a cache should be found of manuscript materials telling of the attitudes toward combat of a representative sample of, say, a hundred men in Stonewall Jackson's army, the discovery would interest Civil War historians." Social scientists certainly could be added to the list of interested parties. Stouffer's cache covers half-a-million soldiers and is a monumental and unique body of evidence on the sociology and social psychology of war. That it was applied research—intended to be useful and practical to the commanders—does not deny the fact that it also provided knowledge on problems of importance for social science and society. No wonder the staff regarded the work as valuable. To be sure, the scientific yield had to be extracted later, at leisure. However, since science often is slow, even the distant prospect of scientific discoveries inspired them.

The Surveys and Their Findings

Now let us consider the content of specific surveys. Even when treated discretely, the November 1943 survey "Liking for the British," as noted earlier, is of interest to students of prejudice and intergroup relations, especially its finding that "liking is greatest among men stationed there the longest." Of equal interest, and a poignant commentary on American versus British race relations of the period, is the "highly favorable opinion which Negro soldiers in England had of the British—more favorable than that of white soldiers" (vol. 1, p. 544). Moreover, since the general topic of intergroup relations was studied repeatedly in surveys in other places and times, the yield to science is enriched. For example, about 3,700 soldiers representative of those stationed in Europe were surveyed at the end of April 1945 on their attitudes toward the Germans to provide "a base-line measurement . . . as part of a continuing study which will index changes in attitudes during the post V-E Day period" (Report no. E-122, 1945, p. 1; some of the findings are reported in vol. 2, pp. 564–565). Done on the eve of victory, obviously it was to give practical guidance to the Army of Occupation.

Dislike of Germans, understandably, was intense and widespread among our soldiers. (Such attitudes toward the British were rare.) But it is the finding of highly differentiated attitudes toward Germans that truly excites the scholar for its bearing on important issues in the psychology of prejudice. In contrast to the 82 percent who reported the extreme attitude "I have a strong hatred towards" German leaders, only 41 percent reported strong hatred of German soldiers, and 20 percent strong hatred of German common people. Congruent with the finding in Britain, and equally interesting to the scholar, was that hatred of German soldiers was least prevalent among our soldiers who had been in actual combat, more common among those who had been under enemy fire but not in actual combat, and most frequent among those with no combat experience at all. In August 1945 the same questions were repeated. The samples were matched in many respects to control the changing composition of the Army and to isolate the changes produced by events and experience. Hatred toward German soldiers had dropped to 21 percent and toward German common people to 10 percent. This finding again is congruent with the data on Britain and surely of interest to students of intergroup relations. Various other findings on hostility toward Germans and Japanese, and surprising findings on the low level of hostility toward the enemy soldiers our combat troops faced, are reported in *The American Soldier*. These findings also enlarge knowledge of the effects of contact on prejudice and bear upon theories of aggression (see vol. 2, pp. 157–167).

The survey findings on race relations between black and white soldiers and with the local civilian populations at home and abroad are so voluminous that the chapter titled "Negro Soldiers" (*The American Soldier*, vol. 1, chap. 10) requires over a hundred pages to cover only the main data collected. These informative surveys, though conducted for practical guidance and policy planning, surely gratified the scientific interests of the staff, which included Lyonel Florant, Arnold Rose, Shirley Star, and Robin Williams—all of whom became notable for their scholarship on race relations.

Findings from only one of these surveys, conducted in May–June 1945, will suffice to illustrate their scientific significance. To set the stage for the dramatic change revealed, a baseline finding from a November 1943 survey of 4,800 white soldiers is presented first. Consonant with Army policy then, 84 percent of the white soldiers answered that "white and Negro soldiers should be in separate outfits." The analysts note that "the overwhelming majority of white soldiers, whether from South or North, and at whatever educational level, expressed approval of separate facilities and separate outfits" (vol. 1, p. 569).

The general policy of segregation persisted throughout the war. However, the great need for infantry replacements in Europe in late 1944 and early 1945 led the Army to accept black volunteers for combat duty from rear echelon units. They were then integrated into white companies with white officers and noncoms within eleven infantry divisions in two different armies, but organized into separate platoons. Each formerly all-white division usually was strengthened with three black platoons, one placed in each of its regiments. Since many Army activities—mess, housing, and so on—operate on a company basis, the new arrangement involved considerable, though not complete, integration, and a radical departure from the standard practice of complete segregation. In March and April 1945 these integrated units were in combat, some in heavy fighting.

A survey to evaluate the new arrangement was conducted in May in seven of the divisions, two of which were predominantly southern in background, among the white officers, white platoon sergeants, and other enlisted men in twenty-four of the integrated companies. For purposes of comparison, white infantry men in nonintegrated companies but in the same divisions, and a cross-section of equivalent white personnel in other divisions without integrated companies, were also surveyed. In the divisions with no experience at all of integration, 62 percent of the men said they would "dislike very much" such an arrangement. Among the infantrymen in the integrated divisions, but not serving in an integrated company, 20 percent expressed that attitude, but among the infantry men serving in the integrated companies, only 7 percent said they would dislike it very much. This latter group was also asked an open-ended question on their initial feelings about serving in combat in a company with black and white platoons, and 64 percent reported "unfavorable" feelings.

> When we note that the proportion of men having no experience with mixed companies who say "they would dislike the arrangement very much" is almost exactly the same (62%) as the . . . proportion of white enlisted men in mixed companies . . . reporting retroactively that they initially opposed the idea, we can get some conception of the revolution in attitudes that took place . . . as a result of enforced contacts." [vol. 1, p. 595]

Other data in the original report, omitted in *The American Soldier,* confirm the findings from the comparative design and the open-ended question on initial attitude. For example, on a question on how the two groups of men "got along together," 60 percent of the white enlisted men in the integrated companies answered "very well." On another question on whether their feelings had changed since serving in the mixed units, about 75 percent of the white enlisted men said their feelings had become more favorable. A most important methodological finding in the original report was that "the opinions reported have developed independently in widely scattered units. In spite of an almost total lack of communication ("comparing notes") among the various companies having colored platoons, striking similarities appear in the attitudes of the white personnel interviewed in the different units" (Report no. E-118, p. 1). These findings are congruent with those from the other surveys in showing the importance of contact in changing attitude.

Surely, the social scientists on Stouffer's staff were fortunate to have this unique natural experiment available for study. In their normal professional lives, they would not have been able to do a large-scale study of interracial contact of a prolonged and powerful nature forced upon white adults. The natural experiments normally inherited usually involve self-selected, favorably predisposed small groups of white adults. They would not have been able to replicate a study six times as Stouffer's staff did via the seven divisions surveyed.

The staff, however, had to be clever strategists as well as good methodologists to conduct the study. Robin Williams, one of the staff, revealed that fact only years later. "The original research could not have been done at all had the research staff proposed a study of racial integration as such. Instead it was arranged to have a request made to the Research Branch . . . to interview soldiers in line divisions about their combat experiences. Once the field teams were accepted within the divisions, it was natural enough to include . . . questions concerning the volunteer black platoons" (1983).

Although this study had a substantial scientific significance, it is ironic that its practical or policymaking significance was negligible, at least in the short run. Despite the findings reviewed and the additional finding that over 80 percent of white officers and sergeants in the integrated units judged the black soldiers to have fought "very well" in combat, the Army returned to its traditional practice after V-E Day, which remained unchanged at least until after President Truman's executive order of 1948.

The many surveys also clarified scientific problems in spheres other than intergroup relations. For instance, the surveys on race relations contributed some of the clues which led, serendipitously, to the basic concept of relative deprivation. "I well remember our puzzlement," Stouffer later wrote, "over the finding that Northern Negroes in Southern camps, in spite of the fact that they said they wanted to be stationed in the North and that they resented discrimination in Southern buses and by Southern police, showed as favorable or more favorable responses to items reflecting personal adjustment in the Army than did those in Northern camps." This discrepant finding continued to disturb the researchers until they finally recognized the utility of looking at deprivation in a relative context. In Stouffer's words:

> Some of our analysts were almost in despair at this discrepancy. They actually held up the report on their study for over a month while they checked and rechecked in the vain hope of finding errors in the data or analysis to explain the paradox. When, eventually, it was suggested that the Northern Negro soldier in the South had very great advantages over Negro civilians in the South and that the advantage over Negro civilians in the North were much less, a clue to the paradox appeared. After a number of such experiences, it became evident that some concept like "relative deprivation" might be useful. [1950, p. 199]

Other illustrations of the scientific implications of the Stouffer studies could be cited. However, to emphasize the point that Stouffer's staff had ample opportunity to gratify their scientific interests I cite the considered testimony of Dan Katz, who, after observing that "the data are often analyzed and presented so that the tie-up with theoretical concepts can be readily made," points to, among other examples,

> demonstrations of the functional nature of beliefs and attitudes; of the importance of primary group standards for the determination and sustaining of beliefs and attitudes; of the significance of psychological

reference groups in the determination of judgment; of the influence of role and position in a social structure on the attitudes and behavior of the people playing these roles; and of the cross-pressure phenomenon of conflicting group membership." [1951, review of *The American Soldier*, pp. 514–515]

There are additional reasons why scholarly members of the staff would not have agonized over their conflicting role as basic versus applied researchers, social engineers, or social scientists. One must remember who they were all those years ago and not think of them in terms of what they became later. They were not yet old, established scholars with a set point of view about science. They were in process of becoming, their views being shaped by the very things they were doing and by their teachers and supervisors. Shirley Star, for example, was 24 and her teacher at the University of Chicago was none other than Stouffer. His conception of science specified high technical standards and special approaches to inquiry, but no particular subject matter. She would have been guided in his path. Similarly, Clausen was in his 20s, in the middle of his graduate training, and a student of Cottrell and Stouffer. Suchman was in his later 20s and had previously worked on radio research with Lazarsfeld, the last teacher in the world to have taught that applied research and scientific research were separate spheres. Brewster Smith was 23 and still a graduate student. These authors of *The American Soldier*, thus central members of the staff, were young and open-minded enough to appreciate their opportunity and to see its scientific implications.

The milieu in which these young academics worked had many of the same novel and stimulating features present in the Division of Program Surveys, compensating for whatever frustrations were produced by the content of their work. The staff represented different disciplines—mainly statistics, sociology, and psychology, with a few anthropologists making the mix even more interdisciplinary—and they reflected different traditions within these disciplines. They worked together in teams, not as isolated individuals. They reaped the many benefits the group provided, but they also paid a price. Reports of the Research Branch and the other wartime survey units were issued in the name of the agency, the individual participants remaining anonymous, and were classified documents. That they worked so hard and well without the classic incentive to scholarship—acknowledged authorship—may suggest the potency of other forces in the wartime setting. As one staff member remarked years later, "Nobody gave a damn about publishability" (Sheffield, quoted in Clausen 1984).

In a paper for a retrospective symposium in 1984, Clausen noted that "no distinctions of rank influenced involvement with research formulation or data analysis" (p. 208)—surprising since the larger institution in which they worked, the Army, was governed by a rigid principle of hierarchy but surely comforting to the young and lowly in the Research Branch. "Ideas and instruments were shared, criticized and refurbished in a give-and-take that might be considered devastating in a graduate seminar but was just SOP [standard operating procedure] in the Branch. We each had something to give to and we each had a great deal to learn from our peers" (p. 209). In preparation for the symposium, Clausen conducted a mini-survey among alumni of the Research Branch who had survived and who could be located. Understandably, after forty years the sample was small, but the testimony on the unique opportunity for learning was weighty and vivid despite the passage of time. "A large number of respondents noted that the training experience provided in doing research could not have been duplicated in any existing academic institution." One respondent reported, "The Research Branch was a high grade university for me." Another remarked, "Contact with Sam Stouffer and an amazingly capable staff was a priceless postgraduate experience which could not have been duplicated in an academic milieu." A third concluded, "I felt that nowhere else in America could I have been part of such an important group in the light of my academic background" (pp. 210–211).

Finally, to understand why the staff were not that frustrated, indeed often were gratified, we must see academic research in realistic, not idealized, terms. Although Stouffer was keenly aware of the perils of applied research, he took a dim view of much of the work done on basic research. In fact, as he once noted, one reason that the pressure for applied research "is difficult to counteract is that so much academic research is sterile" (1950, pp. 201–202). Perhaps he put it too strongly, and perhaps the staff were too young to have learned the difficulties and disappointments of basic research. There is, however, considerable truth in his remark, and even a brief academic career is likely to teach the lessons that basic research is slow and faltering, that problems are puzzling and one's theories and methods and resources are inadequate for their solution, and that only a few are rewarded for their efforts. The goal may be glorious, but the task is tedious. In the wartime surveys the pressing need for answers and the extensive resources available meant that the rewards came quickly, often in the form of having done useful work and sometimes, as the earlier examples indicate, in the form of a scientific by-product of the process.

Samuel A. Stouffer

The staff were recruited with a sharp eye for top-notch talent, with the right blend of skills—commercial, academic, editorial, executive—needed to produce useful, high-quality surveys quickly and to communicate the results clearly and effectively. To accomplish the tasks, that large and diverse staff then had to be motivated and guided to see the utility of the work for the war effort and its larger significance for social science. All this points to leadership of rare ability and brings us to examine the qualities that enabled Stouffer, the civilian director of the Research Branch, to perform his duties so well. It would be wrong to conceive of Stouffer as solely responsible, as a kind of divine, omniscient leader, and surely wrong to cast him in the image of a remote, Olympian figure. That was farthest from his style. Cottrell and Hovland, the civilian chiefs of the two sections of the Research Branch, General Osborn, and many others already mentioned were among the important and effective leaders, but Stouffer, above all, deserves special attention and detailed review.

When Stouffer became the director of the Research Branch at the relatively young age of 41, he had had two different careers already and the unusual interdisciplinary training and work experience that, fortunately, fitted him well for the assignment.[7] He was born in Sac City, Iowa, where his father was editor and owner of the local newspaper. He received an M.A. in English from Harvard in 1923 and, because of his father's illness, became editor and manager of the family newspaper. In 1926 he went on to graduate training in sociology at the University of Chicago, from which he received a Ph.D. in 1930. The clarity of his later writing, his ability to direct the research staff, and his inclination and talent at disseminating the information first in practical wartime publications and later in the scholarly *The American Soldier* rest upon his original foundation in English, journalism, and practical management.

Despite the sociological overlay, Stouffer never lost the look, straight talk, and breakneck tempo of the proverbial reporter. Jacket off, shirtsleeves rolled up, cigarette dangling from his mouth, ashes strewn all over his vest from chain-smoking, bleary-eyed from lack of sleep and working through the night against a deadline—such colorful eccentricities are relevant, albeit not crucial, to explaining his influence on the staff.

Dean Manheimer, who joined Stouffer's branch very early and stayed throughout the war, recalls that "people would laugh at him. One day he came in to work with one black shoe and one brown shoe on. Sometimes he'd work until three o'clock in the morning and just get time to push all the papers on the floor and sleep on the table for the night." Jack Elinson, another early and long-time member of the Research Branch, captures the intoxication that came from working with Stouffer in the atmosphere of the wartime research with one example:

> One day we got a rush request from Isidore Lubin in the White House for information on the troops' attitudes toward the allies. . . . The questionnaire was written on Friday. . . . The data (several hundred respondents) collected in three nearby army camps on Saturday. . . . Sam meanwhile outlined the cross-tabs. . . . We were waiting—Dean and I. . . . The questionnaires arrived Saturday evening. They were coded and sorted into piles and hand tabbed. . . . Sam had already written a prior draft of the report without the numbers. . . . He slept on the desk on Saturday night. Sunday he entered the numbers and revised the prior report. Monday it was typed and delivered to the President.

Stouffer's personal and editorial style reflected his journalistic training and career, but his methods and technical skills derived from his unusual social science training and career. While his teachers at the University of Chicago in the late 1920s emphasized the use of case studies and qualitative description—most of them disparaging statistics and quantitative methods—Stouffer himself was strongly quantitative, but not to the exclusion of the qualitative. One of his teachers, Robert E. Park, whose first career had also been as a newspaperman, urged the methods of the trained journalist. At the dedication of a memorial to Park at Fisk University in 1955, Stouffer reported Park's objection "to sociologists who would count and correlate the trivial, ignoring the important issues." He then expressed his own balanced view: "I believe that quantitative studies will play an ever-increasing role in studies of race relations in the United States. But if so, it will be because the admonitions of Park have been heeded, that we do not narrowly equate the scientific with the measurable and that we do not waste our shining statistical tools on issues which are strategically insignificant" (reprinted in Stouffer 1962, p. 232).

Careful reading of *The American Soldier* will document that he meant what he said: It is based in part on qualitative explorations and informal interviewing and includes case studies.[8] A notable example is Brewster Smith's personal account of his socialization at Officer Candidate School, leading to the provisional concept of "the psychological role of the ordeal" and providing an interpretive background to the quantitative study "Barriers to Understanding between Officers and Enlisted Men" (vol. 1, pp. 389–391). In *Communism, Conformity, and Civil Liberties* (1955), Stouffer made strategic use of qualitative materials to answer the question, "How deeply concerned are the American people, either about the Communist threat or about the threat to civil liberties?" (See especially chapter 3.)

The two teachers who influenced Stouffer most were William Fielding Ogburn, the sociologist, and L. L. Thurstone, the psychologist, statistician, and pioneer in the development of scales by which social attitudes, previously vaguely described in qualitative terms, could be precisely scored. Thurstone reports that "instead of gaining some approval" for his 1928 paper "Attitudes Can Be Measured," he found himself "in a storm of criticism and controversy. The critics assumed that the essence of social attitudes was by definition something unmeasurable" (1952, p. 311). Stimulated by Thurstone, the theory and methods of attitude measurement became one of Stouffer's lifelong interests, revealed throughout the work reported in *The American Soldier*, especially in volume 4, and in his postwar work. One may see a parallel between Thurstone's early career in Carnegie Tech's Department of Applied Psychology, affiliated with the Army development of mental tests in World War I, and Stouffer's attitude research for the Army in World War II.

Ogburn was a pioneer in the use of statistics and diverse, large-scale existing records for social research, no body of survey research data yet existing in that period. Again, a parallel can be drawn between the careers of teacher and student. Just as Ogburn became research director for President Hoover's nationwide study *Recent Social Trends in the United States* (published in 1933) and then coordinated a large staff to produce a comprehensive description of American civilian society (not even one of the twenty-nine chapters is devoted to the military), Stouffer a decade later coordinated a staff and produced a monumental study of American military life.

When Ogburn became chairman of the Social Science Research Council Committee on Studies in Social Aspects of the Depression, Stouffer was appointed staff director and coordinated the activities of the authors who produced thirteen monographs on the overriding practical problems facing society.[9] There is a clear parallel between Stouffer's managerial and practical duties during the Depression and his World War II duties, and the earlier experience was good preparation. Stouffer's scientific stance also parallels Ogburn's: ameliorist in purpose and empiricist in approach, insisting on verified evidence for the advancement of social science and the solution of social problems.

The quintessential Stouffer was revealed in the doctoral dissertation completing his formal training in Chicago. In "Experimental

Comparison of Statistical and Case History Methods of Attitude Research" (1930), the scores of individuals on a Thurstone scale measuring attitudes toward Prohibition were compared with elaborate evidence from life histories that the individuals wrote about the development and present state of their views on drinking and Prohibition. The claims of the two methods were thus tested empirically.

The dissertation, however, was not the end of his formal training. He spent the following year in London on a postdoctoral fellowship studying with the preeminent statisticians Karl Pearson and R. A. Fisher. With this rare training, it is understandable that he was appointed to the Committee on Government Statistics and Information Services (COGSIS), established in 1933 with the support of cabinet officers to meet the critical needs for information created by the Depression.[10] The committee was crucial in reorganizing, coordinating, and improving the quality of federal statistical services and in promoting the development of probability sampling. During his two years of service, Stouffer increased his statistical skills and knowledge of social problems and his experience in dealing with government agencies and top officials.

An assignment a few years later greatly enriched Stouffer's training. When the Carnegie Foundation sponsored a "comprehensive study of the Negro in the United States," Gunnar Myrdal, the director, commissioned Stouffer to prepare one of the monographs. Myrdal returned to Sweden in April 1940 upon the invasion of Norway and was unable to return to the United States for almost a year. Stouffer became the acting director and, Myrdal remarks, "unselfishly devoted all his talents . . . to the task of bringing the research to completion by September 1940, and he succeeded" (Rose, 1964, p. liv). When Carnegie then faced the problems of selecting monographs for publication, a three-member advisory committee was appointed, including Donald Young and Ogburn, and Stouffer served as secretary to the committee.

When Stouffer became the director of the Research Branch in late 1941, he was ideally suited for the task. He plunged into the work with characteristic enthusiasm and brought to it elaborate technical skills, much experience in managing large research staffs, and a deep concern for and knowledge of social problems. He also brought to the task one old-fashioned quality, as his daughter tells us: "My father was intensely patriotic and had a great love of the American heritage. As a youth, he was responsible for saving the oldest log cabin in Sac County" (quoted in Toby 1980, pp. 149–150).

When the war ended, Stouffer moved to Harvard as a professor of sociology and director of the Laboratory of Social Relations, but took a path radically different from that taken by the leaders of other wartime survey research units. Clyde Hart and Elmo Wilson of OWI, and Harry Field of NORC (which had worked jointly with OWI), Rensis Likert of the Department of Agriculture and the U.S. Strategic Bombing Survey—all plunged ahead to expand or establish survey organizations in one form or another, with the aid of their wartime staffs. Through these institutions, they promoted the growth of the field and gave it continuity. None of them, however, paused to codify the findings and methods resulting from the extensive surveys their units had conducted. Stouffer's style, fashioned by his experience with Ogburn, with Myrdal, and with the SSRC studies of the Depression, was admirably suited to create that comprehensive, multivolumed work, *The American Soldier*.

Stouffer's style and priorities, as well as his skills and those of the co-authors, are not the only factors involved in the conception and creation of *The American Soldier*. Foresight and planning were essential, but good fortune cannot be ignored. A strategically located network of parties knew firsthand the merits of the original surveys and provided the support necessary. The conception occurred with speed and efficiency, and without mishap. "Before the wartime Research Branch demobilized, various analysts had been asked to organize digests of materials . . . on which they were particularly well informed" (vol. 1, p. 28). In a letter dated October 1, 1945, Donald Young, by then executive director of the Social Science Research Council and earlier a consultant to the Research Branch, wrote General Osborn expressing the council's view "that it is a matter of national importance that the fullest possible use of the punch card data be facilitated" and asking "that a set of cards be placed on loan for use under council supervision, by responsible social scientists." Osborn, social scientist as well as general, responded quickly and positively. The materials were declassified, and the cards, complete documentation for the studies, and reports were provided. On November 13, 1945, the council was informed that funds had been made available for the analysis of the materials by the Carnegie Foundation, whose president, Charles Dollard, as noted, had been executive officer of the Research Branch. On November 20, 1945, Donald Young wrote General Osborn inviting him to chair a special council committee to oversee the enterprise. Osborn accepted and continued in that capacity after his return to civilian life for the several years needed to see the work come to fruition. A technical subcommittee for the research was appointed at the same time—Cottrell, DeVinney, Hovland, and Stouffer as chairman. During most of 1946, this subcommittee with a dozen other former members and consultants of the Research Branch worked on the materials. The work continued through 1947 and 1948, with additional support of the foundation. The first two volumes were published in 1949 and the last two in 1950.

While Stouffer was a gifted editor and journalist and the co-authors were accomplished scholarly writers, there were difficulties for students and scientists in reading the more than 2,000 pages of *The American Soldier* and examining the numerous charts and tables and complex multivariate analyses, and then extracting the scientific nuggets in this "mine of data, perhaps unparalleled in magnitude in the history of any single research enterprise in social psychology or sociology" (vol. 1, pp. 29–30). The network that had been helpful at the conception now came to aid the reader and to disseminate the findings to the profession. Merton and Lazarsfeld, both consultants to the Research Branch, and Lazarsfeld, a co-author of the formidable, mathematical volume 4, edited and contributed to *Studies in the Scope and Method of "The American Soldier"* (1950). In about 200 pages, a selection of the major scientific findings was presented, as neat an illustration as one might want of Lazarsfeld's concept of the "two-step flow of influence" in which "opinion leaders" provide a communication link between an original source and a mass audience. Thanks to Merton and Lazarsfeld many of the major findings from *The American Soldier* were widely disseminated throughout the social science community.

One further episode in Stouffer's career should be noted. He had brought to the Research Branch of the War Department not only his skills but a patriotism intensified by the war. How sad, therefore, that Stouffer, assigned by the military in World War II to a mission of great responsibility and trust which he executed with distinction, survived the hot war only to become a victim of the cold war. In 1953–54, while directing a nationwide survey sponsored by the Fund for the Republic (*Communism, Conformity, and Civil Liberties*) and continuing his work for the Army as a consultant, Stouffer's security clearance was revoked.[11] The survey for the fund also might have been terminated since Stouffer offered to resign to protect the results from being compromised. In his offer of resignation to Clifford Case, president of the fund, Stouffer pointed out that he had been "a life-long Republican" and never held "any leftist beliefs or affiliations." He goes on to note:

> There is no charge made against me of ever having been a Communist, of ever having been a member of any organization which is on the Attorney General's list, of ever having written or said anything which could be construed as disloyal, or of ever having been indiscreet in any

way in my long and responsible experience in the War Department during a war involving high level security or as a consultant since. Any such charges, even if made, would have had no foundation whatever. The stated reason for the action of the Board is my "close and sympathetic association" with certain persons two of whom are professors at other institutions, but most of whom are professional associates at Harvard, charged with present or past membership in various subversive organizations. Without going into their several cases in detail, I here state that I know of no associate of mine whom I consider subversive or disloyal to the United States." [December 29, 1953, Harvard Law School Library, Manuscript Division]

Perforce, Stouffer would have been closely associated with Harvard colleagues in his own department. Moreover, those colleagues specifically cited in the Stouffer case, notably Talcott Parsons and Gordon Allport, denied their alleged membership in subversive organizations. The association with Ogburn, the professor outside of Harvard singled out in the charge against Stouffer, was inevitable when Stouffer studied with Ogburn at Chicago and continued as a result of their common work on the Depression, some of which was sponsored by none other than President Hoover.

Although the hearings completely vindicated him, his daughter reported, "It would be impossible to describe the anguish he suffered when under personal attack during the McCarthy era" (Toby 1980, p. 150). How ironic. The very study that demonstrated the way McCarthyism had undermined public support for civil liberties might itself have been destroyed by McCarthyism.

Notes

1. Major General Frederick Osborn, of the Information and Education Division, was the titular director above Stouffer and, as will be shown, did in fact make important contribution to the work of the Research Branch. Leonard S. Cottrell, Jr., civilian head of the Survey Section, and Carl Hovland, civilian head of the Experimental Section (the two units of the Research Branch), various executive officers, and many senior staff in charge of smaller subunits all contributed to the direction of the work accomplished by a notable staff of civilian and military personnel. It is with no intention to slight their contributions and only for reasons of brevity that in places my text mentions only Stouffer.

2. Departures from the usual and ideal design did occur because of various

military exigencies. Such instances are reported in an appendix to volume 4 of *The American Soldier*, along with comforting findings from tests of the likely bias in the flawed samples. Experiments and other evidence on measurement error arising from various modes of administering the instruments are also reported.

3. It should be noted that the strategy was not completely successful. The consent of the commanders in the various overseas theaters was required, and this sometimes made the research precarious. In a retrospective symposium on *The American Soldier*, Robin Williams reminds us that "there was always the possibility that particular survey questions, e.g., about enlisted men's attitudes toward officers, might be forbidden, or that an entire research operation might be abolished. Complex maneuvering within the military structure was incessantly necessary to insure continuing work on important questions" (1984, p. 187). John Clausen, another participant in the symposium, notes that "overseas commanders had diverse views on the potentialities of survey research. General MacArthur, for example, stated that his company grade officers could provide their superiors with whatever information was needed about enlisted men's views and concerns. He was willing to have questions asked about recreational preferences. He also acceded to our including in the questionnaire the following item: 'If you could talk to General MacArthur about the war and your part in it, what three questions would you ask him?'" (1984, n. 4).

4. Roper was deputy director of the agency initially called the Coordinator of Information, later renamed Office of Strategic Services. Presumably his OSS mission in London was secret in character.

5. For some, of course, no sacrifice was involved since academic jobs were drying up as students left for the armed services.

6. Understandably, most readers of *The American Soldier* have the impression that the Research Branch employed batteries of conventional, closed questions and scaling methods as the main or exclusive approaches to measurement. In fact, a wide variety of instruments was tried out—for example, a pictorial test similar to the TAT; an inkblot test the results of which were compared with scores on a conventional psychoneurotic inventory. Such wide-open questions as, "If you could talk with the President of the United States, what are the three most important questions you would want to ask about the war and your part in it?" were asked of a nationwide sample of enlisted men in the United States. In studying the reading preference of soldiers for various books distributed in Armed Services Editions, in addition to conventional methods an "unobtrusive method" was developed decades before it had been given that name and was applied to about 1,400 soldiers in the Panama Canal Zone. The collection was displayed in the recreation rooms, soldiers being permitted to borrow books for not more than one day. After four weeks of exposure, ten raters independently

rated the degree of wear and tear of each book in the collection. Such wide-ranging experimental work on methods of measurement quite properly would enhance the staff's sense that their activities were scientific.

7. For more details of Stouffer's career, see Brewster Smith's biography in the *International Encyclopedia of the Social Sciences* (1968), Lazarsfeld's introduction to Stouffer's posthumously published collected essays, *Social Research to Test Ideas* (1962), Jackson Toby's portrait of Stouffer (1980), and my biography of Stouffer in the *Dictionary of American Biography* (1980).

8. In a retrospective review of *The American Soldier*, Williams reminds us of the qualitative methods employed:

    What has been almost totally missed by some anti-positivistic critics of *The American Soldier* is the extent to which "qualitative data," including phenomenological reports, both preceded the "quantitative" surveys and were used in major ways to conceptualize and interpret the statistical relationships found. We practically had a mania for "pretesting," i.e., for open-ended, exploratory interviewing and for "trying out" questionnaires and other instruments prior to larger-scale studies. As I now re-read the chapters of Volume II, *Combat and Its Aftermath*, I am impressed with the extensive use of quotations from interviews, of demographic statistics, of descriptions of formal organization, and of reports of first-hand observations, as well as with the omnipresent tables of survey data. [1983, p. 10]

9. Stouffer and Lazarsfeld co-authored one of the monographs, *Research Memorandum on the Family in the Depression* (1937), thus beginning the enduring association that proved so mutually productive. Lazarsfeld became a major consultant to the Research Branch and developed one of the two new scaling methods described in volume 4 of *The American Soldier*. In return, Stouffer, the story goes, taught Lazarsfeld the fourfold table—the cross-tabulation of two dichotomized variables—which later became central to Lazarsfeld's mode of survey analysis. That auspicious event presumably occurred one day in 1937 in Newark where Lazarsfeld was headquartered when Stouffer drew a diagram on a luncheon tablecloth (Sills 1987). And *Radio and the Printed Page* (Lazarsfeld 1940b), the first book published by the Office of Radio Research, which Lazarsfeld directed and later transformed into the Columbia Bureau of Applied Social Research, contained a major contribution by Stouffer. In that book, Lazarsfeld also notes that Daniel Katz, a central figure in the other wartime survey research units whose role is described elsewhere in our history, conducted "a valuable pioneering study for the Office of Radio Research," also incorporated into *Radio and the Printed Page* (pp. 207–213). The repeated criss-crossing of paths by the small band of

pioneers in survey research, and its importance for the growth of the field, is a theme mentioned frequently in our history.

10. In their *Revolution in United States Government Statistics, 1926–1976*, Duncan and Shelton stress the importance of the committee. "COGSIS brought about a revolution in the way Government agencies thought about statistics. . . . By destroying an outgrown concept and substituting a new way of thinking, it achieved important, immediate, and positive results" (p. 31). "The research activities stimulated by COGSIS and by ex-COGSIS personnel . . . eventually really had revolutionary results in the development of the theory and applications of probability sampling" (p. 30). Through the committee, Stouffer developed close connections with other statisticians and social scientists important in the development of survey research. For example, another member was Stuart Rice, a pioneer in attitude measurement, and at various times president of the American Statistical Association, assistant director of the Census, and assistant director of the Bureau of the Budget for Statistical Standards.

11. Professor Sigmund Diamond of Columbia University, whose history of the relations between the FBI and the universities during the McCarthy period will be published in 1991, has generously provided me with previously unpublished materials on Stouffer's hearing before the Eastern Industrial Personnel Security Board—an extreme and grotesque example of guilt by association.

· 4 ·

The Bombing Surveys: Germany and Japan

On November 3, 1944, following a directive from President Roosevelt, the secretary of war established the United States Strategic Bombing Survey of Germany. Although the organization employed 850 officers and enlisted men and depended for essential services on the Army and Air Forces, it was not attached to any branch of the military. Advisedly, it became an autonomous agency under civilian control within the secretary's office and was given freedom of inquiry. The 300 civilian members were led by an eleven-member directorate with Franklin D'Olier, then president of the Prudential Life Insurance Company, as chairman and Henry C. Alexander, a vice president of the Morgan Bank, as vice chairman. The directors of the divisions assigned to evaluate various physical and economic effects of bombing included George W. Ball, John Kenneth Galbraith, and Paul Nitze. Thus the vested interests of the Army and Air Forces in the question of the effectiveness of what was then a new weapon, given its first massive wartime test, could not compromise the findings and reports, which were written without censorship by civilians. The responsible and elite leadership gave added stature to what turned out to be an impressive and consistent body of evidence.

The appointment of Rensis Likert as director of the Morale Division,[1] established "to determine the direct and indirect effects of bombing . . . upon the civilian population, with particular reference to its effect upon the willingness and capacity of the bombed population to give effective and continued support to the German war effort" (U.S. Strategic Bombing Survey 1946, vol. 1, p. iv), began a new and important chapter in the history of the sample survey. That was the main, though not exclusive, method used by the Division. The actual surveys, of course, could not be conducted until Germany was defeated and occupied, but by November 1944 that was in the foreseeable future. However, planning and the inquiries based on supplementary methods began immediately.

When, if ever, has survey research addressed a question of greater importance for future military and political policy, with moral implications so grave, a question so persistent that it plagued policymakers twenty-five years later during the Vietnam War? To that question the Morale Division surveys gave an emphatic answer. That those who made policy in the Vietnam War rejected the answer adds an ironic and tragic ending to this chapter, as well as a reminder for researchers that even the most useful survey findings are not always used. Those policymakers surely were informed of the findings since Ball, Galbraith, and Nitze all held high office in Kennedy's or Johnson's administrations. Nitze, for example, served as secretary of the navy from 1963 to 1967 and as deputy secretary of defense from 1967 to 1969, and Ball served as undersecretary of state from 1961 to 1966; and Galbraith and Ball were outspoken public figures in the later years of the Vietnam War.

Although the chapter ends on a note that must sadden all survey researchers, in other respects the chapter will encourage them. It demonstrates compellingly the power of the survey method to solve seemingly intractable methodological problems, if ample resources are provided. Thus, the Bombing Surveys have an important place in the annals of survey research.

Like Stouffer's *The American Soldier*, the Bombing Surveys enlarge our knowledge of the sociology and social psychology of war. When we abstract from that oppressive problem, they also illuminate a variety of other scientific problems that otherwise could not have been studied under such extreme and revealing social conditions: the importance of relative versus absolute deprivation, the psychodynamics of resentment and aggression and their modification by cognitive processes, social cohesion as it is shaped by external threat and strains within society, the ways ideology and commitment sustain the individual against severe deprivation and fear, and—when the comparative findings of the later Japanese survey are examined—the relative insignificance of culture and the importance of social ecology in shaping some psychological patterns. The bombing of the two populations and the accompanying surveys may be seen as giant natural experiments. Their gruesome and tragic content makes it more, not less, important for social scientists to study the findings for the unique knowledge provided and to learn why the experiments should not be repeated.

In contrast to the Stouffer studies, whose methodological and substantive findings were codified and published in *The American Soldier,* and then clarified and condensed by Merton and Lazarsfeld (1950), the findings of the Morale Division surveys were not brought to the attention of social scientists in the same scholarly and dramatic ways. After the original mimeographed reports were declassified, a fairly comprehensive review of the basic findings (two volumes on Germany and one on Japan) was published by the U.S. Government Printing Office in 1947,[2] but it does not stress the implications, substantive or methodological, for scientists. Sadly, scholars as well as policymakers seem to have ignored it. Fragments did appear later in occasional scholarly writings by former staff members, but these have been lost in memory in the forty years since their publication.[3]

The Recruitment of Likert's Team

My account begins in November 1944 when Likert's cable inviting me to join the Morale Division reached me in New York City. Although I had not worked for him in more than two years, I was excited by the prospect, and after only a brief conversation I promptly accepted. The episode tells as much about his magnetism as it does about my impulsiveness. To be sure, I was also lured by the prospect of working again with Krech and Crutchfield, my former associates in the Methodology Section of Program Surveys, and with Katz, my former collaborator in OWI, who had also received invitations. The four of us were the nuclear team to whom Likert planned to entrust his new and challenging mission. None of the others, however, rallied round him immediately. Katz, and perhaps the others, had a conflicting commitment to resolve, and all three were more wary than I. So I sat in Washington for about eight weeks, struggling as the sole member of the Division to make progress toward a conceptualization and research design, suffering over the long string of difficulties the survey would present to even the most skilled staff, and the staff were nowhere in sight.

Where, for example, could we recruit a large field staff, composed of Americans fluent in German and skilled in open-ended interviewing? Army regulations and our own judgment dictated against the use of German nationals even after V-E Day, and the open-ended interview seemed the method best suited to the problem and the one Likert favored. Would German respondents, by then defeated and occupied, give honest answers about their support of the German war effort to American interviewers clearly identified by the uniforms prescribed for them as members of the occupying forces? Indeed, would Germans speak freely in any interview, no matter what its structure or personnel, given all the years of Nazi surveillance and control of the population? If they were to speak freely and candidly, could they possibly recall experiences that dated back several years, especially experiences so horrendous, so prone to repression, as being bombed? Could they discriminate between the effects of being bombed and all the other wartime experiences that affected their morale, or could we separate analytically the morale effects of bombing? How could we conceptualize and trace all the important direct and indirect effects that bombing might have on the willingness and capacity to support the German war effort?

Despite this sea of troubles—surely enough to drown me or any man in worry—no cares seemed to afflict Likert. As always, his faith in the power of the sample survey seemed boundless; his confidence in the abilities of his trusted staff seemed endless; and although they were still nowhere in sight, he never seemed to doubt that Krech, Crutchfield, and Katz would arrive in response to his call. And finally they did, and not just because he was lucky. In 1944, Katz had taken on the responsibilities to chair and revitalize the psychology department at Brooklyn College and felt that he could not drop the responsibility. So Likert visited Katz personally, and then persuaded the president of the college to grant Katz a leave of absence for the duration of the survey. Although Krech was in the Army assigned to an OSS unit screening secret agents, he, too, joined us in London in March 1945.

Many such personal experiences with Likert conveyed a characteristic style and entrepreneurial spirit: his willingness to undertake risky ventures, his confidence that he had the resources essential for success, his capacity to get support for his enterprises, his talents at recruiting a staff and commanding their loyalties and best efforts, and then, when the staff was securely in service and hard at work, his restless spirit, which led him on toward the next risky venture. Likert's style with the staff added to his appeal and effectiveness, although it may seem incompatible with the spirit of the conventional entrepreneur. The standards he upheld were those of a scientist, not a businessman, and attracted us. The nature of the surveys he undertook created heavy pressures, but he personally rarely made demands. Whenever the resources permitted, he recruited ample, even excess staff to share the work, and offered more rather than less pay. He was democratic in his social relations, friendly not distant, and simple not slick in manner. To me, his only serious and chronic fault seemed to be irresponsibility in promising more than we could safely deliver, but this I attributed to his earnest and high purpose, his incurable optimism, and perhaps his better judgment.

So it was understandable that the nuclear team Likert set out to recruit to design, conduct, and analyze the survey finally joined up with him again in the new mission. Some may wonder why he waited for us and did not recruit from the plentiful and capable staff available to him in Program Surveys. His entrepreneurial spirit is the explanation. Although Likert was no orderly manager or administrator, he was prudent in protecting his major enterprise while embarked on foreign adventures. If he had recruited Charles Cannell or Angus Campbell or others, Program Surveys might have been put in jeopardy. Campbell remained behind and in charge. By recruiting Katz, Krech, Crutchfield, and me, formerly but no longer members of Program Surveys, Likert obtained a team he had tried before and still trusted but at no cost to his major enterprise.

The fact that he detached Cartwright from Program Surveys, but only temporarily to help us in the planning stage, also suggests Likert's prudence in protecting both his enterprises. The two other senior analysts added to the nuclear staff, Helen Peak and Howard Longstaff, were then recruited from the outside. With the addition of William G. Cochran as the sampler, the senior staff was immeasurably strengthened and complete. Cochran was not a full-time member of the Division, but was a frequent consultant; he, too, had been tested many times and could be trusted to overcome the host of difficulties in sampling that were anticipated. Given the chaotic, immediate postwar situation in Germany, no one knew what kinds of sampling frames would be available to design the sample or what logistical problems would be faced in carrying it to completion. Cochran's proven ingenuity and flexibility in dealing with practical problems, in addition to his theoretical preeminence, and his congeniality as a co-worker made him an ideal choice. Likert worked his usual magic, and Cochran joined up.

Planning the Research

The senior staff for the sample surveys thus complete, we moved to our main headquarters in London, where we developed the detailed plans and made practical preparations for the research. The dependent variables—will and capacity to support the German war effort—and the independent variables—direct and indirect exposure to various kinds and magnitudes of bombing and to the threat of bombing, as well as the deprivations and damage experienced, observed, or communicated—were conceptualized. Intervening variables and accompanying conditions which, depending on their presence or strength, would aggravate or attenuate the effects of bombing also had to be conceptualized. These included German propaganda promising a secret weapon that would turn the tide of war; playing upon fears of the calamities of defeat and the brutality of the Allied occupation; police control; punishment for unauthorized absence from work; air raid protection; relief measures following raids and indemnities for those suffering property loss and casualties in the family; patterns of obedience to authority and devotion to work; and evacuation, with its threefold implication as a direct disruptive effect of bombing, as a protection against future exposure, and as an indirect effect of bombing on the unbombed hosts, who learned from their guests about its horrors and were disrupted by their unwanted presence.

This intricate formulation, the research and sampling design, and the corresponding instruments and questionnaires were developed in the first four months of 1945 and tested in pilot studies in April in the cities of Krefeld and Darmstadt, by then occupied by our troops. Then and later, the work was facilitated by a gifted group of officers and enlisted men: former pilots, Air Force Intelligence, military psychologists, and former interrogators fluent in German retrained by us in survey interviewing and given supervised practice during the pretests. Some of these interviewers served later as coders along with other German-speaking military personnel assigned to those duties.

While we were planning, Likert, with the aid of Katz, was recruiting other essential personnel. The civilians fluent in German and knowledgeable about the society who formed the core of the field staff, expanded to necessary strength by the retrained interrogators, came from many quarters and often through past academic connections. A more exotic group would be hard to imagine, but following special training most developed fine competence in intensive interviewing and often went far beyond the call of duty. Among the luminaries were W. H. Auden, the poet, who in his spare time prepared an excellent study of the July 20 attempt to assassinate Hitler; James Stern, the British writer, whose sensitive postwar account of the experience will be drawn on later;[4] Nicholas Nabokov, a distinguished composer and cousin of Vladimir; and Franz Plunder, Swiss by birth, a sculptor and professor at St. Johns College, whose knowledge of Tyrolean dialect made him an ideal member of the field staff in Austria.

Likert was also busy recruiting staff for the nonsurvey section of the Division. Even though a series of independent surveys of contrasted design was planned to provide mutual checks and strengthen the major body of evidence, it was also decided to use two nonsurvey sources of evidence. Then the overall conclusions would not rely exclusively on surveys, which might be vulnerable to memory and other types of response error and which would be inappropriate for measuring variables outside the common knowledge of many respondents—for example, the absenteeism of industrial workers or the ways the bombings were presented in German propaganda.

To offset such problems, official German documents and records of various kinds were to be analyzed. For example, the *Stimmungsberichte*, periodic reports on morale filed during the war by local German intelligence agents, though subject to special limitations and biases, were examined critically.[5] One such monthly series for a particular region documented changes from February 1942 to October 1944. Press and radio content for the entire 1939–45 period was analyzed. Country-wide government records and managerial records from selected major war plants covering extended periods provided evidence on absenteeism and its causes. Time series of statistics on arrests for such crimes as looting and labor offenses were also analyzed. All such records were contemporaneous.

Interviews with local officials and other key informants—for example, plant managers—in all the cities in the sample were the second check on the survey data. Such evidence, in principle, was subject to memory error, but the informants often had records they consulted, and the considerable number of informants used to prepare the background report on each city attenuated the error from an especially forgetful informant.

In recruiting the senior staff for the nonsurvey section, Likert again showed his talent. Among the skilled social scientists recruited were Otto Klineberg and Theodore Newcomb, who had monitored German media for our Foreign Broadcast Intelligence Service; Charles Loomis, with extensive research experience in prewar Germany (in one of the towns which he described in a field report he had maintained contact with the families for more than eleven years); and Gabriel Almond and E. L. Hartley, who had analyzed intelligence on Germany for the Office of War Information.[6]

A third source of data not subject to memory and other response errors that might affect the surveys was collected and analyzed by the Survey Section and therefore required no additional staff. Letters written by German civilians during the war and captured prior to German censorship were the basis for two large-scale studies. The novel design and the unusual methodological checks used in these two studies will be reviewed in detail later.

As we contemplate the roster of social scientists, one question seems to demand an answer: Why would so many men of scientific bent devote themselves to the practical question of the effect of strategic bombing? Why would humane scholars be willing to study something so inhuman as the bombing of civilians, the findings potentially serving to make this destructive weapon even more devastating in the future? For an answer to these questions the reader must transport himself back to an earlier era. It was World War II, not the Vietnam War. All of us were anti-Nazi and anti-fascist. Some of us were Jewish, and some of the interrogators and civilian interviewers were German refugees who knew firsthand the wrath of Hitler. Our headquarters were bombed-out London in early 1945 when Hitler's ultimate secret weapon—the V-2 rocket which gave no warning to the civilians in its path—was devastating the city. And many of us remembered that the history of the bombing of civilians began with Hitler's bombing Warsaw, Rotterdam, and Coventry in World War II and Guernica in the Spanish Civil War.

After all these years, my reconstruction of our feelings at the time can be only speculative, but I am sure of one thing. I can recall no instance where I ever felt or heard any of the senior staff express conflict about the work we were doing.[7] This does not mean that we felt no sympathy for the German civilians who had been bombed—those terrible experiences reported vividly in the course of interviews—but it did not prevent us from conducting the surveys in which we felt deeply involved. That sympathies sometimes hampered the performance of some of the interviewers is revealed in a poignant passage from Stern's book *The Hidden Damage*. He had none of the insulation built up from prior experience as a professional survey interviewer and was taxed to his very limits in the interview he describes.

> "It is difficult for me to tell you how I'm getting along under the Occupation. You see"—and promptly like a pricked balloon all the life that was in the meagre dress under the ancient cloche hat seemed to collapse. Only the arms—like a drowning person's arms as they quickly rise before disappearing for the last time—came up to hold the dropped head while the words gurgled out as from a body saturated in water. "Oh, I'm sorry and ashamed, I really am, but you see, all my men, all

I still had to live for, my husband, my boys, my husband's brothers and all their boys—all my men, you see, are killed or missing," then, "killed or missing," she repeated several times like a chant, like a chant that had stamped itself indelibly and forever on her brain from having seen it too often in the newspapers or in the dreaded official telegrams.

He reports his reactions:

Well, what do you do and say, you damned Gallup poller? You, with your fatuous Fragebogen, its questions about prices and taxes, about wartime domestic problems, the military and political leaders already dead or jailed, about what plans she and her family have for the future, that charming rosy little hell called the future? What do you do and say with all that Galluping nonsense on the table to be answered and across the table the forlorn life with nothing to live for and not the courage to take it because as long as the heart goes on beating life is dear or because someone said long ago that this in the eyes of almighty God is the greatest sin. What do you do and say, you who are no physician or priest or psychoanalyst but a human worm with a full stomach and a wife and home and future and friends next door and a nervous system like a coil of taut and quivering copper wire? What do you do and say? [p. 230]

That other interviewers were tougher, perhaps even untouched by their experiences, is also clear from Stern's conversation with a former military interrogator on the field staff about the ways to handle such taxing situations.[8]

I once summoned up the courage to ask a tough, square-faced sergeant that, after he'd been knocking what he called "the bullshit outa crying Krauts." I asked, not because I knew he was a psychologist by profession but because I knew he was a different kind of a worm and I wanted to try and learn a lesson. "What did I say," he said, as though what he said was all there was to be said. "Why, I said, Madam, you better quit that blubbering quick, we gotta long way to go yet and they ain't gonna keep my dinner warm on accounta you, that's what I said, and Jesus, was my dinner cold, no sirree." [p. 230]

The Design of the German Surveys

From the cumulative records of the British and American air forces, all the cities and towns in the British, American, and French occupied zones of Germany and Austria were stratified in terms of tonnage and character (day or night, early or late in the war, and so on) of the bombing they had experienced, and also in terms of population and region. (The Russian occupied zone was out of bounds for the surveys, producing an awkward situation for one of the Austrian field teams, which surveyed only half of the small city of Steyr, the other half being under Russian occupation.) Thirty-four places in Germany were drawn from the strata so as to represent communities of various sizes and locations that had been exposed to no bombing at all, or to "light," "medium," or "heavy" bombing. Then, in each place, in ways to be described later, a probability sample of individuals was drawn and interviewed, their morale and the damage, deprivation, and injury personally sustained from bombing being measured by multiple indicators. The total number of interviews in Germany was 3,711. The heavily bombed cities, on the average, had been exposed to 30,000 tons of bombs, the figure going over 40,000 tons for Hamburg, Cologne, and Essen. The equivalent design was applied in Austria, where about 750 individuals were interviewed in eight communities contrasted in severity of bombing. However, none of the Austrian cities had experienced anywhere near the tonnage dropped in Germany. The most heavily bombed city in the zone, Linz, had been exposed to about 8,000 tons.

This quasi-experimental design served to answer critical substantive questions. Individuals in unbombed towns might well be reflecting the indirect effects of bombing stemming from knowledge (sometimes communicated through evacuees) that raids were occurring elsewhere, that others and the war effort were suffering, and that their own turn might be coming. Thus, what the military strategist or a person of humane disposition can find out from those towns and individuals is how much psychic damage can be achieved without bombing everyplace and everybody. What we learn from all the bombed towns and all their residents is how much or little more is gained by direct exposure to raids, whether or not the individual and his family and property were specifically affected. What we learn from comparisons of light, medium, and heavily bombed communities and residents contrasted in the severity of their personal exposure is how much or little more is gained by massive increments of bombing that damage or destroy more and more families.

The design also answered critical methodological questions that had perplexed us initially. Civilians throughout Germany experienced not only bombings, but all the other consequences of war—for example, the death of family members in the military services, the battle victories of the allies, the deprivations and controls in a wartime economy and society. Their morale was certainly sensitive to these forces. How could they distinguish for themselves or we dissect the causes of their morale and misery? Whatever the level of bombing, everyone experienced these diffuse conditions and their effects, and thus the differences observed in the contrasted communities could not reflect these other constant factors and represented the effects of bombing. We might say that the individuals in the unbombed and lightly bombed towns revealed how much could be achieved by waging a war with little bombing.

There were, of course, individuals who wished to falsify their true feelings, to posture as more or less war-weary than they were, as better or worse patriots, and those who had deceived themselves or could not remember the flux of their feelings. The design provided a basic protection against such error: There is no reason to think that such errors varied between the groups of towns and cities. That, too, should be a constant not obscuring the comparisons between levels of bombing. The assumption implicit in the design, that the initial levels of various kinds of morale were the same prior to bombing, seemed warranted for the groups of towns in the sample and for most variables, although it did not hold for special kinds of variables that entered into particular analyses—for example, crime—and for particular specialized communities. Cautions were applied in these instances, and there was much internal evidence in the surveys and independent evidence in the nonsurvey materials to check on error and on the conclusions about the specific effects of bombing.

No quasi-experimental design is perfect. One could not expect—one would never want—the generals to drop thousands of tons of bombs on some tiny towns in order to create an elegant, true experimental design. The heavily bombed communities were large cities of strategic importance, but there were also other large cities that received medium or little bombing. Thus city size was subject to some control and, as noted, created a technical problem only in the analysis of special variables with which it was correlated.

The surveying of the total sample of about 4,500 respondents was, in fact, designed as four surveys of equivalent subsamples. One survey was conducted in June 1945, a second equivalent one in July, when each field team returned to the same set of communities it had covered the previous month. If memory and the overlay of events following defeat and occupation affected the reports of morale, it would be revealed in the comparison between the two subsamples. The comparison not only reduced concerns about memory errors—as did other checks on the problem[9]—but yielded evidence on the candor of the respondents. The interview began with a battery of open questions on attitude toward the Occupation and expectations about the future, the questions making no mention of bombing. These questions—on the surface unrelated to the bombing—were indeed relevant to our substantive and methodological problems and designed with that in mind. They also were intended to provide general information on the administrative problems of the Occupation—an objective, as we shall see, that was part of a larger design that Likert, the farsighted entrepreneur, had in mind.

In the June survey, 85 percent of Germans expressed a favorable attitude toward the Occupation, the most frequent reason given by 24 percent being their relief that the bombings had stopped. The majority also reported that the Occupation was much better than they had expected. If this reflected attempts to ingratiate themselves with their conquerors rather than honest relief that the war and bombing had stopped and that the American troops were not as bad as they had been led to fear, the same pattern should have been observed in the July survey. Instead, the proportion who reported a favorable attitude toward the Occupation had dropped markedly, down from 85 to 58 percent. Similarly, the proportion who reported favorable expectations of their future welfare had dropped from 49 percent in June to 28 percent in July. The reasons for the dissatisfaction and doubt about the future, increasingly reported from June to July, were the shortages of food and the inability to find work. These genuine worries had dissipated the initial relief from the worries about the war and bombing which had been reported in June. The trend findings hardly suggest lack of candor and desire to ingratiate oneself with a conquering army.[10]

The Questionnaires

Just as the overall survey was divided into the June and July surveys, these in turn were subdivided into two surveys using different instruments. One third of all the respondents in the bombed communities were interviewed with questionnaire A, questionnaire B being used for the other two thirds and for all respondents in unbombed communities. Both questionnaires used open-ended questions and probes. However, A asked directly about bombing and solicited a narrative account of the respondent's experience beginning with the first raid and his or her reactions and judgments of the morale changes produced specifically by bombing. Since the conclusions about the effects of bombing could not rely exclusively on memory and subjective judgment, questionnaire B used a radically different approach. No inquiry about bombing was made until near the end of the interview although it might, of course, have been mentioned spontaneously by respondents, suggesting the saliency of the experience and the way it had invaded their thoughts. The indirect approach was devised in order to compare the morale of unbombed, lightly bombed, and heavily bombed people when they themselves did not know the purpose of the interview.[11] Morale was measured by a variety of questions about war weariness, willingness to accept unconditional surrender, fear and terror, confidence in leadership, sense of deprivation relative to other Germans, illegal listening to Allied broadcasts, absenteeism from work, and so on. Indeed, questionnaire B was rich enough to yield eighty-nine coded items within the domain of morale during the war from which a composite index was constructed, and this index as well as the discrete items were correlated with bombing exposure to estimate the effects.

Both questionnaires ended with a battery of questions on evacuation; a battery of factual items on deaths of family members as well as property damage, injury, illness, and deprivation of food or water or utilities sustained by the individual as a result of bombing; a battery of background questions including such unconventional items as membership in party organizations and a residential history during the war;[12] and, finally, a set of interviewer ratings on rapport, truthfulness, and Nazi ideology.

Those skeptical about the honesty of the respondents and the validity of the inquiry will find reassuring, indeed compelling, evidence in the comparison of the survey estimate of Nazi party (NSDAP) membership with the figures from official German records obtained by American and British authorities during the Occupation. When the survey estimate was projected with an appropriate adjustment made for our sampling being restricted to the Allied zones and to civilians under age 70, it was very close to the official count, suggesting that few respondents falsified so telltale a fact as their party membership. That the Nazis felt relatively uninhibited in the interview is also clear. When asked the question about whom they blamed for the bombings, 68 percent of the Nazis (in contrast to 26 percent of non-Nazis) answered, "the Allies," and 11 percent of them "expressed bitter hate and intense anger often accompanied by cursing and verbal abuse" (Peak 1945, p. 18) to our American interviewers in uniform.[13]

As can be sensed, the two surveys, using radically different instruments, worked together to buttress and enrich the findings. The narrative reports obtained with the open-ended questionnaire A enlarged our understanding of the dynamic processes underlying the effects of bombing. Unlike Survey A, the surveys using questionnaire B did not rely on the power of individuals to remember and weigh the causes of their morale. That was determined by comparing the morale of individuals living in communities contrasted in severity of bombing, as measured by independent, objective information on the bombing history of the place and external evidence on the damage it sustained. Since that was a gross measure of exposure not necessarily applicable to every inhabitant, variations in morale were also correlated with the refined measures of the damage and deprivation the respondent and family members suffered from the raids.

Our initial worries that memory errors might afflict Survey A, however, turned out to be unwarranted. Bombing was an unforgettable experience, a finding of substantive as well as methodological importance revealed by the clarity and comprehensiveness of the narrative accounts of respondents. A lengthy extract from an A interview with a young housewife describing her experience during the October 1944 raid on Duisburg, the site of Thyssen war factories which had been heavily bombed for two days, conveys the sharpness of memory some nine months after the event.

Question 10. When did you first experience a big raid?

That was in October 1944. There were attacks throughout 2 days, the fourteenth and the fifteenth.

Question 11. How did you fare at that time? What were your experiences?

On the fourteenth we had an early alarm about 6 A.M. but no planes came. I stayed up and did my housework. At 9 A.M. a preliminary alarm came and then a full alarm almost immediately thereafter. My baby, who was only a few weeks old, was in his carriage. I snatched him out and rushed to the cellar. The other people in the house were also in the cellar and there was much crying and praying because almost immediately large bombs began to fall directly on our section of the city. The house shook so that the men had to hold the timbers that propped up the walls and floor above to keep them from falling. We opened holes in the walls into the next cellars and called out to see if the people there were alive. People were crying and praying. They said that we had to thank our Fuehrer for this. The Party leaders had their safe bunkers and most of them were in Berlin. We usually went to bunkers, but this time the attack came too quickly. . . . That night we took turns keeping watch, listening for the alarms across the Rhine. The alarm came about 2 A.M., but it was too late to go to the bunker. We went to the cellar, where again there was a fearful scene of crying and praying. After about 15 or 20 minutes of bombing there was a pause. My sister and I put our babies into their carriages and with my father ran to the bunker. Many phosphorous bombs were dropped, and everywhere houses were in flames. We hurried until we were completely exhausted. All the while my father was shouting to us to hurry. Finally, I took my baby out of the carriage and ran on with him in my arms. By the time we reached the bunker bombs were falling on all sides. I was completely exhausted and said I could never go through this again. We stayed all this night in the bunker. After we went home there were still continual alarms. We did not have time to wash our children or eat. All that day we were running from the house to the bunker and from the bunker to the house. The night that followed we stayed all the night in the bunker and the babies got some sleep. Father remained at home and he brought us something to eat. About 4 A.M. we went home. Our house was damaged and there was no water running, but we brought some from a pump and washed ourselves and the children. Then we got some soap from the Nationalsozialistische Volkswohlfahrt [N.S.V.] and for 8 days thereafter we got food in this way. Our flat was badly damaged but we could live there. . . .

Question 17. Did these repeated raids have any other effect on your state of mind?

I always thought I would surely be killed. I lost the desire to live. The smut and dirt covered everything and it was impossible to keep anything clean. There was always so much work to do. Life was no longer beautiful. [vol. 1, pp. 113–114]

Another woman's description of the heavy raid on Bremen on October 6, 1944, also reveals the clarity of memory after an eight-month interval. Again, a lengthy excerpt is required to convey the amount of detail that is recalled.

An alarm came at 7 P.M. I was at home. I stayed at home usually because I did not want to be sitting in the public shelter while my house was possibly burning. My mother and sisters went to the shelter. I stayed upstairs because our house has no cellar. The first wave of airplanes passed overhead and nothing happened. My hope grew that this time nothing would happen. Then a second wave came. I knew by the sound that it dropped incendiary bombs, although none landed in our neighborhood. I also knew that after incendiary bombs, demolition bombs were dropped. Therefore I ran to join my family in the air-raid shelter. All the people scolded me and said that if I again came so late they would not let me in at all. While I was in the shelter, a third wave of planes came over and by the noise I knew that there were nearby hits. Some fell on the shelter itself. A great deal of panic arose in the shelter when that happened. Downstairs I could hear that our air-raid fighters were called up, so I knew that our neighborhood had been hit. I insisted on going out with them and finally succeeded although I had an exchange of words with the official at the gate, who was unwilling to let me leave, being a woman. Outside all was a sea of flames. The house next door to ours was in flames. You couldn't see that there were any flames in our house because of the air-raid curtains. It was difficult to get to my house because of the air raid and across the way a house had had a direct hit and was blocking the entrance somewhat. I got inside and ran upstairs. As I got in, a wave of smoke met me. Several incendiary bombs had penetrated the attic. I threw sand on them and extinguished them. Also a bed had caught fire. I threw it out of the window. I had to go downstairs then because it was difficult to breathe up there. Downstairs I got a wet cloth to hold on my nose; luckily the water was running. I ran back to the shelter to get my mother because I could not handle the whole situation alone. Again I had difficulty with the official at the gate. He said, "Either in or out!" Nevertheless, I succeeded in causing him to make another exception in my favor. Then I went back home with my mother, for whom I had also brought additional wet cloths. When we got home a new wave of bombers passed overhead, but we went ahead with our fire fighting. My mother found and extinguished some incendiary bombs that I had missed, or rather we both extinguished them. The windows were blown open by the pressure from the demolition bombs which had struck earlier, and showers of sparks from the surrounding flames had set fire to the curtains and rug. I tore down the curtains and threw them out the window. My mother ran and fetched water from the bathtub which we always kept handy and with that she put out the fire in the rug. After we had things under control, my mother went back to the bunker and I stayed home as long as I could stand it, but the air was so hot from all the flames everywhere that I got dizzy and got a headache, so that I went to the bunker where the air was better. And so I went back and forth between the bunker and my house all night long like a pendulum. In our street one house after the other burned. [vol. 1, p. 120]

Sampling and Field Work

In one respect, sampling for the German surveys was simple and facilitated by wartime conditions. Like the Stouffer surveys of American soldiers, the surveys of German civilians were an inquest, an inquiry enforced by the authority of the American Army. After the sample of individuals in each community had been chosen from local lists of names and addresses of the population, "appointments . . . were made in advance by Germans placed at the disposal of the team leader. For this job teachers, rationing officials or policemen were used" (vol. 1, p. 128). The respondents then traveled to the central office, where all the interviews were conducted, or in large cities, where transportation was poor, to the nearest neighborhood office of several that were established. Under such conditions, refusals and not-at-homes were a negligible problem, although other problems caused by migration or inefficiency on the part of the German officials occasionally arose.

In some towns, a recent military government registration provided the list; in other towns ration card registrations—normally updated monthly and from which the individual obviously would not want to be excluded—were used. Despite the disruption in the immediate postwar period and the movement of population, the estimates indicated that the lists were more than 90 percent complete. Individuals were selected within age-sex strata, excluding those under age 16 or over age 70. (Those with military service were screened out later.) Travel to a central office was too difficult for old people since many would have had to walk long distances given the disruption of public transportation, and children under age 16 were found in the pilot studies to have too much difficulty in answering the questions for themselves. Understandably, the sex ratio of the civilian wartime population was very unequal. For example, among 20- to 45-year-olds, only about 28 percent were men. The stratified design ensured the correct representation of various age-sex groups.

Although in one respect the sampling was simplified, in all other ways it was intricate and difficult. To ensure accurate stratification of communities by severity and character of bombing—that being crucial to the quasi-experimental design—various logs from the several air forces had to be carefully checked against each other. The population of the communities had to be carefully determined to allocate the right number of interviews per stratum (or to apply the correct weight) so that the estimates of aggregate effects on the total civilian population would be accurate. The size and organization of the field staff, the logistical problems in covering the communities, the need for four subsurveys—this and more had to be taken into account in designing the sample. On these and other problems, Cochran was monarch of all he surveyed. The final design and the occasional minor flaws are reviewed in detail in the report and need no further treatment here.[14]

The novel organization of the field work necessitated by the wartime situation, however, is not reviewed in the printed report and deserves discussion. Ten field teams, each composed of five interviewers plus an officer who dealt with the local military authority and was responsible for the team's welfare, constituted the staff. The normal load per interviewer was two interviews a day. Thus a team could complete 50 interviews, the average allocation per community in June or July, as well as travel to the next place within one week, and still cover the four communities normally assigned to it within the one month allowed for each survey.[15]

The officers in charge of the teams, fortunately, were skilled in managing logistical problems and gaining local cooperation. They also ensured the welfare and good morale of the team, often by unusual resourcefulness. On a visit to the team assigned to Bavaria, which included Auden and Stern and an especially gifted officer, I found them on Starnberger See, an Alpine lake south of Munich, temporarily resting from their duties and Auden's self-imposed extra assignment of studying the July 20 conspiracy against Hitler. They were ensconced in an elegant villa with well-stocked wine cellar, those ideal quarters carefully chosen by the officer. Auden and Stern were relaxing on the terrace, edified by the sight of the Alps, restoring themselves for the next phase of interviewing.

My next stop took me to Linz to review the work of some of the teams assigned to Austria, where I happened to observe accidentally an ironic outcome of bombing. Because of Hitler's emotional attachment to the city, Linz was especially well defended against air raids. One of our bombers had been shot down near the churchyard where Hitler's parents were buried under an impressive monument.[16] The pastor had provided burial places for the crew in the adjacent plots, their names shown on temporary markers. The eternal rest of Klara and Alois Hitler had been invaded not just by Americans but by non-Aryans—every name conveying that irony to the observer.

Surveys of Foreign Workers

In addition to the four subsurveys of German civilians, surveys were conducted among French, Italian, and Russian "displaced persons" (DPs) who had worked in Germany during the war and experienced the bombings. Eight million slave laborers had contributed to the Nazi war economy and had to be surveyed. Morale changes in such a huge, albeit coerced, component of the total labor force could not be ignored in reckoning the total effect of bombing.

An equally compelling reason for these surveys was that the DPs had been

> witnesses to the conduct of the German people . . . they worked in every German city and in innumerable German war factories. While they themselves experienced bombing, they were also able to observe the German reaction. Information has been obtained which serves as a check on the findings in the main cross sectional study of German civilians. . . . All the major conclusions . . . have been substantiated by the DP data, and there are no significant discrepancies in German and DP reactions to bombing not clearly explainable by . . . differences in . . . background or the slave-labor circumstances in which the DPs experienced bombing. [vol. 2, p. 15][17]

These "circumstances" included denying the DPs equal access to the air raid shelter that was provided to protect the German population, the large majority in all three nationality groups reporting such discrimination and almost every Russian mentioning it. Nevertheless, the DPs were more likely than the Germans to report habituation to the raids with time. This paradoxical finding suggests the way cognitive processes modified the emotional reaction to bombing. To a loyal German, bombing signified defeat. To a foreign slave laborer, it spelled liberation. The large-scale evidence of the way in which so powerful an emotional experience as bombing was attenuated should interest psychological theorists.

In May and June 1945, the DPs in camps throughout the American, British, and French zones were given a self-administered anonymous questionnaire in the appropriate language version, under the supervision of an interviewer fluent in the language. The instrument used mainly closed questions, eleven of which asked about the ways Germans reacted to the bombings. About 400 Italians, 800 French, and 1000 Russians were surveyed, the majority in each group having spent most of the war in heavily bombed communities. The agreement among the groups on most of the findings added confidence to the conclusions and the occasional discrepancies—taking into account the differential opportunities the three groups had to make observations—served to qualify the conclusions.[18]

While this design, involving so many interlocking surveys, as well as the studies of captured mail to be reviewed below, might seem too taxing for the staff, especially given the pressure to produce the findings quickly to guide the bombing of Japan, the sizable senior staff were highly motivated and had often operated under similar time pressures in their earlier work on wartime surveys. Our prime concern was practical, not scholarly, and we believed from past experience that we could be quick without being hasty, thoughtful without becoming obsessive, thorough without engaging in interminable analysis. It never would have occurred to us back then that a survey researcher needed six months or a year to design a survey and another year or two to analyze the findings.

The work also was speeded by a large staff of coders and assistants recruited from the Army and Air Forces.[19] From a new headquarters at Bad Nauheim, a spa near Frankfurt, in one of the spacious—once grand—hotels, the field work could be supervised easily. The processing, analyzing, and writing of reports progressed rapidly in the summer of 1945.

One summer morning, when the analysis was far along but not yet finished, an episode occurred which again reveals Likert's spirit and relations with staff. That particular day was an Army holiday, and all of the senior staff had taken off except Dan Katz and me. I answered Likert's phone call from London to be told that we must analyze everything and summarize it in time for presentation at a meeting in Washington the next day, when further strategy for the bombing of Japan would be reviewed. His response to the fact that Dan and I had no one to help with the mountain of data was to suggest that we do the best we could. By way of help, he would fly over that afternoon in one of our transport planes, with a GI typist aboard. He would pick us up, which would give us the extra six hours of flying time to Prestwick, Scotland, to analyze additional data and dictate the findings to the typist. There we would meet an Air Force general and go on to Washington for the meeting.

Dan and I were not paralyzed by the message; it was the way Ren functioned. No task, however impossible for us, was inconceivable to him. Our irritation was mixed with wry amusement over his apparent innocence about survey analysis despite his long experience. I was thrilled at the thought of a sidetrip home, reading that prospect into the ambiguous message that "we would fly to Prestwick, then on to Washington," and we were carried along by the importance of the mission. So Dan and I worked feverishly and had a memorandum ready in time for the flight. At that point, either out of exhaustion or having reached the limits of his tolerance toward Likert, Dan decided to stay behind and I boarded the plane with a pile of additional material for review with Ren during the flight.

A stranger setting for survey analysis would be hard to imagine. The C-47, military transport version of the DC-3, was not outfitted for comfort or contemplative work. We sat on a contoured metal bench along the side of the cabin. No insulation dampened the noise of the motors, and Ren and I reviewed the memorandum by yelling over the noise. His string of ideas for further analyses and additions to the memorandum involved my going over the data, then running the full length of the plane to the typist—the only other passenger—and dictating changes. Backing and forthing, I seemed to be running the full distance from Germany to Scotland. The noise and the bucking of the plane in the bumpy weather were no minor obstacles to progress.

During the entire trip, Likert never sat back in his bucket seat. He shared the hard labor and the excitement, and a satisfactory memorandum—considering the circumstances and the wealth of data—was ready when we arrived at Prestwick. Ren introduced me to the general, thanked me profusely, and then said he would see me in Bad Nauheim upon his return from Washington. My hopes for a visit home were suddenly shattered and I was furious at Ren, but my fury did not last. The thought that he had duped me never crossed my mind. I realized that my fantasy precipitated by the ambiguity of his message—not his duplicity—was the real source of my frustration, and I believe that the other staff would have perceived the situation in the same way. The honesty, amiability, and high purpose we sensed in Likert strengthened our bonds and outweighed his irresponsibility. In my frustration, I made an absurd, inspired request. I deserved better from Ren for all my labors. If I could not fly with them, at least the general could order our transport plane and pilot to fly me to Paris for a brief vacation before returning to Bad Nauheim. The request did not seem absurd to Ren and I was promptly rewarded and flown to Paris in solitary splendor. Whatever resentment I felt was soon dissipated by the royal treatment he had arranged.

Studies of German Civilians' Uncensored Letters

The reassuring findings on memory error were not yet known at the time that the German civilian surveys were being planned. Therefore, two complementary studies of the morale effects of bombing were conducted, based on contemporary evidence in letters written by civilians in July–November 1944. The analyses were done in early 1945, while we planned and waited for the surveys that could not begin until the Occupation.

Only a brief summary of the basic design is presented, since the details and the variation between studies to compensate for the limitations in each are presented in the report.[20] From all the uncensored mail captured by Allied troops as they advanced into Germany, about 25,000 letters were selected at random. From that large pool, about 2,000 letters satisfying special criteria were used in the two studies. The reports in these letters, of course, were addressed to other Germans, not to American interviewers as in the surveys. The letters came from all regions of Germany and could be classified by the cumulative weight of the bombs dropped in the area or city of the letter writer up to November 1944 (the end point of the period sampled). Thus, as in the design of the surveys, the writers' morale revealed in the letters could be correlated with the severity of the bombing, as measured both by the objective—but gross—data on tonnage and by personal reports in the letters of closeness of exposure and of disruption, damage, injury, and death in the family.

The results of the quantitative analysis will be presented later to accompany and confirm the survey findings, but I will note and illustrate the value of the studies now. The reading of hundreds of contemporary letters and the retrospective interviews from the later surveys clearly show that the experiences when recollected were no more tranquil despite the passage of time. That conclusion, of course, has substantive as well as methodological implications. Two excerpts from interviews and two from letters illustrate the point and provide qualitative evidence on the trauma from bombing, which will be confirmed by the later quantitative findings. A respondent recalls the experiences in her first big raid:

> I saw people killed by falling bricks and heard the screams of others dying in the fire. I dragged my best friend from a burning building and she died in my arms. I saw others who went stark mad. The shock to my nerves and to the soul, one can never erase. [vol. 1, p. 19]

Another respondent recollects:

> It was in March 1944, the first large raid on Ulm. My husband was at his job at the auto works and had raid duty when a phosphorous bomb fell directly on him. He burned like a torch. His nerves were burned all along his back. It was terrible pain that he had to suffer before he died. [vol. 1, p. 19]

A worker in a war plant in Hamburg wrote in July 1944:

> So far I'm all right, momentarily we have a terrible attack behind us. Kiel was the target. You may well imagine the fright I experienced. For days and nights we are on duty and soon I shall not be able to stand it any longer. I believe that in time I shall collapse. [vol. 1, p. 20]

A woman in Bingerbruck wrote:

> We have alerts day and night. . . . It really is a misery. . . . If this war does not come to an end either our nerves will be ruined or else we all shall be dead. It's becoming nearly impossible to work or to even prepare lunch at noon time. On Sundays we can't go visit the cemetery. We scarcely receive any milk deliveries at all. If we go to town for milk there is a constant alert on. People here are about to lose courage. In Mainz and Bonn they possess less courage yet. There they are in the process of moving and going away. [vol. 2, p. 9]

Although the letters studied had not been subjected to official censorship, the analysts assumed that some writers would exercise self-censorship and others would distort their true feelings in a variety of ways.

A mother writing to her son at the front may have minimized damage caused by bombing at home, or she may have suppressed her anxiety over future raids in order not to upset the recipient of the letter. It is also probable that some writers withheld information because of fear of possible reprisal, or through a genuine desire not to spread news of raids, since such news would impair the morale of others. On the other hand, there were those people who tended to over-dramatize and over-emphasize bombing and its effects. It is plausible that some, in order to identify themselves more fully with the war effort, tended to exaggerate their sufferings in order to convince others that they, like the soldier, were making sacrifices for the war. [vol. 2, p. 43]

The findings, however, were unlikely to be jeopardized by such sources of error for the same reason as those in the surveys. The assumption seemed warranted that suppression and distortion as well as the diffuse influences of war should be constant in all the places from which the letters originated. Then the differences in morale that were documented would reflect accurately the effects of bombing. The assumption was tested empirically. A series of correlations were computed between the bomb tonnages dropped on the area and the proportion from the area mentioning various bombing experiences in their letters. The correlations were uniformly positive and high. For example, the correlation between tonnage and proportion mentioning personal damage was .89. "In other words, writers tend to report experiences that correspond to the amount of bombing the town actually experienced" (vol. 2, p. 43).[21]

The Findings of the German Surveys

The morale effects of bombing must be seen against the background of the objective, physical effects on the population: damage to property, deprivation of essential needs, disruption of families from evacuation, injuries, and deaths. The survey estimates, when projected to all of Germany, were that 22 million civilians (about one third of the population) were directly exposed to raids. Injuries numbered about 780,000; deaths, 305,000; homes destroyed or damaged beyond repair, 1.9 million; those evacuated, about 5 million; those deprived of electricity or gas or water for some period (often temporary), about 20 million; and those suffering some loss of property, about 14 million. The sample-survey estimate of homes destroyed was validated against an official German figure of 1.96 million—suggesting the overall accuracy of the sampling and measurement procedures (vol. 1, p. 9). Since relative as well as absolute numbers are essential to interpretation, one should note that about 1 percent of the total civilian population of about 70 million were injured, about .5 percent killed, and about 7 percent evacuated.[22]

Strategic bombing indeed took a heavy toll—unprecedented in magnitude in that era—but two points should be noted. Considering the number of raids and the heavy bombing (about 1 million tons in all), the gross effects were far below the expectations of the extreme advocates of strategic bombing. Moreover serious "involvement" (injuries, deaths, or property damage) did not increase in proportion to the severity of bombing. "Only 5% more people were involved where 30,000 tons of bomb had been used than with 6,000 tons" (vol. 1, p. 30). This finding of diminishing physical effects with increased bombing parallels a major finding on morale effects.

That bombing was a horrible experience and depressed morale cannot be doubted. The passages from interviews and letters quoted earlier convey, albeit qualitatively, the intensity of the experience and the depth of the psychological effects, and the sample-survey results document quantitatively the extent of such effects. Among those exposed to bombing, 38 percent reported traumatic emotional effects. Their "terror transcends the immediate raid to such an extent that it is reinstated by the next alert" (vol. 1, p. 19). Among all those directly exposed, 69 percent experienced some emotional effects, and a majority—52 percent—reported that they did not become adapted or habituated to bombing, 28 percent stating that their fears increased with time. One respondent reported: "I never became accustomed to the raids and bombing. . . . I was always afraid and shaking and nervous" (vol. 1, p. 20). Another said: "One can't get used to the raids. I wished for an end. We all got nerves" (vol. 1, p. 20). A letter written from Dresden in October 1944 tells the same story: "Believe me we are trembling. The fright from the last time is still in our system" (vol. 1, p. 19).

In the survey which directly asked people exposed to bombing to describe the effects (questionnaire A), 60 percent said that "they did not want to go on with the war because of bombing" (vol. 1, p. 15). This finding was corroborated in the other survey, which determined the effects of bombing indirectly, by comparing communities (questionnaire B). Among residents of bombed towns, 58 percent answered yes when asked, "Did you at any time during the war come to a point where you did not want to go on with the war?" In Table 4.1, the comparisons of people in bombed and unbombed towns on

Table 4.1   The Morale
of Residents of Bombed and Unbombed Towns

	Percentage of People in Towns	
	Unbombed	Bombed
Willing to accept unconditional surrender	51%	58%
Believing that leaders had best interests of people at heart	62	49
Believing that people like them got along worse than other groups	49	57

NOTE: Adapted from vol. 1, pp. 16–18. The size of the two groups varies slightly from question to question. Approximate Ns: unbombed towns, 538; bombed towns, 1,812.

a number of indicators reveal the lowered morale of those who had been bombed.

The hypothesis that bombing improved morale by arousing hatred for the Allies was examined. As Table 4.1 shows, bombing turned people against their own leaders, not against the Allies. On the direct question, "Did you blame the Allies for the air raids?" (questionnaire B, no. 36), there was no difference between bombed and unbombed towns, and a slight majority of the total sample stated without qualification that they did not blame the Allies. About one third categorically blamed the Allies, the remainder voicing qualified blame—for example, saying they could not see the justice in bombing innocent women and children.

The main cognitive process that underlay the findings was that this was war. The Germans had bombed the Allies and in return they had to expect it. As Peak reports: "Again and again they said in effect, 'Our leaders told us proudly of bombing England and other countries. They bragged about the complete destruction of Coventry. We knew we would get it sooner or later. It is just war' " (1946, p. 5). Understandably, resentment would be turned against the German leaders who had started the chain of events. Confidence in them would be undermined by the fact that they had promised that Germany would not be bombed and then could not protect the people from such attacks and their devastation. To counteract these ideas, to turn the blame away, a directive from the party chancellery as early as 1942 stated: "The concept of 'terror raid' is intended to reflect the criminal behavior of the enemy . . . therefore a German attack must never be called 'terror raid.' Counter measures of the German Air Force are to be designated as 'retaliation measures' " (vol. 1, p. 75). Such attempts to shape German thought about the bombings obviously did not work.

The hypothesis that the experience of bombing creates a sense of unity among people sharing the hardship of war with each other and with the soldiers at the front is also not borne out by the findings in Table 4.1. Indeed one strategic gain from not bombing every town—apart from its humanity—is that suffering then is not equally shared. Qualitative evidence also showed that those who bore the brunt resented their countrymen who had been favored by the fortunes of war, and even experienced malicious pleasure rather than sympathy when the wheel of fortune turned. "Many people in the Rhineland, for example, were pleased when the bombs began to fall upon Berlin" (vol. 1, p. 18). Krefeld, the site of one of the pilot studies, was a Rhineland city bombed early in the war. The intelligence report on January 21, 1943, by the local security police states:

> The news of the bombing of the capital has been the talk of all parts of the population. Without exception especially great satisfaction that the loud-mouthed Berliners have at last got it again could be noted in all conversation. The satisfaction derives from the feeling that Berliners are said to have shown little understanding thus far for the suffering of the population in the Rhineland. There was veritable indignation that after this one light attack on Berlin retaliation attacks were immediately launched against England, while after raids that destroyed at least parts of such cities here as Cologne, Duisburg, Düsseldorf and Mainz allegedly no plane was made free from the eastern front for such a retaliation attack. It is hardly possible to reproduce the number of statements of this sort. Frequently it could be heard said that it would be fine if the British flew more frequently to Berlin so that the inhabitants there would get a taste of how we in the west are feeling. People are very curious as to whether the population of greater Berlin will get extra coffee rations for this trifling attack. One often hears it said that the whole thing proves unequivocally that we in the west are regarded as second class people and that the whole Rhineland has already been written off. [vol. 1, p. 18]

The practical implications for bombing strategy are clear, and the implications for scholars concerned with problems of relative deprivation and reference group theory should be noted.

That strategic bombing was a powerful weapon in reducing civilian morale was demonstrated by a great deal of evidence, only some of which has been presented, but this last finding should deter the strategist from wholesale bombing. Those strategists who conclude from the other findings that bombing should be applied with ever-increasing force must look more closely at additional crucial findings in the original reports.

Low morale, to be sure, was more prevalent among people in the bombed towns, when examined without finer distinctions in severity, but often it was also widespread among people living in unbombed towns. As Table 4.1 shows, willingness to accept unconditional surrender was only 7 percent higher in bombed towns. The paradox is quickly resolved. "All of the unbombed communities had repeated alerts and many expected that sooner or later they would be the target. Moreover, these people had heard much about the devastating consequences of raids from the evacuees in their midst" (vol. 1, p. 16). Again, we see that morale can be reduced without extensive bombing.

When we examine the variations in morale by levels of bombing, the findings are unusually consistent and perhaps unexpected. Table 4.2 presents a few of these results. (The composite index is based on a large number of morale measures.) "The greatest rate of decline in morale tends to occur between unbombed towns and those subjected to total average bombing of about 500 tons. There is some further decline when bombing is stepped up to 6,000 tons. There is very little change or, in some cases, slight improvement in morale as a result of increasing bombing up to 30,000 tons" (vol. 1, p. 22).

Thoughtful readers might well conclude that it is not only wasteful but immoral to inflict more damage than is needed to achieve a strategic purpose. Other findings underscore this conclusion. "There is some evidence for the notion that severe raids increased apathy. . . . Under these conditions, resentment against leaders, which was stimulated by light bombing, might give way under heavy raids to preoccupation with personal matters, apathy, and reduced interest in political affairs . . . people in this state of mind are more easily manipulated and controlled" (vol. 1, p. 22).

The pattern of diminishing returns from increased bombing was so important to establish that it was tested in various ways. The pattern was revealed again when cities were classified by amount of physical destruction, rather than by sheer tonnage dropped. When cities with as much as 40–60 percent of their buildings destroyed (or even 60–80 percent) were compared on eleven different measures of morale with cities less destroyed, no consistent decline in morale was observed. On some tests, morale even improved! Person-specific measures of severity of bombing were employed for a parallel analy-

Table 4.2   Variations in German Morale
by Magnitude of Bombing

	Inhabitants of Unbombed Areas	Inhabitants Exposed to		
		Light Bombing	Medium Bombing	Heavy Bombing
Not wanting to go on with war	71%	79%	79%	72%
Willing to accept un- conditional sur- render	51	54	59	59
Believing that leaders have best interests of people at heart	62	52	44	48
Scoring "high" on composite index of morale	59	51	42	44

NOTE: Adapted from vol. 1, pp. 23–26. Approximate Ns: unbombed, 538; lightly bombed, 278; medium bombed, 599; heavily bombed, 935.

sis. When individuals contrasted in the magnitude of personal deprivation following bombing (the lack of food, water, utilities, transportation, sanitary facilities, contact by phone and mail) were compared on twelve morale measures: "On almost half of the measures there is a tendency for morale to remain at the same level or to improve where deprivation is the greatest. In other words, there is evidence here . . . that beyond a certain point further increase in deprivation has very little additional effect in depressing morale" (vol. 1, p. 28). Even among those whose own houses were damaged by bombing but who sustained no personal injuries or deaths in the family, there was no consistent evidence of declining morale, and on some tests there was improvement. Only among those Germans who sustained personal injuries and/or deaths in the immediate family was there a consistent decline in morale, but on some measures that decrement is small in magnitude (vol. 1, pp. 27–28). This last stark finding might suggest to some a strategy of unlimited bombing. But apart from calculations of feasibility and costs in personnel and dollars, the outcome is problematic since severe personal consequence, as noted earlier, "does not increase in proportion to the weight of bombs dropped. . . . Only 5% more people were involved (sustained injuries or casualties and property damage) where 30,000 tons of bombs had been used than with 6,000 tons."

The two studies of captured, uncensored mail provided independent, contemporary evidence that confirmed the basic findings of the sample surveys.[23] Bombing did depress morale. However, when the morale of writers in communities varying from no bombing to very heavy bombing was examined (the same design as in Survey B), there was no evidence of a decline in morale with increased tonnage. When letter writers who reported being in close proximity to raids were compared with those who reported being more distant or having had an alert but no bombs, the differences on various morale indicators were small—sometimes as small as 1–3 percentage points. When writers who reported continuous raids were compared with those who reported exposure only in the past, "continuous bombing of people" was found "to add little to the morale changes produced by recent or past raids" (vol. 2, p. 10). Finally, when writers were scored (as in the survey analysis) on an index of severity of personal consequences following bombing (property damage, disruption of essential services, injuries, deaths in the family) and then compared on various morale measures and a composite index of morale, the pattern of diminishing returns was again revealed. "Above a certain level of severity the decrement in morale seems to taper off" (vol. 2, p. 13). Given the scoring system for severe personal consequences used in the mail studies, the bombings would have to go far to achieve maximum effect, but not to the ultimate limit.

These were the effects on German civilians generally, no reference having been made until now to differential effects in some subgroups. Many characteristics were examined, but only a few produced differential effects. Vested interest, specifically defined as the belief that they had more to gain from a German than an Allied victory, helped sustain the morale of individuals even under heavy bombing, although the bombing did have a negative impact on them. Such a belief should not be confused with vested interest that comes from advantaged position in society. Its illusory source is illustrated in this young stenographer's answer to the question of what she expected if the Allies won the war and occupied Germany:

I and all of us could only believe what we were told in the newspapers, etc. I believed that all men up to the age of 65 would be taken away to work elsewhere. I believed that we who remained behind would have to do hard manual labor in a slave status, breaking up stones, removing rubble and so on. I feared we would be moved about arbitrarily from one city to another. I feared we would not get enough food to support life. I feared rape and general violence and disorder. Also I feared severe limitations on civilian movements. I expected to be allowed out of doors only 2 or 3 hours a day. On the other hand, I expected freedom from air raids; that was a partial consolation. [vol. 1, p. 117]

Beliefs in the adequacy of the defense measures against bombing and in the power of the promised secret weapons produced small differential effects. However, "personal identification with the Nazi cause was by all odds the most important" factor in sustaining morale. "Ardent Nazis subjected to heavy bombing retained better morale, as a group, than did non-Nazis who were not bombed at all. This was true for all aspects of morale with the possible exception of the purely emotional reactions of fear and terror brought on by the raids. Nazis seem to have been frightened almost as much as other Germans." Bombing indeed depressed the morale of Nazis. However, "their initial morale was so much higher that bombing was insufficient to bring it down to the level of the non-Nazis" (vol. 1, p. 33). Among ideological Nazis (not merely party members), the diminishing effect with increasing bombing was dramatically demonstrated. Those experiencing the heaviest tonnage showed better morale than those exposed to lighter bombing. And, as noted earlier, the bombings were far more likely to produce resentment and hatred of the Allies among Nazis than among other Germans. Thus, although bombing substantially dented the spirit of the Nazis, it was never sufficient to obliterate their support of the war or alienate them from their cause, and at the heaviest level the effects on them were counterproductive. These differential findings suggest the ironic conclusion that bombing harmed the innocent more severely than the guilty.

In observing and offsetting the morale effects of bombing, German officials distinguished between *Stimmung* (literally "mood," referring to inner feelings) and *Haltung*, "deportment" (referring to behavior that might be held in check or released). *Haltung* was crucial, since low morale that was not translated into behavior would not endanger the war effort. Given the findings on the decline in commitment and the rise in hostility, the officials could not rely on people's self-imposed internal controls and instead imposed harsh external controls. Our studies paid special attention to the distinction between feelings and behavior, and findings on the behavioral effects of bombing were obtained.

Absenteeism of industrial workers was measured by a battery of questions in the surveys, by a critical analysis of German statistics, and by interviews with multiple informants in bombed and unbombed towns. For many reasons demoralized workers would be expected to have high rates of absenteeism. Among those expecting defeat, work would no longer serve any patriotic purpose. Monetary incentives for working were weak because there was little to buy, and many people received indemnities for bomb damage. Getting to work became more difficult as bombing disrupted transportation; authorized absence to repair a damaged home, to find a new home, and to search for missing relatives, or because of injuries or illness, increased with bombing. Offsetting these forces, however, were the official controls and severe penalties for unauthorized absence.

Despite the controls, all the evidence consistently showed that bombing increased absenteeism. The rate specifically labeled "sickness" increased so markedly that malingering is the only reasonable interpretation of the trend. However, the rates also were abnormally high in unbombed towns and increased over time, suggesting that "absenteeism thus appears as a wartime phenomenon, quite apart from bombing" (vol. 1, p. 55). Although the effects were larger in heavily bombed cities, absenteeism "was also serious in lightly bombed cities and in relatively undamaged plants in heavily bombed cities" (vol. 1, p. 60). This evidence and other evidence on tardiness and declines in productivity (see vol. 1, chap. 2) establish behavioral effects but again suggest diminishing returns from increasing bombing.

Other behavioral effects were also documented. The surveys revealed that listening to Allied broadcasts, behavior specifically prohibited, was more prevalent in bombed than unbombed towns, but the difference was modest and listening was equally frequent in towns experiencing light and heavy bombing. Looting was studied through crime statistics and informants' reports and was found to increase markedly after air raids. From official records and interviews with local informants, estimates of the amount of subversive behavior (sabotage and underground activity) and disruptive behavior (black market activity, riots, and demonstrations) were computed for all communities in the sample and correlated with bomb tonnage and physical damage. For various technical reasons reviewed in the original report (vol. 2, chap. 1) but too intricate to be treated here, some ambiguity clouds the interpretation of the moderate positive correlations obtained. The effects of heavy bombing on such behavior were, at most, modest, and these findings are congruent with the general pattern of diminishing returns from increasing bombing.

The Design of the Japanese Surveys

While we were completing the analysis of the German surveys, and while Likert was making a futile attempt to establish a permanent survey research unit in occupied Austria,[24] we began the preliminary planning of the Japanese surveys, authorized by President Truman on August 15, 1945. Krech directed the planning in the United States; I helped only part time because of my commitment to Dan Katz to teach at Brooklyn College. In October, pretesting began in Japan, the revisions of the instrument, final design, direction of the field work, and later analysis becoming the responsibility of Burton Fisher, originally a member of Program Surveys and during the war a member of Stouffer's research staff.

Since with the end of the war many of the German survey staff had returned to their normal civil careers, replacements, especially those with knowledge of Japanese society, culture, and language, were needed. The staff that were recruited again showed Likert's talents and strategy. Cochran was replaced by Morris Hansen, a distinguished sampling statistician from the Census Bureau. The training of interviewers, a delicate matter for reasons to be described, was entrusted to Waldemar Nielsen, a former supervisor of the Program Surveys field staff who later had served as a naval officer in the Pacific theater. As in Germany, the policy was to not use native personnel and to identify the interviewers as representatives of America; only Americans of Japanese ancestry were recruited, not merely for fluency in the language but in order to maximize rapport. About one third were civilians; the others were military personnel. Since none had previous experience in open-ended interviewing, they required intensive training, accomplished partly during the three pretests in Japan necessary to develop satisfactory instruments.[25]

In applying survey methods that had been proven in the West but untried in Japan, sensitivity to cultural differences was essential and ensured by the anthropologists recruited for the senior staff. Jules Henry brought that sensitivity, as well as long experience in survey research with Program Surveys and with the Surveys Division of OWI, and was aided by Ruth Benedict and Clyde Kluckhohn, both of whom served as consultants. Alexander Leighton, an anthropologist and psychiatrist who had directed a program of survey research among Japanese-Americans interned in our war relocation centers, served on the senior staff and was rejoined by Conrad Arensberg, who had been associated with the research on internees. Other senior staff included the social psychologists Donald Adams and E. L. Ballachey, sociologists Raymond Bowers and William Sewell, and political scientist David Truman. The experience Bowers, Kluckhohn, and I gained in the Bombing Survey aided us when we served in 1947 as an "expert mission" recruited by the Occupation to help train the Japanese public opinion researchers and stimulate fledgling survey organizations just beginning to flourish in postwar Japan. Unwittingly, the Bombing Survey had this benign effect, which came about through the deliberate efforts of a former associate at Program Surveys and the enlightened goals of the Occupation.

The basic design of the German surveys proved satisfactory and was used again in Japan, although some of the earlier components were dropped and some new ones added. Some sixty cities and places contrasted in the magnitude of bombing and yielding a sample representative of Japan, excluding the northern distant island of Hokkaido and the island of Shikoku, were chosen, and about 3,200 civilians aged 16–70 were interviewed in November and December 1945. Given the late timing of the field work and the earlier reassuring German evidence on the vividness of memory, studies of mail and separate surveys for each of the two months were not conducted. Only one questionnaire form was employed, which effectively combined the two instruments used in Germany and covered all the same essential variables. "In the prescribed introductory structuring, and up to question 26, not a word about bombing occurs. The interviewer should never use the words 'bombing' or 'air raid' or similar terms unless the respondent himself brings them up" (Krech and Ballachey 1948, p. 190). After question 26, a battery of questions asked of respondents living in bombed areas elicited the narrative account of their experiences that questionnaire A had obtained in Germany. Understandably, Hiroshima and Nagasaki and rural areas adjacent to them were included, as a separate stratum, and questions about the atomic bombing were asked of those residents and also of all others in the survey. Thus comparisons of the morale of people in or near Hiroshima and Nagasaki and those far removed from the atomic bombings and between those conventionally bombed and those unbombed could be made, and the effects inferred from the quasi-experimental design.

The Japanese survey, like the German, was an inquest enforced by military authority. In the company of a local policeman or other municipal official, the member of each field team who was a Caucasian but Japanese-speaking officer located the predesignated respondents and arranged appointments for interviews, which were conducted in a local headquarters for the unit. That central facility enabled a new auxiliary procedure to be used in the Japanese survey. A subsample of interviews (about one in seven) were sound-recorded as a check on interviewer performance and to provide full narrative accounts of experience. A small number of long, clinical interviews was also conducted as another check on validity. As in Germany, informants were interviewed and documents collected to produce a background report on each community in the sample, to measure special variables, and to provide independent, external evidence to supplement and check the survey findings.

The Findings of the Japanese Surveys

From a theoretical perspective, the comparable German and Japanese surveys could test whether there were uniformities in the morale effects of bombing despite the contrasted conditions.[26] Excerpts follow from interviews with two Japanese women describing their experiences under bombing.

> On the night of the 23rd of May, I opened the window and looked out, wondering if it would be safe tonight. . . . Three planes came over together; two of them circled overhead and then passed by while the third let loose with its bombs. There wasn't very much time to prepare for it, since the air raid warning didn't go on until the planes were practically overhead. I ran out with my two children. As we stepped out, flames enveloped us. Flames fell on my chest and in back of me. I was terrified. The child that I was holding got caught in a little hole; so instead of extinguishing the flames that were burning my chest and face, I gave the child a yank and she pried herself loose. The child cried in fear and started to put out the fire. Between us we extinguished the flames. It was driving me mad. My whole face ached with pain. I couldn't see very well. I did put out the flames on my chest but did not succeed too well with the fire on my back. We fled from one place to another. It seemed that the fire was trying its best to swallow us. [p. 35]

The second excerpt:

> Each time there was a raid our town was spared, but I had made preparations. As I took the last piece of furniture to the shelter, the planes came over and I heard a noise and looked out and smelled gasoline and the houses were burning. I was going to fight the fire, but the fire was too strong so I left the burning area. At that moment everything was in a turmoil and I wished I were dead or the war would end soon so I wouldn't have to go through this again. [p. 35]

If you had not known the respective nationalities of the two German respondents quoted earlier and these two Japanese respondents, you would not have been able to tell who was German and who was Japanese. If the United States had been bombed, might you not have thought that American women were describing their experiences? From these quotations one senses that bombing penetrates far beneath layers of culture to produce uniform emotional effects.

The Japanese survey again revealed a pattern of diminishing returns from increasing bombing, but it also showed that the morale effects in all communities were much worse than in Germany. The uniformity in the pattern of effects in two contrasted societies is a compelling finding, and the severity of effects in Japan is a surprising finding when we learn that the magnitude of bombing was much less in Japan. The geography, social ecology, and wartime situation together provide the explanation of this perplexing finding and will be reviewed shortly. First, consider the magnitude of the bombing.

The tonnage dropped on Japan was so much less than in Germany that some of the Japanese cities classified in the analysis as "heavily" bombed received only 500–1,000 tons of bombs. Many German cities classified as "medium" bombed received larger tonnages than practically any of the "heavily" bombed Japanese cities. Most of the German cities classified as "heavily" bombed received two to five times the tonnage dropped on the most heavily bombed Japanese cities, and this despite the fact that the Japanese cities were far larger in population. We must therefore think of the cities at the high end of the Japanese comparisons as equivalent to the middle or low points in the German comparisons. Thus, in interpreting the Japanese finding on the relation between severity of bombing and decline in morale, we must realize—taking into account the transformation onto one scale of magnitude—that the test reveals only what moderate, not truly heavy, bombing can do to the people of a second and different society. We learn that bombing did not have to reach even a modest level to depress morale substantially.

Despite the lesser bombing, the damage, disruption, and toll over all Japan were greater than in Germany even though the Japanese civil population was slightly smaller. The survey estimates were: injured, 1.3 million; killed, 900,000; evacuated, 8.5 million. The homes of about 15 percent of the population were destroyed and the homes of an additional 5 percent were badly damaged. One medium-sized city exposed to 1,500 tons of ordinary—not atomic—bombs was 99.5 percent destroyed, according to physical inspection. Another medium-sized city exposed to less than 900 tons suffered 74 percent destruction. The corresponding estimate for Hiroshima was 68.5 percent destruction. Clearly, great destruction can be done by "moderate" conventional bombing of relatively vulnerable communities and structures such as those in Japan, and the effect of a "little" bombing was even greater than it was in Germany.[27]

The heavy toll in cities that were exposed to only moderate or light bombing helps explain the pattern of diminishing returns. As well, the indirect effects of bombing on unbombed communities were so severe that there was hardly any additional decline in morale in bombed and badly damaged communities. Geography and ecology explain those indirect effects. In a country as small as Japan, people, no matter where they were located, whether rural or urban, could not avoid exposure to the threat of bombing.

> Despite the fact that the principal targets were the 66 cities subjected to urban area attacks, few Japanese lacked contact with the air raids. The nature of the intensive attack against a nation small in geographic area, with American planes criss-crossing the skies as they went their unchallenged way to their targets, meant that even the most isolated Japanese frequently saw the American B-29s in the sky . . . 57% of even the native rural population had experienced air raids and alerts, and about one-sixth said they had actually been bombed. Indeed . . . rural people ascribed loss of confidence in victory and depressed work capacity to the air attack almost as often as did urban people. . . . Those of the more than 8,500,000 people who left the heavily bombed cities went to live with their friends and relatives in rural and other urban areas scattered throughout Japan, and told of the terrible destruction caused by bombing. [p. 55]

The diffusion of effects throughout the society helps explain the finding that when individuals were contrasted in terms of "damage to home and property by bombing, a composite index of home and property damage plus death and injury in the respondent's family . . . most of these measures were not consistently related to morale . . . nor did they generally show differences in morale" (p. 44n). When individuals who had no experience of bombs falling in close proximity to them are compared with those who had experienced such personal proximity once versus more than once, and the groups are compared on a variety of discrete morale measures and on a composite index of morale, those with no personal experience had only slightly higher morale. Repeated personal exposure almost never produced a further decline in morale. When residents of cities varying in tonnage and physical destruction were compared, parallel to the German analysis, those in unbombed communities showed higher morale but the differences were generally less than 10 percent. Among bombed communities contrasted in severity the differences generally were small (usually between 5 and 10 percent) and sometimes inconsistent in direction. These and other findings led to the conclusion that "the effects of bombing in depressing morale were pervasive and affected the entire population, not merely those who personally experienced raids or lived in heavily bombed places" (p. 2). "Throughout the small nation the effects of the bombings were remarkably uniform" (p. 6).

Apart from the pervasive, indirect effects of bombing, the depths to which Japanese morale sank everywhere reflected two additional forces of war. One of these was the acute shortages of food as the war progressed which led to widespread fear of starvation.

> By 1943 imports of rice had fallen 50%; by 1944, 70%; and by 1945 they had virtually disappeared. . . . By 1945 the quantity of fish available for food had fallen 35% below normal because of wartime restrictions on oceanic fishing. Rice rationing was begun in April 1941. By 1942 it became necessary to mix barley and wheat with the rice ration. Starting with 4%, this adulteration had increased to 18% by 1945. The net result of this situation, the mass of evidence shows, was widespread under-nourishment, nutritional disease, social conflict, and depression of the will to resist.
>
> Almost uncontrolled inflation permitted inequities to develop in the distribution of the limited amounts which were available. . . . With rationing and the decrease in the food supply, the black market flour-ished. By March 1944, 4% of the rice and wheat, 36% of the vegetables, and 39% of the fish consumed were being bought on the black market at fantastic prices. And those who could not pay simply did not eat. [p. 17]

The inequality of sacrifice created feelings of relative deprivation and hostility to those who were advantaged and thus weakened social cohesion. The wife of a small businessman in Osaka described her feelings.

> Our leaders told us to work hard, cultivate every bit of land, and grow as much as we could. Those crops that were grown were taken away for rationing purposes; those were usually gobbled up by the upper class people. . . . Oftentimes, when ladies got together, we used to talk about Tojo and his cohorts, wondering what kind of clothes they wore and what kind of food they ate. We were darn sure it wasn't the kind of food we ate. [p. 213]

The second factor that produced a pervasive decline in morale was the military reverses later on in the war. Earlier defeats occurred far from home and the news did not reach the ears of many people because of effective censorship. Later, when the news of the chang-ing tide of victory reached the people, the effects on morale were severe, and thus bombing was not totally responsible for the depths to which Japanese morale sank everywhere. Inadequate air raid protection heightened the fear and demoralization from bombing and weakened confidence in the government. The statement by a machinist in Funabashi, a small city that suffered almost no bombing and destruction, conveys the pervasive effects of bombing and the deprivations of war:

> Yes, I reached the point when I was unwilling to go on with the war. It was when the air raids became severe and our homes and factories were destroyed but there was no opposition from our planes. I felt as if we were fighting machinery with bamboo. Also, my food ration was not enough to keep me working. I could hardly stand it. The government told us we would defeat the U.S. forces when they landed in the homeland, but since my house was burned, my clothing gone, and I had no food, I knew I could not go on. [p. 49]

Of the many other discrete findings, one more will be noted to suggest the uniform effects of bombing in the two societies. The German survey had established that the demoralizing effect of bombing was less consequential among those who believed they had more to gain from German victory than from defeat. In Japan, a larger proportion of the population held and were sustained by such beliefs. Although they wished that the war would be over and the bombings cease, they believed that an American victory might bring even worse suffering down upon them. "The propagandists throughout the war instilled . . . a fear of the dire consequences . . . until the overwhelming mass . . . expected anything from enslavement to annihilation if they were to lose the war" (p. 23). Thus, however demoralized, the Japanese persevered. The fact that almost three quarters of the sample felt free to express such uncomplimentary views of America to the interviewers again suggests the validity of the surveys.

The Lessons of the Bombing Surveys

The experience in conducting these large and complex studies had taught the staff a great deal about the methodology of survey research. That surveys, despite the many obstacles, could yield valid and potentially useful results increased our confidence in the method. That the method had worked so well in Japan and Germany, among people whose experience with surveillance and repression seemed to make it inapplicable, seemed compelling proof that survey research could be conducted in many countries. Indeed, the confidence and experience that Katz, Krech, and I had gained led us to train survey researchers and help conduct the first postwar surveys in Japan, Turkey, Norway, and elsewhere against the frequent objections that the method would not work.

Some of the methodological principles we had learned were reviewed in the literature although, as noted earlier, these reports were only fragmentary. Not even that much can be said about the substantive findings and the moral questions they raised. I, for example, described the diminishing returns with increasing bombing in *Survey Design and Analysis* (1955), but only to illustrate the methodological principle that an explanatory variable should be examined over a wide range of magnitude rather than dichotomized, the crude practice common in much survey analysis in that period. It is a telling fact that I never remarked that heavy bombing inflicted more death and destruction than was necessary to achieve the strategist's goal of demoralizing the population. Nowhere did I ever publish any of the extensive evidence of the horrors experienced under bombing.[28]

This is not to suggest that I or other staff members had become callous. We could never forget the harrowing content of the interviews, but it remained lodged in our minds, not brought to the attention of others. Moreover, the moral issues posed by the bombing of World War II prior to the knowledge produced by the surveys seemed to me difficult to appraise. Almost twenty-five years later, during the bombings of the Vietnam War, the evidence from the World War II surveys seemed to me thoroughly relevant to our policies and to give an unambiguous answer to the moral issue. By then our government knew, or should have known, that massive bombing was inhuman and that its intensification did not serve the strategic purpose of reducing morale. So I could not understand how the secretary of the Air Force, Dr. Harold Brown, could recommend in March 1968 "the intensification of the bombing . . . to erode the will of the population by exposing a wider area of North Vietnam to casualties and destruction" (*New York Times*, July 4, 1971, p. 17:1). Later, I could not understand how President Nixon could renew and intensify the bombing to such a level that by the end of 1972, 2 million more tons of bombs had been dropped on Vietnam than on Germany and Japan put together, even though Japan alone had a larger land area than Vietnam and twice as many people. Then, during our massive bombings of Hanoi in December 1972, when our Defense Department dismissed North Vietnam's assertion that these were "terror bombings," I could not help recalling the statement quoted earlier (p. 39) by the Nazi party chancellery, rejecting the very same term of "terror raid" for the German attacks on England.

As the bombings continued and passed the mark of double—finally triple—the bomb tonnage of World War II, I felt compelled to report the substantive findings of the Bombing Surveys, to remark on the immorality of bombing civilians when one knew it served no strategic purpose, and to speculate on the reasons for such massive bombings despite the contrary evidence in our own official and authoritative surveys. Over a considerable period, I submitted an article seriatim to various popular magazines, hoping my offer to have it edited in any way needed to simplify its style would ensure its publication and the circulation of the facts to a wide audience. The article was rejected by the *New York Times Sunday Magazine*, the *Atlantic Monthly*, *Harper's*, the *Saturday Review*, the *Scientific American*, as well as a few other less well-known magazines, not with intent to suppress the facts I had tried to make available, but, as they said, because the bombings were stopping and the article was no longer needed. In the course of that period, whenever the bombings resumed, ironically, it was too late since the article had already been rejected. Finally, I gave up.

Notes

1. Franklin D'Olier's assistant, Colonel Guido R. Perera, called President Conant of Harvard for someone to direct the Morale Division. Conant referred him to Leonard Carmichael, president of Tufts, who recommended Likert. [Ed.]

2. U.S. Strategic Bombing Survey, Morale Division, *The Effects of Strategic Bombing on German Morale*, 2 vols. (1946, 1947); and *The Effects of Strategic Bombing on Japanese Morale* (1947). In addition to the three main volumes, two volumes on the effects of bombing on health in Germany and Japan and a volume on the effects of atomic bombs on health in Hiroshima and Nagasaki bear upon the general problem of morale effects. These volumes were also issued by the U.S. Government Printing Office.

3. Henry 1946; Hyman 1955; Katz 1950; Krech and Crutchfield 1947; Loomis 1946; Peak 1945, 1946. A mimeographed compilation of the materials from the Japanese Bombing Survey showing the progressive changes in the questionnaire, sample design, and interviewing procedures in the course of planning and pretesting was edited by Krech and Ballachey and used by them as a syllabus in courses at the University of California at Berkeley. This valuable and detailed case study of the methodological difficulties and progress in the development of a survey had limited circulation, has long been out of print, and included none of the analysis of data or findings. See Krech and Ballachey 1948

(mimeo). Janis reanalyzed many of the findings of the Bombing Surveys, notably the interviews with survivors in Hiroshima and Nagasaki, in a study for the U.S. Air Force on problems of civil defense against a future air attack. He does not review, however, any of the methodology of the surveys and his monograph also was published more than thirty years ago. See Janis 1951. Another reanalysis of substantive findings from the Bombing Surveys was conducted in the 1950s by Iklé. Since that study also was supported by the U.S. Air Force, it is further evidence that policymakers during the Vietnam War were familiar with the survey findings from World War II. It is worth noting that Iklé was later appointed as an undersecretary of defense. See Iklé, 1958. A more recent but still brief fragment was included in Boyd and Hyman 1975.

For a review of the U.S. Bombing Surveys and the controversial issue of the effects of massive bombing, see Converse 1987, pp. 174–180; MacIsaac 1976; and Wilensky 1967, pp. 24–34. [Ed.]

4. J. Stern 1947.

5. On the biases to be guarded against and the evidence in these sources, see vol. 1, pt. 2, chap. 1, especially p. 42.

6. Likert also had to recruit staff for a Medical Section of the Division which examined direct and indirect effects of bombing on mental and physical health, such impairments reducing the will and capacity of the population to support the war effort. The staffing presented no difficulties since the few personnel needed to analyze hospital records and interview expert informants were obtained from medical branches of the service. Colonel Meiling, an Air Force officer who had studied medicine in prewar Germany, became chief of the section and was aided by a few other officers and civilian psychiatrists. The occurrence of various symptoms such as insomnia, headaches, and "nerves" was also determined by questions in the survey. However primitive these measures may seem, the estimates from the sample could be generalized to the population, whereas hospital records are limited in this respect and present other ambiguities. For example, the English reported an increased admission of cases of senile dementia after bombings, explained by the fact that families who had been caring for their impaired elderly prior to the raid were no longer able to provide the care. This, to be sure, is a disruptive effect of bombing, but the unwary might have concluded that a slow progressive disorder afflicting some old persons was all at once created by bombing.

7. Brewster Smith's autobiographical account (1983) of his experience with Stouffer's unit supports my analysis:

The intervening trauma of Vietnam makes it hard for younger generations to realize that while ostentatious patriotism was out of style, there was very strong social consensus in support of the Allied war effort against the Axis powers. The contribution of psychologists was desired in the war, and psychologists wanted to contribute. . . . Psychologists in the war were not trying to prove how scientific they were; rather, they were trying to use all the science they knew—and everything else, too—to cope with urgent problems. [pp. 169–170]

8. That strong beliefs about the war defended interviewers against the trauma they might experience, but on occasion could bias their interviewing, is suggested by an excerpt from another of Stern's interviews:

"Did I blame the Allies for the air raids? Ha, why naturally, we never once raided America. England? England started them. England."

"England started the air raids," I repeated, dropping the smile now and barely asking the question. "England started the bombing of open cities and villages? England, I suppose, started that before the Germans flattened Guernica in . . ."

"I don't know anything about Guernica . . . and . . ."

"No, of course, you wouldn't."

"I know England started the air warfare against Germany by bombing Freiburg and Karlsruhe in 1940, in May 1940 and . . ."

"And Germany, of course," I said, managing the smile again, "bombed Warsaw and Rotterdam in 1941! And, of course, Germany never declared war on England . . ."

"Of course not, the English declared war on us."

"Well, well," I said, "That's very interesting, just why did England declare war on Germany?"

"Why? Why, how would I know? [Aus Feindschaft gegen uns] From hatred of us, I suppose."

I let the laugh out and said, "Did you ever listen to the Allied radio?"

"The . . . Never" was spat out like venom striking tin.

"Never?"

"Never, I said."

"Oh, well," I said calmly, smiling, "Oh, well, that explains a lot." [p. 236]

9. The pilot studies conducted in Krefeld and Darmstadt in April 1945, shortly after those cities had been bombed, furnished a check on the memory errors that might have affected the June and July surveys.

10. For detailed findings on the trend in attitudes toward the Occupation between June and July, see vol. 1, app. B, pp. 130–131.

11. That the respondents in Survey B did not know the purpose of the inquiry assumes that they were not "contaminated" by the respondents in their communities who had been interviewed in Survey A. The danger of respondents in the two surveys communicating with each other, or even of respondents interviewed early talking to respondents interviewed late within each survey, was minimal. Within each community, a very small number of respondents was interviewed—on the average fifty in June and fifty in July, only one third of whom were A respon-

dents. Especially in the large cities that was an infinitesimal fraction of the local population. The respondents were not drawn from clusters within neighborhoods, since that conventional economical procedure in American surveys was not necessary, and therefore were unlikely to know each other. All the interviewing within a community was deliberately done very quickly, averaging five working days per place in June, and another five days on the return in July, thus reducing the opportunity for communication between respondents already interviewed and those not yet interviewed.

12. The critical reader may wonder about the misclassification of respondents. The respondents were drawn from the 1945 residents within a community, but their exposure to bombing might have occurred in a different city where they were living during the war, from which they had migrated or been evacuated. The residential history for each respondent permitted us to reclassify respondents into their correct bombing strata, no matter where they had been interviewed. For example, the respondent whose report of being bombed in Duisburg is presented below was interviewed in Detmold, to which she had fled after the October 1944 heavy raid.

13. For the detailed findings on party membership, see Peak 1945, pp. 37–38, 43–44; and for more evidence on the candor of the Nazis, see pp. 19–20. For the complete questionnaires in an English translation, see vol. 1, app. A, pp. 109–112. However, this appendix does not include the item on Nazi membership or other factual questions.

14. Vol. 1, pp. 121–129.

15. Many interim mimeographed reports covering all phases of the work were prepared by the Morale Division, and not all of this information could be incorporated into the final two-volume publication by the U.S. Government Printing Office. My summary of the field work is taken from the interim report, *The Cross-Sectional Interviewing Study*, issued on August 27, 1945. Some of the mimeographed reports may still be extant in government archives, but, no doubt, others have vanished in the course of forty years. The fact that the average take per community, large or small, was 100 interviews over the two months may confuse the reader trying to understand how the representativeness of the total sample was achieved. The proper weight for each bombing stratum nevertheless was assured by varying the number of communities sampled for each stratum.

16. Although Hitler was born in Braunau, his parents moved to the village of Leonding on the outskirts of Linz when he was 9 and when he was 16 his mother resettled within Linz proper. Adjacent to the house in Leonding was the cemetery and village church where his parents were buried.

17. The major difference in background was that the slave laborers were mainly men (over 90 percent among the French and Italians and about

70 percent among the Russians). The sex composition of the German civilian population during the war was disproportionately women. This demographic factor was taken into account in the comparative analysis of the DP and the German surveys.

18. Heinz Ansbacher, a social psychologist of European background working as a member of an OWI unit surveying German prisoners of war, critically reviewed the DP study after publication and suggested that the interpretation of the discrepancies by the original analysts was arbitrary and reflected a preconception about the Russian DPs. See Ansbacher 1950. For the original interpretation, see vol. 2, pp. 17–18.

19. Considering the wartime conditions, the reader may wonder how the data from those large-scale surveys were processed so quickly. Mobile IBM installations and trained operators, which the Army normally used for administrative purposes, were made available to us. In a few instances, German machine installations and German employees were used. In one ironic case, machine records valuable for our analyses were found on file and tabulated for us by the German personnel who had been ordered to destroy all such records in case of defeat. The IBM cards, however, had taken on an almost sacred aura and the personnel could not bring themselves to such a wanton act. Perhaps the same sentiments would have governed IBM personnel in other countries, the worship of the machine not being unique to Germany.

20. Vol. 2, chap. 2, pp. 7–13; app. A, pp. 43–45.

21. The methodological appendix to the "mail studies" demonstrates not only the validity of the reports in the letters, but also the reliability of the coding. For example, the consistency in judging morale was tested by coders recoding a sample of their own material after a one-month interval. The coefficient of agreement on the judgment of "desire for peace" was .79. A sample of material was also coded independently by a different coder. The coefficient on "desire for peace" was .78. See vol. 2, pp. 44–45.

22. Aside from the actual physical effects—whether presented in relative or absolute terms—a third essential basis for interpretation is the perceived physical effects. Rumor and panic in both the unbombed and bombed areas led to greatly exaggerated beliefs about casualties and damage. The methodologically minded reader may also have wondered about the inevitable bias produced by the fact that those Germans killed by bombs obviously could not be included in the survey. As noted, this group was only .5 percent of the population, and the bias—even if their prior attitudes were radically different from the survivors—therefore was infinitesimal. A similar question about possible bias might be raised for those who fled voluntarily or were evacuated from bombed cities. Those who had returned to their former cities by the end of the war were bound to be sampled without any special procedure, and special procedures were employed to sample those who had not returned. See vol. 1, p. 128.

23. Occasional inconsistencies were observed in the findings of the two mail studies, which reflect the different designs employed. My summary, however, is faithful to the overall results. For the detailed findings, see vol. 2, chap. 2.

24. Likert proposed to General Mark Clark, the commander of the American Occupation in Austria, the idea of a permanent survey unit attached to his headquarters to aid in the administration of the Occupation and the reeducation of the population which had suffered years of Nazi control and indoctrination. With his usual persuasiveness, Likert had obtained General Clark's tentative agreement and had persuaded Krech, Crutchfield, and me to direct the unit, obtaining our firm commitment with no difficulty.

   A small-scale survey was conducted in August 1945 as a sales piece to obtain Clark's definite commitment. In line with the avowed educational goals of the Occupation and the hypothesis that the years under Nazism might have insidiously influenced political thought, the survey examined in depth beliefs about the ways a democratic regime would and should operate. The findings revealed that favorable attitudes toward democracy were widespread but often did not imply endorsement of the specific institutional practices normally operative in a parliamentary democracy. The practices that respondents expected or preferred often were totalitarian or authoritarian in character. The report tendered proved informative and persuasive and Clark's commitment seemed assured. Our plans to move our families to Salzburg and to organize the unit went ahead. Then suddenly in October, for reasons never made known, the final decision was negative.

25. The difficulties in training were compounded by the fact that the appropriate vocabulary and syntax in Japanese varied with the status of the person being addressed. Consequently, and contrary to normal survey procedures, the interviewers had to be given latitude to depart from the standardized questionnaire and yet taught to maintain uniformity in meaning over all respondents and avoid bias.

26. I refer here only to the effects of conventional bombing, the atomic bombing of Hiroshima and Nagasaki, of course, having no counterpart in the German experience. And in the rest of this discussion, I do not review the special studies conducted on the effects of nuclear bombing, because of its uniqueness in the past and, one hopes, in the future. Readers interested in those special studies are referred to the special report and to incidental, passing references in the general report.

27. Although physical destruction in some Japanese cities exposed to even small amounts of conventional bombs exceeded the physical destruction in the atomic bombed cities, this is not to say that conventional bombing produced more casualties. Indeed the casualties were much higher in Hiroshima and Nagasaki, the estimates indicating that deaths were three to four times higher per unit area than in conventionally bombed cities.

28. Years later, Richard Boyd and I included a brief summary of the Bomb-
     ing Surveys in a chapter on survey research in the *Handbook of Political
     Science* (1975). Although the bombings and the war, fortunately, were
     past and the summary thus might have seemed a futile academic exer-
     cise, it communicated a lesson to social scientists. The most useful sur-
     veys, even when conducted with care and objectivity and with the
     original intention to be of service, may fail to be used.

PART TWO

The Postwar Years

· 5 ·

The Establishment of the National Opinion Research Center

Soon after the war ended, I joined the National Opinion Research Center and remained there for more than ten years. In that period, NORC moved to the University of Chicago, long famed for its social science division and its empirical social research. NORC expanded, attracted social scientists and graduate students, contributed to training and scholarship in the social sciences, and over the years conducted many varied and useful surveys. NORC's history illustrates how survey research became established in universities and integrated with the social sciences, thus creating a new academic career of surveyor-scholar-teacher. My own experience at NORC illustrates the way the conventional careers of social scientists of my generation were radically altered.

The postwar development depended on the foundation built during the war years. But it had been envisioned even before the war by Harry H. Field, who in 1941 founded NORC at the University of Denver. This was the first nonprofit, public-interest survey facility affiliated with a university that employed a national field staff, whose services were offered at cost to noncommercial clients. The graduate department and program of training and methodological work to be established were to foster, as the brochure proclaimed, "the new science of public opinion measurement." However visionary this may seem, it hardly describes the full range of Field's vision.

Surprisingly, this bold design for the future—for survey organizations dedicated purely to social and scientific purposes—was conceived by a man with no academic background whose earlier experience had been solely in advertising research and commercial polling. Field died at the age of 49 in an airplane crash over Belgium in September 1946, and thus did not live to see NORC grow and change into a great academic center of survey research.

I joined NORC at the end of 1945, in time to participate in its early growth and the dramatic change that followed. Between 1942 and 1944 NORC conducted the field work for our Surveys Division in OWI. Although I was not then employed by NORC, I had close and continuing association with Paul Sheatsley, who directed the field staff from NORC's adjacent office. In fact we were colleagues and became friends, and I soon learned to respect his conscientious, fine work and the larger organization and its staff. Sheatsley, whose association with NORC continued uninterruptedly from 1942 until his death in 1989, wrote a brief history of NORC, "The First Forty Years" (1982), on which I have drawn liberally.

NORC's Origins

Harry H. Field was born in Yorkshire and joined the British army in 1914 at age 17, thus terminating his formal schooling; he served throughout the war and was cited for distinguished service. He came to the United States in the 1920s and worked first as a door-to-door salesman, an unorthodox but perhaps useful background for field work and surely one that increased his understanding of the American public. He moved into the business side of newspaper work and then into advertising, joining Young and Rubicam, where he worked with George Gallup, the director of its research department.

In 1936, Field went to England and organized the British Institute of Public Opinion, Gallup's first foreign affiliate. In 1939, back in the United States, he established his own independent survey organization, the People's Research Corporation. The name is a significant symbol of the man. It suggests "Field's populist philosophy," to use Sheatsley's phrase, which found its full expression two years later in the National Opinion Research Center.[1]

Other pioneering jounalistic and political polls also described and justified themselves as a new institution for measuring and communicating the public's views. Gallup, for example, titled his earliest book *The Pulse of Democracy* (1940). How much of this common usage was pure sales pitch to ensure support and create legitimacy we shall never know. But Field, like Gallup, surely believed what he said. Between 1939 and 1941 he put all his energies and skills behind the establishment of the first nationwide organization whose surveys would serve public and scientific interests exclusively, yielding him no private profit since they were provided at cost to noncommercial clients.

The leaders of the wartime survey units were gifted in many ways. All of them had to promote new ideas and find supporters for untried ventures. Some had to locate and recruit promising staff before there was a large, established pool from which to choose. Then they had to train them in new skills and orient them to a new style of work—not necessarily onerous but certainly new. And they had to sell their services to users and create demand for a novel product.

Field was well endowed for these tasks. He was highly intelligent and persuasive, with a flair for public relations and selling. He was charming. In his dress and speech he seemed the proper Englishman, which gave him an air of distinction. The finishing touch was his English bulldog, which endeared him, at least to dog lovers like me.

Field's previous business and professional association with Gallup and the heads of other early commercial polls was especially valuable. Sheatsley stresses the "strong support from the leaders of the then-small world of public opinion research. Gallup, Elmo Roper, and Archibald Crossley . . . knew and respected Field as a colleague. His proposed research center would not compete with their business and could only help the fledgling field of public opinion research" (p. 7). Gallup introduced Field to Hadley Cantril of Princeton University, who in turn introduced him to Gordon Allport of Harvard and Samuel Stouffer, then at the University of Chicago. They supported Field's plan, served on the first board of trustees at NORC's founding, added academic luster, and gave guidance in the early years.

There are many instances in the early history of survey research where commercial and noncommercial, business and academic branches intertwined to support its spread and growth. This intertwining recurs in the Bureau of Applied Social Research, more than once in NORC, and in the OWI and War Department units. As Sheatsley suggests, they intertwined when the parties did not see themselves in competition and also saw something to be gained from cooperation. Field, formerly in commercial research, did not distance himself from his past. He skillfully used his former business contacts to advantage in establishing NORC and later was the prime mover in creating a common professional association to unite all the branches of survey research.

Although he had much in his favor in founding NORC, nevertheless, it took "many months of intensive effort and negotiation. Harry Field finally found the two sources of financial support that he needed" (Sheatsley 1982, p. 7): The Field Foundation (no relation) agreed to provide three years of seed money at approximately $30,000 a year;[2] the University of Denver offered housing and a $5,000 annual subsidy. In October 1941 NORC was incorporated as a nonprofit organization under the laws of Colorado. Despite Field's past associations, the seven-member board of trustees included no one from market research or polling organizations. In addition to the three external trustees from academia already mentioned, two represented the Field Foundation and two the University of Denver. Thus NORC was protected from any hint of commercial control.

Field had already assembled his senior staff in the summer of 1941. Douglas Williams, from Roper, became the associate director; William Salstrom, the sampling director; and Anne Schuetz, the field director, came from Gallup. Apart from the editor for the digests, news releases, and reports—the organs to disseminate public opinion free of charge or at nominal cost in the spirit of NORC's stated purpose—these three were the original senior staff. They "immediately boarded trains leaving Denver's Union Station to travel around the country recruiting and training interviewers in the newly selected NORC sampling points" (Sheatsley 1982, p. 7). This expensive, stringent training method, eccentric in an era when Roper was the only pollster to practice it, suggests Field's high standards.

Field, understandably, had recruited his triumvirate exclusively from commercial polls. When the need for a New York office to service OWI (initially the OFF) arose in the fall of 1941, he recruited John F. Maloney, again from Gallup, as director. Maloney joined the Navy after Pearl Harbor and was succeeded by Sheatsley, once again recruited from Gallup.

It was no ordinary time. The needs of the military and civilian wartime agencies were creating a general scarcity of skilled personnel—witness the departure of Maloney and, a bit later, Williams, to join Stouffer's branch of the Army. Field turned to the small pool that was accessible and familiar to him, given his background in polling.[3] However, wisdom as well as familiarity and expediency governed his strategy. He needed experienced personnel, already practiced in training interviewers and the chain of operations involved in surveys. I noted before and stress again that the universities were not yet providing formal trainings in survey research. Indeed, a major reason for establishing NORC was to provide such training in a new graduate department.

If the war had not intervened, the Denver staff would most likely have reached and maintained Field's goal of serving the public interest by conducting many high-quality surveys on important issues and then disseminating the public's views accurately and effectively. The staff were well suited for those tasks. Like Field, they had the sensitivity to identify social problems of importance and the skills to conduct surveys carefully and report the findings clearly and precisely.

The surveys and reports in the first years exhibit those good features. For example, a series of surveys explored opinions on postwar problems and policies, using lengthy batteries of closed questions with provisions for qualified answers and comments and some open-ended questions. The focus was on American measures to ensure peace and on the role of international organizations. Another survey explored opinions on race relations and integration, using a lengthy interlocking series of closed questions and a considerable number of open-ended questions, which provided the battery and a baseline for the long-term trend studies Sheatsley and I conducted later (1956, 1964). Another survey measured support of civil liberties for political nonconformists with a battery of questions developed after intensive interviewing on the issues and was one source for our later paper on such long-term trends and for the historical summaries included in Stouffer's monograph on the problem (1955). During the 1944 presidential election, NORC conducted the first nationwide panel study involving preelection and postelection interviews with a sample of over 2,000 cases.[4]

The early surveys also incorporated various sophisticated measurement devices. Interviewers' questionnaires were collected to test whether the interviewers' own opinions biased the answers obtained. Split ballots were used on equivalent subsamples to estimate question wording as a measurement error. The reports and releases used free answers, volunteered comments, and interviewer reports liberally to blend qualitative and quantitative description, the latter refined by extensive breakdowns showing the differentiated views of various segments of the population. Trends based on the continuing repetition of questions on the big issues of the period were presented frequently to describe changes in the pattern of public opinion. Findings from related questions in the battery often were juxtaposed to describe the profile of attitudes, and occasionally the cross-tabulation of such questions presented a more dynamic or explanatory analysis. Periodically, comparisons with relevant findings from Gallup and Roper were presented, any contradictions noted and clarified by thoughtful examination of the respective methods.

All these practices suggest that the Denver staff very likely would have achieved the social and political goal Field had set for NORC, but not Field's other goal: to establish a graduate department to train students, conduct methodological research, and link survey research and the social sciences. They lacked the academic credentials that would have legitimated them as faculty and created the aura of prestige necessary to attract graduate students. Although they were exceedingly sensitive to the needs and problems of the great society, they did not see that their surveys could, and indeed did, illuminate many classic problems in the social sciences and that the findings should be translated into scholarly publications. Instead, they channeled their reports into the larger stream of journalistic writing and debate on public matters, perhaps giving the public a stronger voice and weight in politics, but muting NORC's voice among social scientists.[5]

One other feature of the early NORC reports supports my prognosis. Although open-ended probes often revealed the reasons for opinions, and the frequent demographic breakdowns and occasional other cross-tabulations often suggested explanations, multivariate analysis was not used to provide rigorous and refined explanations of the opinions. The Denver staff emphasized refined description, not refined explanation. The former admirably served NORC's social and political goal; the latter was needed to advance its scientific goal.

My prognosis for the scientific future of NORC, however sound the argument, is bound to remain speculation. We shall never know what might have happened to NORC in its first years if the war had not shattered the original agenda and timetable. "Only three or four surveys a year were issued from Denver during that period, the headquarters staff languished" (Sheatsley 1982, p. 8). Instead, NORC's energies were invested in the war effort and devoted to the work done under contract for OWI directed from the New York office.

I am not suggesting that the war was detrimental to the long-run welfare of NORC. The OWI contract provided a continuing source of funds to supplement NORC's modest endowment.

Exposure to the thinking and practices of the OWI survey directors . . . was immensely educational to the NORC staff, most of whom had been accustomed to the polling tradition. The OWI staff, moreover, was concerned about the quality of the survey data. They welcomed methodological experiments and often suggested new methods of interviewer training and supervision. The OWI work also produced a strong, national field staff, accustomed to questioning people about sensitive topics, handling complex questionnaires, and responding to sympathetic supervision. [Sheatsley 1982, pp. 8–9]

And, as already noted, the war created the new breed of skilled survey researchers who also had the academic training and credentials needed to achieve the scientific goal Field had envisioned. It forged the interpersonal links between Sheatsley and me, between us and Clyde Hart, and between Hart and Field that at a later date brought us together again at NORC.

NORC's Postwar Development

In 1945 Field began building his scientific enterprise on this fine foundation. The end of the war provided a new opportunity and potential staff for Field, but it also created a crisis. The OWI contract was terminated, and the New York office no longer had funds to continue or an essential function to serve. Fortunately, a new contract with the State Department for a series of surveys to be directed from the New York office resolved that organizational crisis and led to a long program of research that provided a more effective channel for public opinion on foreign policy and also contributed to social science.

Field also faced critical problems in Denver. He needed to recruit staff and an associate director to strengthen NORC's survey research and integrate its activities with the university's social sciences. As a result of recruiting and arranging a joint faculty appointment for Don Cahalan, the surveys were quickly strengthened, and the student training and methodological studies Cahalan then initiated ultimately became a larger, longer program with which I later became involved.

Cahalan had the right background for these roles. In 1937–38, he had been a graduate student at Iowa of Norman Meier, one of the few social psychologists in that period interested in public opinion polling and a friend of a fellow Iowan, George Gallup.[6] Cahalan began his professional career with Gallup, joined Program Surveys as a member of the field staff, and then served as a naval officer from 1943 to 1946 in a special unit concerned with compiling the opinions of civilians (not naval personnel) on matters of special interest to the Navy.[7] The source materials were mainly published polls augmented by occasional surveys done under contract by private agencies. His practical experience in the commercial and wartime agencies combined with his academic training and inclinations prepared him well for his later duties at NORC.

Field's progress in recruiting an associate director was much slower. His prime candidate was Clyde Hart. "The job appealed to Hart but he was reluctant to settle in Denver and asked for more time to consider" (Sheatsley 1982, p. 9). But in the meantime in the spring of 1946, with NORC progressing, Harry Field began to think of other ways to promote the development of survey research. He organized a conference, held in July at Central City, a ghost town high in the Colorado Rockies once famous for its silver mine. Under the auspices of NORC, some seventy individuals from all branches of the field met to discuss common problems, to promulgate technical and ethical standards, to promote the uses of surveys, and to develop some permanent form of organization to carry on those activities. Field's background and desire to unite divergent branches of the field were reflected in the invitations sent to representatives from the national and state polls, market and media research, government surveys, and academia, and from abroad, and the invitations to the entire NORC staff reflected his democratic spirit.[8]

The American and World Associations for Public Opinion Research—AAPOR and WAPOR—were conceived at that meeting in the form of resolutions to be implemented by a continuing committee. The births occurred one year later at the second conference in Williamstown, Massachusetts. The first officers of AAPOR suggest the mixture of strains in the early history of the field and the importance of the wartime government agencies. Clyde Hart was elected president unanimously, Elmo Wilson was the vice president, and Julian Woodward was the secretary-treasurer. Other officers were Philip Hauser, then at the Census Bureau, Daniel Katz, Hadley Cantril, Rensis Likert, Paul Lazarsfeld, and George Gallup.

In late 1946 Field focused on another distant goal, the development of academic survey centers in Europe. In pursuing that mission he died in an airplane crash, just after having suffered a period of almost four months of semi-blindness and regaining his sight following a difficult operation for detached retinas.

NORC's Move to Chicago

The death of Harry Field led to the appointment of Clyde Hart as director in 1947 at age 55, to the relocation of NORC in Chicago and its affiliation with the university, and to a radical change in its character. Sheatsley summarizes the transition:

> Before taking the job, he had persuasively argued to the NORC Board of Trustees the case for moving the Center out of Denver to a larger and more prestigious university where it could attract the scholars necessary to carry on NORC's work. Hart had a vision of NORC somewhat different from that of Field. Whereas Field had come from the

world of advertising, market research, and political polls, Hart had been a university professor and scholar. Wheras Field saw NORC as a sort of nonprofit public interest polling center, Hart envisioned a major social research institution, with academically trained social scientists pursuing their interests under government or foundation grants and contracts. [p. 11]

Hart's biography helps explain the move to Chicago and is vivid proof that the wartime experience had created a new breed of surveyor-scholars. He was born in southern Illinois and did his graduate studies at the University of Chicago in the 1920s, becoming a close friend of members of the sociology department and strongly identified with the empirical tradition in which it led the field. Hart taught at the University of Iowa from 1923 to 1942. He probably would have remained there all his days—happy, secure, and teaching the scholarship he had learned—if the war had not brought him to Washington, first to OWI and then to the Office of Price Administration (OPA), where he became involved with survey research. Although an empiricist before the war, his early attitude toward "the survey" was not especially favorable, as indicated by a passage from his *Introduction to Sociology*, co-authored with E. B. Reuter in 1933:

The survey is an extension rather than a refinement of the common-sense procedure. In practice it has been chiefly the collection of a large body of factual data in regard to easily observed phenomena. The enumeration procedure of the federal census is the survey in its most extensive form. Often the procedure is invalidated by the fact that the data are collected to serve as evidence in support of some reform campaign. The survey is in its nature preliminary. It may serve to locate a problem to be stated and defined for scientific study by other means. So far not much success has resulted from the effort to develop the survey as a valid research tool. It lends itself admirably to investigation; it seems to have limited value in scientific research. [pp. 18–19]

Hart's discussion clearly is in terms of the classic social survey, not the modern sample survey, which developed after that date. Hart's wartime experience with the new form and uses of the survey changed his conception and attitude. At OWI, he had directed a staff[9] which synthesized survey data from many sources for regular reports on wartime attitudes and morale. At OPA, he commissioned surveys (conducted by our OWI Surveys Division) on public knowledge and attitudes about and compliance with rationing and price controls, the findings increasing the effectiveness of those programs which depended on the voluntary actions of consumers.

NORC trustees had explored other possibilities before making the decision to resettle in Chicago. Columbia, Cornell, Michigan, Pittsburgh, Princeton, and the University of Wisconsin also expressed interest, and the University of Denver wanted to keep the center.[10] The continued interest of Denver was served by maintaining an affiliated center under the direction of Don Cahalan, which made an important contribution to the program of methodological research that NORC began in 1947. No doubts were raised about maintaining the New York branch office. It was essential to service the State Department contract, a major source of income, and to keeping Sheatsley and me on the staff, both of us being deeply attached to the city.

In 1947, Hart needed to find staff with scholarly interests and knowledge and technical skills in order to achieve NORC's new goals. The war had solved the shortage of such strategic personnel, producing others like him with academic backgrounds and inclinations who had become trained in and devoted to survey research. When the wartime units disbanded, that pool of talent became available. Hart recruited Shirley Star immediately and somewhat later, Jack Elinson, both highly skilled from their wartime surveys with Stouffer. Again the old-boy network came into play, Star having introduced her war buddy to Hart. Eli Marks was recruited somewhat later, his career having followed a slightly different course. He had completed his training in social psychology during the Depression, and then luckily had found a position at Fisk University, where he worked with Charles Johnson on an early survey of rural black youth in the South. He greatly enlarged his survey experience during the war at various government agencies and after the war at the Census Bureau.

Hart also had a pool of potential ability in close proximity to NORC—graduate students at the University of Chicago—who at first required training in survey research on the job. From that pool, Hart recruited Jacob J. Feldman, who stayed for many years and became director of research; Selma Monsky, who became director of the field staff; and Josephine Williams, as a study director.

My Departure from and Reentry into Survey Research

With my work on the Bombing Surveys terminating, I faced a return to the peacetime academic career for which I had prepared before the war and to which I had long aspired. I felt lucky to be invited by Daniel Katz to join him at Brooklyn College. Academic jobs in social psychology had been scarce before the war. To land immediately in a department where the chairman was my wartime colleague, collaborator, and friend seemed lucky indeed, even though teaching survey research and doing it were not part of my duties. Survey research seemed to me a wartime interlude, but not part of the long-run, normal academic career. It was not in the prewar curriculum and had not yet invaded the postwar curriculum, and my expectation was shaped by that reality. Similarly, Krech and Crutchfield gave up their jobs without complaint—albeit saddened—and returned to their former academic careers at Swarthmore. Katz resumed the chairmanship he had interrupted to join the Bombing Survey. Although I had adapted to the facts of life in that era, found the academic work gratifying, and counted myself lucky to be doing what I always thought I wanted, I was far from happy. I was heading toward a personal crisis that seemed to have no easy solution.

I missed all the exciting features of survey research—the fast pace, the grand scale, the stimulating milieu of work, the quick and socially useful payoff from the findings and the apparent impact in high places, the foreign travel and the exotic encounters in the course of field work. A job in market research was not the solution. I was addicted to survey research but not so addicted that I was ready to sacrifice my identity as a social psychologist in order to feed my habit. But I also was not satisfied to remain in the traditional academy.

So when Sheatsley offered me a part-time post to help design and analyze the U.S. State Department surveys, I quickly accepted. Since there seemed no way then to merge academic work and survey research into one organic career, I oscillated between the two careers and had the benefits of both at a price that seemed a bargain to me in those days—being crushed in the subway as I rode back and forth between Brooklyn College and the Madison Avenue office of NORC. The long program of surveys begun under that regime and continued under less onerous conditions after I joined NORC full time, was confidential in character, and most of the analyses have remained unpublished. The program produced much of methodological and substantive value and shows the institutional constraints but also the opportunities surrounding survey research in that period.

The Foreign Affairs Surveys for the State Department

In August 1945 NORC began a series of confidential surveys on the public's interest in, knowledge about, and opinions on foreign affairs, conducted under contract for the State Department. The surveys operated on an almost monthly cycle: interviewing a nationwide quota sample of about 1,200 cases; processing, analysis, and report being completed around the time that the questionnaire design and pretesting for the next survey began, after a planning session in Washington with State Department officials on the topics to be covered the following month. The contract was renewed again and again. When it was finally terminated in 1957, 104 such surveys had been conducted on most of the specific international problems America confronted in the postwar period and on the general patterns of opinion formation, persistence, and change during that important period.

This contract, creating such good fortune for NORC and me and such rich findings, came to us through Hadley Cantril. He had conducted confidential, indeed clandestine, surveys throughout the war for various military agencies, the White House, and the State Department. At the war's end, he was eager to return to teaching and research. To meet the State Department's continuing needs, he arranged with Harry Field to take over the department contract (Cantril 1967). It is understandable that the findings of his wartime surveys as well as those of OWI and Program Surveys would have to be confidential: Publication might have jeopardized delicate relations with our allies and provided clues to morale on the homefront for enemy intelligence.

That the State Department's sponsorship and purchase of survey research was kept secret is hard to understand from the perspective of the present, when survey research has become a legitimate, routine activity of government agencies and is also used by Congress and the White House. But in this instance it was necessary because of the secret character of the contract.[11] The State Department paid NORC out of the secretary's confidential funds, which did not have to be accounted for in detail to Congress. Thus Congress could not exercise ultimate control over the operation.

Indeed, the department was more concerned about the confidentiality of the contract than about the confidentiality of the findings, which they allowed NORC to release at intervals after the policy issues had been decided—but with no reference to the department's sponsorship. Occasional mimeographed reports presenting marginals and breakdowns on various topics were distributed by NORC (see Series FA, nos. 1–4, 1953–57). The last of these, through a chain of accidents and distortions, led to a fight in Congress about the research program and to the cancellation of the contract.

As Clyde Hart described in a memo to NORC interviewers dated July 30, 1957:

> An official of the International Cooperation Association [the agency mainly concerned with foreign aid] was struck by the continuing popu-

lar support of the government's foreign aid programs shown by our surveys and persuaded a *New York Times* reporter to publicize this fact in a special news story. This the reporter did, in a story which appeared on the front page of the *New York Times* (March 17) and which was subsequently inserted in the *Congressional Record* by a pro–foreign aid Senator. A California Congressman, whose own inclinations, combined with the mail he received from those of his constituents who took the trouble to write him, were opposed to the administration's requested appropriation for foreign aid, saw in this newspaper story an attempt on the part of the State Department, the ICA, and the administration to put pressure on Congress and to rally public opinion behind the foreign aid bill.

The resulting fight came to center on the way the surveys had been funded, and after considerable argument between a congressional committee and representatives of the State Department, it was decided that if they were to be continued, they would in future have to be paid for an explicit budgetary allocation. And so the twelve-year series of surveys on controversial foreign policy issues came to an end.

When the State Department surveys began in 1945, the NORC New York office consisted of Sheatsley, a secretary, and an assistant. The tiny staff, through hard and efficient labor, had ably supervised the field work for the OWI surveys. Clearly, they could not carry a series of surveys all the way from design through analysis and report writing on a monthly cycle, and Sheatsley asked me to share his burden. While the burden might seem unmanageable even for the two of us, the OWI surveys had demanded a very fast pace and sharpened our skills, and Sheatsley's original career as a newspaperman had made him a quick and facile writer. The monthly surveys also compensated us in many ways for the pressure we had to bear. There was endless opportunity to replicate or reject earlier findings, to improve procedures and correct mistakes, to sense general patterns and determinants of opinion on many issues, and to observe anomalies, departures from the usual pattern which could be explored fruitfully in later surveys. Serendipity might come our way only once in a hundred surveys, but it was our good fortune to conduct more than a hundred surveys! Additional, less obvious compensations will be mentioned later.

Considerable time was saved, as in the OWI surveys, by using open-ended questions selectively, in judicious combination with closed questions and as probes to explore the reasons behind opinions and to determine the specific meaning of vague general policies that respondents had endorsed. Despite the pressure, other qualitative material was used routinely and systematically to enrich and clarify the findings from closed questions. Volunteered comments recorded by the interviewers were examined, and the interviewers' reports after each assignment were summarized and used as checks on ambiguities and misunderstandings of questions, artifacts produced by wording or sequence, and as evidence on the interest, knowledge, and motives underlying specific opinions.

Another set of factors expedited the surveys. Since the sample size averaged only 1,200 cases and about ninety interviewers were used, they could easily complete their small assignments within the deadline of one week. Generally they took only three or four days, since these were quota samples and interviewers were not obliged to call back on predesignated respondents who initially were not at home or were uncooperative. The risk in quota sampling—so obvious to its critics—that interviewers, given freedom, approach only accessible and friendly respondents and that the obtained sample is badly biased in unknown directions by substantial loss of those initially hostile or away from home must be played off against the benefit, far less obvious to critics, that it expedited surveys on urgent problems. And when the putative bias was evaluated empirically by Stephan and McCarthy (1958) in a survey in the series, one fact was clear. The NORC interviewers spent a good deal of time approaching households where no one was at home or respondents refused them, but nevertheless met their deadlines.

Another factor expedited the surveys and improved their quality and utility. The State Department clients were gifted men with both academic and foreign affairs training, and easy and effective working relations developed over the long period of the program. In Cantril's day, John Sloan Dickey, later president of Dartmouth, directed the branch involved. In NORC's time, the directors were S. Shepard Jones and H. Schuyler Foster, both with doctorates in political science.[12]

With these factors favoring us, we were able, despite the pressure, to conduct careful surveys, to analyze the data in some depth, promptly report findings of practical value, and periodically produce valuable scientific by-products most of which, alas, remain buried. Only a few examples taken from the tattered carbon copies of the original confidential reports can be presented. In one 1948 survey, two questions of concern to the department seemed likely to be affected by the order in which they were asked. The split-ballot experiment indeed documented a dramatic effect. Our passing reference to the results in a 1950 paper, omitting any reference to the State Department (Hyman and Sheatsley), led Schuman and Presser to replicate the experiment twice in 1980, obtain the same basic result, and conclude that "the comparison . . . raises issues for attitude surveys that are of profound importance" (1981, p. 28).

In most of the surveys, we embedded the specific knowledge, involvement, or attitude items under study in a larger battery of items in the same psychological domain. For example, in a 1946 survey devoted to Palestine, a question on knowledge of the Anglo-American report on Palestine was accompanied by knowledge questions on the Acheson-Lilienthal Report on Atomic Energy and several other events, none of which were subjects of the survey. A question on interest in Palestine was accompanied by questions on interest in Franco Spain and the atomic bomb. In a survey on satisfaction with the State Department, satisfaction with the War Department and the Interior Department was also measured. In a survey on satisfaction with the handling of the Japanese Occupation (that itself measured by a battery) questions on the handling of the German Occupation were asked. Thus we built some statistical norms into each survey, and over many surveys built an entire library of norms for evaluating the oddity or typicality of whatever phenomena were under study.

This strategy, learned on the job and found to be so useful then, was helpful to me later in writing *Survey Design and Analysis* (1955). There I recommended it as a basic principle in designing descriptive surveys (see "The Inclusion of Related Phenomena," pp. 126–137). I illustrated its widespread value by citing State Department surveys and published surveys by others who had also invented the same strategy, the nature of the work leading us all independently toward the same solution, though not necessarily to its codification and explicit formulation. Such processes of independent invention were not uncommon in the history of survey methods.

The batteries within a survey often were used for indexes or typologies to describe a constellation of ideas, the general attitudinal position, level of knowledge, and involvement in foreign affairs. Tabulations across the domains of the composite measures of discrete items were used to reveal the dynamic relations between interest, knowledge, belief, and attitude. Such findings in a series of 1945 and 1946 surveys led to our 1947 paper, "Some Reasons Why Information Campaigns Fail." There we described the "chronic know-nothings," whose ignorance of a series of prominent, recent foreign events was so pervasive that a generalized predisposition or characteristic of such people, rather than the availability of information, seemed to be the explanation. Cross-tabulation of scores on a composite index of interest and on the index of knowledge provided empirical evidence that lack of motivation was indeed the source of the ignorance.

These and other findings reported in the paper were scholarly by-products of the earlier practical analyses for the client. That they were of more than trivial scientific value is suggested by the many reprintings of the paper over the years.[13]

Many of the methodological refinements and substantive findings in these surveys were never used by us in scholarly publications. Apart from the few papers cited, the materials from these postwar surveys, like the material from the wartime surveys, were neglected, and probably for the same reason.[14] Two last illustrations will suggest how much valuable material remained buried.

The State Department, understandably, was concerned that the public had a stereotyped, and negative, conception of the American diplomat, and the problem was explored in a preliminary way in one question in a 1945 survey ("Stereotype of 'an American Diplomat,' " January 9, 1946). We decided against a checklist of traits, as in classic social psychological studies of ethnic stereotypes. One needed prior research to construct a nonarbitrary list, and any closed-question method might have pressed respondents with no conception at all into a definite answer, thus overestimating stereotyping. Instead, an open-ended question asked respondents for the words they thought of to describe an American diplomat, and the answers were classified under a detailed and elaborate code. (For statistical norms, respondents also described "an Admiral" and "a Judge.")

Our caution seemed well warranted, since 35 percent of the national sample were unable to report any trait. Although the single, wide-open question created the opposite danger of underestimating stereotyping, it seemed "clear that plain lack of knowledge of what an American diplomat is, does, or looks like" (p. 2) accounted for the finding. Among the grammar-school educated, or those who did not know what the State Department was, about 50 percent reported no description at all of the diplomat. Ironically, when such individuals had conceptions, they were likely to be favorable. The educated, involved, and informed were far more likely to have a conception, but the tone was less favorable. The conceptions, however, were highly varied. In that sense, there was little stereotyping. An index of "uniformity," modeled on Katz and Braly's classic study (1933), showed little uniformity over the whole population or in any sub-group, although the less educated were a bit more likely to stereotype or to share a uniform conception. This is not to deny the array of expected and colorful descriptions—"smooth-talker," "bull-thrower," "fancy pants," "caviar and high hat"—but the scatter was wide. Alas, this suggestive study was never pursued in depth or repeated at a later date.

In November 1946, a battery of nine questions on disarmament was included in a survey which also contained questions on confidence in the UN, on optimism about and support of programs for reeducation of Germany and Japan, on freedom of information between Russia and the United States, and on expectations of war. Under conditions of reciprocal agreements and an effective system of international inspection, about 90 percent of the population were found to favor reduction of our armed forces. Why a tiny minority were still opposed despite such guarantees led to a special analysis, "The Enemies of Disarmament" ("Public Attitudes Toward Disarmament," December 20, 1946). After finding that "analysis of the group in terms of the usual population characteristics is almost completely unrevealing" and getting nowhere by elaborate cross-tabulations, "we selected a random sample of half such cases and studied them qualitatively" (p. 17), examining their answers and comments on the entire questionnaire and also the interviewers' reports on the survey. I slight the substantive findings, noting only that the group had a rigid and extreme "point of view that is sometimes almost pathological" and was "rabidly isolationist and nationalist" (p. 16), since the illustration is purely for methodological purposes. The need to clarify puzzling findings on an important problem that resisted quantitative analysis inevitably led us to a qualitative method, codified and formulated later by Kendall and Wolf as "deviant case analysis" (1949). My intent is not to claim priority, but simply to document another example of independent invention in survey research stimulated and guided by the nature of the work.

One last feature of the program of surveys should be noted. The State Department's need often could be met by a relatively short instrument, leaving space and time for other questions to be asked with minimal change in the total cost, a large portion of which is fixed. As Sheatsley notes, "the Department of State had no objection to the sale of additional questions . . . to other clients" (p. 12), the costs then being distributed and saving everyone money. Thus began the "amalgam" or "omnibus" type of survey, only one of many innovations and experiments by NORC to reduce costs without sacrificing quality and thus make survey research available to a variety of clients, poor as well as rich (see Sudman 1967). Periodically, Sheatsley and I felt like rich clients, since the surveys that were not packed permitted questions of scholarly interest to us to be piggybacked at no cost to anyone. Over the many months of the program, the free rides we took more than compensated us for our labors and resulted in our early trend study of desegregation (1956, 1961) and other studies.

In 1947, Hart was eager to recruit me for a full-time appointment at NORC directing a long-term methodological project that seemed likely to help NORC's finances and scientific reputation. (Coincidentally, at about the same time Likert tried unsuccessfully to persuade me to join the Survey Research Center at Michigan.) Hart had known of Sheatsley's and my work on the State Department surveys, but had also known me from the war years, when I was the study director of some of the OWI surveys for OPA. In accordance with Elmo Wilson's innovative administrative practices, Hart and I were in direct contact on those studies. The work had been fruitful and the relationship gratifying. That wartime foundation set the stage for his new offer.

His proposal was irresistible. He had been invited to nominate one of the three members of an "expert mission on public opinion and sociological research" to work in Japan for about three months at the request of the Army of Occupation. He would nominate me, if upon my return I would agree to switch from a part-time to a full-time position at NORC. My teaching career, well under way, would have to be terminated for some unknown but lengthy period. That sacrifice, involving the loss of Daniel Katz's companionship, was carefully weighed against the pleasures and benefits I anticipated. My addiction to survey research, the chance to pursue it for a while in exotic Japan, later under Hart's congenial regime in Sheatsley's pleasant company, and working on an exciting project won out. I resigned my appointment at Brooklyn College and left for Japan in March 1947 to join Raymond Bowers, the sociologist, and Clyde Kluckhohn, the anthropologist, the three of us having worked before on the Japanese Bombing Survey.

Upon my return in June, I began full-time work at NORC on the methodological project whose auspices and funding symbolized the new status of survey research after the war. In the interim, Sheatsley had recruited Charles Herbert Stember to share the work on the State Department surveys and on the new project. He had been drawn out of the same pool as the rest of us, having started at Program Surveys and later in the war moving to Stouffer's unit.

This analysis of the process of recruitment omits a crucial element: Hart's personal qualities. He had good judgment in selecting promising candidates from the pool of applicants. But he needed something else to attract them to join the staff and, equally important, to remain at NORC. Hart was very different from other early leaders, and yet most effective. He did not communicate the sense of sacred mission that attracted the flocks to Likert and Stouffer. He did not have the dashing, romantic air that made fans for Elmo Wilson. He had no eccentricities like Stouffer's or Lazarsfeld's, which fascinated and amused the staff. He did not entrance with cascades of ingenious ideas. What then was the secret of his leadership?

His character was so abundant in virtues and his style and personality so endearing—gentle, humorous, nonauthoritarian, helpful —that the staff felt absolutely secure and comfortable under his trustworthy and lovable regime. Above all, he was tolerant, almost saint-like in his patience, in coping with the staff's problems and demands. Star versus Hart is the best case to cite. Shirley Star was as temperamental and bellicose as she was brilliant.[15] At no provocation, she would fire a nasty memo at any one of her old friends on the staff. But she reserved her sharpest weapon for Hart. She had placed on file a standing, permanent letter of resignation. Over the years, at the slightest irritant, she threatened to use it. Hart suffered this permanent state of war and continued to treat Shirley graciously, sympathetically.

The NORC Studies of Interviewer Effects

That survey research had achieved a new status by the end of the war was proved by the decision of the Social Science Research Council and National Research Council in June 1945 to establish a joint Committee on the Measurement of Opinion, Attitudes, and Consumer Wants. These prestigious bodies, representing the broad interests of the social and natural sciences, saw by then, as their proposal stated, that "research in this area has been greatly expanded during the war," that "increasingly wide use will be made of sample surveys . . . by business and industry, government, and independent natural and social scientists,"[16] and that there was "the need for intensive work on methodological problems" (SSRC Proposal, June 1945).

The committee represented all sectors of the field—polling, commercial, government, and academic survey facilities—but the same figures appear here as elsewhere in the early history of the field. Stouffer was appointed chairman and S. S. Wilks, the mathematical and sampling statistician from Princeton, vice chairman. With Likert and Frank Stanton they served as the executive committee. Cantril and Lazarsfeld also were among the eighteen members of this large and varied committee. Likert received his invitation in Europe, while still serving on the Bombing Survey. He accepted with alacrity in a reply dated August 2, 1945, despite the fact that Crossley, Gallup, Roper, and several market researchers from industry and advertising were also members of the committee. The fundamental research on the agenda of the committee and the scientific auspices of the SSRC, in this instance, outweighed his feelings of distance and antagonism toward commercial research and polling.

The committee sponsored three major projects, all quickly supported by grants from the Rockefeller Foundation. A study of panel methods was conducted by Lazarsfeld and the Bureau of Applied Social Research. The study of sampling methods was conducted by Frederick Stephan and Philip McCarthy (1958) of Cornell University. The study of "interviewer effects," conducted by NORC and aided by a grant of $42,100, was the long-term methodological project for which Hart had recruited me full time.

"Interviewer bias"—error caused specifically by the interviewer's own opinions or ideology affecting his performance or the respondent's reactions—had long been a matter of concern to polling organizations. An early analysis of the magnitude of such effects in Gallup polls had been conducted by William Salstrom when he was still a research assistant at the Princeton Office by Public Opinion Research (see Cantril et al. 1944, pp. 106–112). NORC, guided by that tradition, regularly asked the interviewers working on the early surveys to complete and mail back the same questionnaire to be used for respondents before they began their field work. The results obtained by interviewers with divergent opinions could then be examined, controlling for differences in the localities and groups to which they were assigned. Interviewer effects caused specifically by the group membership of the interviewer, especially among respondents from disparate groups, had also long concerned survey researchers. Katz had studied the effects of the class of the interviewer in 1941; and during the war NORC, together with the OWI Surveys Division, had studied the effects of the interviewers' race and their status as strangers or residents in the town in which they worked.

NORC's new study, in contrast to these earlier discrete studies of particular effects, was intended to be a long-term, systematic, and comprehensive program of research: exploring the wide variety of interviewer effects, evaluating the magnitude of such errors, and developing methods to minimize the effects in future opinion and attitude surveys. And in contrast to the surveys for the State Department and the wartime surveys, where the urgency of the client's needs demanded all possible speed, the developmental character of this program demanded, and the character of the sponsor encouraged, a leisurely pace.

Consequently, although interviewer effects were my major responsibility from July 1947 until 1954, when the collected studies were published (Hyman et al.), I often worked on surveys during those years, some of which were important enough in NORC's and my personal history to be described later. Under Hart's beneficent regime, I was even given periodic leaves for new adventures here and abroad which will be described later.

The leisurely pace also permitted other NORC staff to work on the project regularly without impeding their other duties. Feldman, Hart, and Stember carried a major share of the work, and Sheatsley made substantial contributions. In 1946, Cahalan had begun a series of studies of interviewer bias at the affiliated Denver center as part of his effort to revitalize the methodological research and training program for graduate students (Cahalan, Tamulonis, and Verner 1947; Cahalan 1948). These studies contributed to our later program. Cahalan and other staff at Denver also collaborated on the field experiment conducted in Denver in 1949 in which randomized assignments to a large field staff permitted accurate estimates of differences among interviewers, and criterion data on fourteen factual questions permitted comparisons of the validity of the work of different interviewers (see Feldman, Hyman, and Hart 1951; Parry and Crossley 1950; Cahalan 1968). After thirty-five years, Presser remarked that the study "still ranks among the most extensive investigations into the validity of survey data" (1984, p. 344) and reanalyzed the data to determine whether invalidity was a generalized tendency of respondents. As a result of the collaborative, albeit part-time, work of the regular staff and the affiliated staff over an extended period, only one new staff member, William Cobb, had to be recruited for the program. He, too, functioned part time, making fruitful contributions not only to the work on interviewer effects but to other NORC surveys, especially the sampling.[17]

There is no need to summarize here the many findings on interviewer effects; they were reviewed in detail in the 1954 book. However, the strategy that was useful then and may still be valuable for other inquiries deserves note. Although the earlier literature was our first source of guidance, our theorizing and planning were not limited by it. The program of research began with a qualitative method, intensive interviewing of interviewers and respondents to free us from preconceptions and to give deeper understanding of the way the survey interview is experienced by the two parties, which in turn broadened and revised our theorizing about interviewer effects. The theorizing was then translated and tested in a series of quantitative studies. In presenting the findings, we reviewed the unique benefits survey research derived from using interviewers, these needing to be weighed against the errors they produced for a balanced appraisal. We also reviewed the magnitude of interviewer effects and the inattention to such errors in nonsurvey research so that the reader would not unfairly condemn survey research. That seemed to us the proper context for the detailed confession of error we were about to make.

Seven years passed before the book appeared. So that the profession and NORC would not have to wait so long before reaping benefit from the research, our strategy was to publish findings from discrete studies promptly throughout the period. By 1954, eighteen papers written by various members of the team had appeared;[18] these were consequential for NORC. From its founding, NORC had hoped to contribute to the scientific development of survey research and to strengthen its position in a university so that it could contribute to graduate training. That mission had passed from Field to Hart, who hoped to achieve it in the new location at the University of Chicago. The many articles helped to validate and enlarge NORC's reputation among social scientists at Chicago and elsewhere. The book further enhanced that reputation, especially in the places where it counted. The University of Chicago Press published it, and it was still in print thirty years later. As the first scholarly book for which NORC could take complete credit, it nourished the center's reputation at Chicago during critical, early years. The publications also pleased the SSRC and the Rockefeller Foundation, and they continued to sponsor and support NORC's activities.

The publications, of course, also enhanced my reputation, but what is worth noting here is the way they contributed to redefining my public image and my identity. I had started out as a social psychologist in the traditional prewar mold. Now I was, conspicuously, a survey "methodologist," a fancy label I did not mind displaying. Inevitably, not by my design, my career was being rechanneled. Attractive opportunities and offers for a "methodologist" came my way and were hard to refuse. Indeed, they led me to spend most of my professional life in sociology departments, although my formal training and origins had been in psychology. In such ways, survey research reshaped the careers of my generation.

Other Surveys During NORC's Early Years at Chicago

In addition to the continuing program of State Department surveys and the program on interviewer effects, NORC conducted such a wide variety of surveys in the early years at Chicago that only a small assortment can be presented. Those exploring a novel substantive area, showing some significant methodological feature, or inaugurating some long-term continuity in social research deserve special, if brief, mention.

UN Campaign   In 1947 NORC conducted a panel study on an area sample of the general population of Cincinnati to evaluate a six-month campaign to increase knowledge of, interest in, and support of the United Nations. Like some of the State Department and wartime surveys, it revealed the social and psychological factors that impeded information campaigns (see Star and Hughes 1950).

The study's valuable methodological by-products were also exploited. The variability in the measurement of stable background characteristics (for example, age) when the respondents were reinterviewed by different interviewers contributed to the interviewer effect studies (see Hyman et al. 1954, pp. 247–252), and other by-products were used by the Lazarsfeld study of panel methods.

Animal Experimentation   In 1948, out of concern that the anti-vivisection movement, abetted by the Hearst press articles on the brutal treatment of animal subjects, would impede medical research through laws and other means, the National Society for Medical Research, with funds from the Rockefeller Medical Foundation, sponsored NORC's nationwide survey on the public's knowledge about the procedures of animal experimentation, beliefs about its value, and sentiments and attitudes about it. A distinguished group of medical scientists acted as advisers, and the managing director of the National Anti-vivisection Society also reviewed the questionnaire for its objectivity. The design and the topic were unusual and important. Complementary surveys were also conducted among two strategic groups, high school teachers and physicians, who might influence various publics. Although a detailed mimeographed report ("Animal Experimentation," Report no. 39, February 1949) was given to the client, no scholarly publications ever appeared. In this instance, NORC missed the opportunity to make scientific contributions on a central and neglected topic in social psychology—the social and moral sentiments—and on the effectiveness of a social movement and a prolonged mass media campaign in mobilizing mass support.[19]

Prestige Ratings of Occupations   In March 1947, while NORC was still in flux following Field's death, its location and future still uncertain, NORC conducted the first nationwide sample survey on the prestige of occupations, Don Cahalan serving as study director in collaboration with Paul Hatt and Cecil North representing the client. The President's Scientific Research Board was concerned specifically and exclusively with the prestige the public accorded scientists in government employment, it presumably having declined and hampered recruitment. The survey, however, wisely obtained ratings on ninety widely varied occupations. To avoid anchoring effects on the judgments, the sequence in which sets of occupations were presented was rotated. The prestige ratings would have satisfied the client, but NORC added a battery of questions, some open-ended, on the desiderata in choosing an occupation, on the value attached to education, on occupational choice and its determinants, and on father's as well as respondent's occupation. And in addition to the sample of adults, a complementary national sample of youth aged 14–20 was surveyed, their educational plans, ratings, and occupational choice still being fluid.

Despite NORC's difficulties and the untimely death of Paul Hatt, this survey, intended originally to serve the client's narrow, practical problem, became a classic source on social stratification[20] and was the basic source for my secondary analysis, "The Value Systems of Different Classes" (1953). Then, in 1963, when the survey was replicated on national samples of adults and youth, it became the baseline documenting the stability of the prestige hierarchy of occupations over that considerable period (Hodge, Siegel, and Rossi 1964).

Attitudes Toward Commercial Radio (1945)   In 1945, from Denver and under Harry Field's direction, NORC conducted the first nationwide survey on the public's attitudes toward the institution of commercial radio: its programs, commercials, and regulation by government. In fact, three surveys were conducted in close succession, the two smaller supplementary ones to correct for crudities and oversights in the first questionnaire. The analysis was then done cooperatively with the Bureau of Applied Social Research and presented by Lazarsfeld and Field in *The People Look at Radio* (1946), the first scholarly book on NORC's list of publications.[21]

Attitudes Toward Commercial Radio (1947)   In the fall of 1947, after NORC had moved to Chicago, a second comparable nationwide survey was conducted to measure stability or change and to deepen understanding of the public's attitudes by the inclusion of additional new questions. To prevent the crudities and oversights that had occurred in the 1945 survey and to eliminate the need for supplementary surveys, the 1947 questionnaire was revised nine times under the scrutiny of an advisory committee and pretested in what seemed like an endless process. Such caution seemed essential to offset any stigma that the inquiry was biased in favor of commercial radio. That criticism had been voiced by some social scientists after the first survey, understandably since both surveys were sponsored by the National Association of Broadcasters. The "final" questionnaire was then reviewed with the earlier critics, and some further changes made in light of their suggestions. The analysis, by Lazarsfeld and Kendall, was reported in *Radio Listening in America* (1948),[22] with the subtitle *The People Look at Radio—Again;* Appendix D presents the final defense against the claim of bias. A reasonable explanation was given for every change made from the 1945 questionnaire, thus undermining the accusations that some items omitted or changed were those that had elicited public criticism of commercial radio in the earlier survey and that other items too blunt to elicit criticism in 1945 were left unchanged. I retell this cautionary tale for the benefit of innocent analysts who decide to conduct new surveys on highly controversial social issues. One respondent's unforgettable answer—"I like the commercials because they break up the monotony of the programs"—will also caution analysts against projecting their own attitudes onto respondents.

Attitudes Toward Commercial Broadcasting   The idea of periodic surveys of public attitudes toward radio had been proposed originally by Frank Stanton. In 1960, the Columbia Broadcasting System, of which he was then president, made a grant to the Bureau of Applied Social Research for a third study in the series. The focus by then was television, which had supplanted radio; but putting that distinction aside, we may conceive of the series as a study of trends in public attitudes toward commercial broadcasting. Two equivalent national samples were drawn and interviewed independently, one by NORC and the other by Roper (the sponsorship of CBS never being mentioned). This was an early, but not the first, test of what later came to be called "house effects." The comforting findings of that test were reported in Appendix A of Steiner's *The People Look at Television* (1963). In 1970 the fourth survey in the series was conducted; Robert Bower and the Bureau of Social Science Research were responsible for the analysis and Roper for the field work, and the results were reported in *Television and the Public* (1973). And in 1980 the fifth survey was conducted, the analysis reported by Bower (*The Changing Television Audience*). By then the series provided a picture of American attitudes toward the institution of commercial broadcasting spanning thirty-five years, beginning with the 1945 NORC survey.

Attitudes Toward Jews   Between 1945 and 1957, under contract with the Division of Scientific Research of the American Jewish Committee, NORC conducted at least twenty-seven nationwide surveys in which a battery of questions or the entire questionnaire measured beliefs and attitudes toward Jews. In addition, two elaborate and large-scale local surveys were conducted, one in Minneapolis–St.

Paul with a sample of 3,800 respondents, and the other a panel study in Baltimore involving a probability sample of about 1,000 cases reinterviewed after a six-month interval. The surveys were identified as NORC studies, no reference being made to the sponsorship by the American Jewish Committee, which might have inhibited respondents from expressing anti-Semitic feelings. The surveys were designed jointly by the New York staffs of the division and NORC, but the analyses were done exclusively by the division staff and used only internally, to guide the policies and practices of the American Jewish Committee.

The staff of the division were highly qualified; the composition again reveals the importance of the wartime experience and the tight little networks in the development of survey research. It was directed by Samuel H. Flaverman and included Eunice Cooper and Helen (Schneider) Dinerman from the OWI Surveys Division and earlier from the Bureau of Applied Social Research, Marie Jahoda from the Bureau of Applied Social Research and earlier Lazarsfeld's collaborator in Vienna, and Dean Manheimer from Stouffer's wartime unit. Lazarsfeld served as a continuing consultant.[23]

The surveys served useful social purposes in aiding the committee to combat anti-Semitism, but, sadly, their value for the larger scientific community remained dormant because the substantive findings were not published in those years. Indeed, the twenty-seven surveys spread across twelve eventful years, as well as another dozen NORC had conducted during the war either of its own volition or under contract from the committee, and questions on anti-Semitism asked by other agencies over that period probably contained the longest string of replicated tests on the correlates of various components of anti-Semitism; and they contained the most massive evidence on the changes in attitude produced by such stirring and soul-searching events as the rise of the Nazis, the Holocaust, World War II, the Cold War (when the names of Jews figured prominently in the trials of spies), and the founding of the state of Israel. And surely the problems of prejudice and intergroup relations are central to social psychology and sociology.

Fortunately, in 1959 the American Jewish Committee commissioned Charles Herbert Stember, who had worked on the surveys in NORC's New York office, to reanalyze these voluminous materials for publication. In 1961, his monograph on the effects of education in reducing various forms of prejudice against Jews (and against blacks, in order to establish its generalized effects) appeared. In 1966 his second monograph on trends in various forms of anti-Semitism and their correlates and causes appeared. His findings were consistent, powerful, and, in many respects, unexpected.[24] Thus the scientific value of the surveys ultimately was realized.

Social and Psychological Effects of Disasters   In 1951, NORC received a contract from the Army to organize a mobile field team, ready to move quickly into communities where the civilian population had been exposed to a disaster in order to conduct studies of the social and psychological effects and of the conditions that aggravate or reduce the devastating effects. Clearly, the problem concerning the sponsors was future disasters in times of war, made all the more real by the bombings of civilians in World War II. Such effects, of course, had been studied thoroughly in the Bombing Surveys, described in chapter 4. Since, fortunately, Americans had not experienced strategic bombing, and since the disasters of war seemed past, the closest analogy was the disasters of peacetime, which unfortunately occur all too frequently.

Indeed, over the next four years, the NORC team traveled to Arkansas, California, Colorado, Illinois, New Jersey, New York, and elsewhere to study such major disasters as earthquakes, explosions, floods, tornadoes, and a variety of "minor" disasters such as airplanes crashing into communities, building collapses, and fires. The findings, of course, had immediate, obvious applicability to such common and dreadful afflictions, however remote and shaky their applicability may be to the disasters that enemies might afflict on the United States in future wars. And these surveys, like the Bombing Surveys, had implications for basic as well as applied research, yielding unique evidence on the ways populations and communities and organizations react to, cope with, and can be helped in emergencies. Experimental and clinical studies of stressful experiences are either weak analogies to true disasters or, at best, limited to small numbers drawn from specialized groups, sampled in a haphazard way. Such considerations enhanced the appeal of the disaster research program for NORC.

Under the efficient direction of Eli Marks, Shirley Star, and Charles Fritz, the field team generally arrived within three hours to three days after the event and remained on the scene for one to three weeks, the intent being to observe the immediate and short-term effects and the adjustments made. The research clearly fell within the tradition that later came to be called "firehouse" research. However, despite the rush and the disorganization following disasters, samples of the population of the communities were carefully selected, usually by some combination of purposive and area sampling. In fact, in the study of an Arkansas county devastated by a series of tornadoes, a strict probability sample was designed and the completion rate was an extraordinary 94 percent. A supplementary sample of informants from the relief and rehabilitation agencies usually was interviewed. Nondirective, intensive, tape-recorded interviews, averaging about one and a half hours, were completed. That procedure clearly is not in the survey tradition labeled "polling." Indeed, the protocols obtained in the Arkansas survey were so rich and nondirective (the opening probe was, "Tell me your story of the tornado") that they were used later for a secondary analysis of class differences in modes of communication and patterns of thought (Schatzman and Strauss 1955).

The disaster program, more than any other in the early years, seems to have had a magnetic attraction for graduate students and to have been the best bridge between the center and social sciences at the university. Graduate students joined the team, based theses and dissertations on the studies (Bucher 1954; Quarantelli 1953; Krauss 1955; Schatzman 1960), and produced a series of published papers (Bucher 1957; Marks and Fritz 1954; Bucher, Fritz, and Quarantelli 1956a, 1956b; Quarantelli 1954, 1957; Schatzman and Strauss 1955, 1958). Disaster research, aided by funds from the military and encouraged by a committee of the National Academy of Sciences and the National Research Council, also struck the same responsive chord in individuals and centers at other universities and produced a substantial literature.[25] Somehow, the topic must have connected with their deep concerns, aroused their humane impulses, and seemed of both practical importance and theoretical significance for the social sciences. Other projects also meant jobs and money. This project had an extraordinary appeal that cannot be explained simply. If one is seeking the magic ingredients for the future survey project to capture students and scholars, one would be well advised to reexamine the history of the disaster program.

The Threat of Communism and the Threat to Civil Liberties   In May 1954, the Fund for the Republic, at the suggestion of Elmo Roper, one of its directors, sponsored a survey to examine whether the threat of communism raised by the cold war and McCarthyism had ramified so far as to undermine support for the civil liberties of other nonconformists such as socialists and atheists, as well as for the civil liberties of admitted and suspected Communists. The survey was directed by Stouffer, advised by a committee which included Lazarsfeld and Frank Stanton. Three unusual features of the survey deserve special attention. "First, it relied more heavily than many surveys on what are called free-answer or open-ended questions. . . .

The first twenty minutes or so of the interview were devoted to a general discussion of whatever things the respondent had most on his or her mind, without any hint as to the ultimate purpose of the survey" (Stouffer 1955, p. 19). The answers to these questions were used most effectively by Stouffer to show that neither the Communist threat nor the threat to civil liberties was of deep concern to the public in 1954. Although we must credit the heavy use of open-ended questions mainly to Stouffer, that feature of the survey shows that "polling" is not necessarily confined to the use of a few closed questions.

The second feature of the survey was that two equivalent nationwide probability samples, each with about 2,500 adults, were drawn and interviewed with the identical questionnaire during the same time period, one by NORC and the other by the Gallup Poll. Moreover, the two agencies were sharply contrasted in character: The Gallup Poll was commercial, had a very large staff of interviewers trained by mail, and did a great many brief polls, whereas NORC was noncommercial, with a small personally trained field staff accustomed to asking open-ended questions. Careful inspection of the house manuals for interviewers indicated additional differences in the practices recommended to the interviewers. The Gallup interviewers also were more conservative politically than the NORC interviewers. This was the first carefully controlled, large-scale test (involving about 600 interviewers) of what later was labeled "house effects."

The occasional comparisons Stouffer presented provided comforting evidence that the way each field staff conducted the prescribed interviewing had negligible effects on the findings. However, Stouffer had limited his comparisons to the closed questions. Stember, sensing Stouffer's omission and sensitized to the problem from his work on the NORC study of interviewer effects, seized the opportunity to make a thorough study of house effects on the many open-ended questions and then used the findings for the doctoral dissertation he had not completed earlier (1955).

The third feature of the survey was that a sample of some 1,500 community leaders, those who held specific offices in municipal government and in a set of specified local organizations in all the middle-sized cities in the national sample, were asked the same questions, again by the two field staffs. This elite group, by virtue of their strategic positions, could translate their opinions into action and influence others. When Stouffer compared elite and mass opinion in the same cities, his dramatic finding was greater tolerance toward political nonconformity among the elite, including the officers of conservative organizations. Those findings were not vulnerable to house effects.

However, it should be stressed and often is neglected that the elite interviews were structured so that the leaders expressed their personal opinions, not the views they might have endorsed if cast in their roles as official representatives of organizations and governments.

The 1954 study gave me a new opportunity to observe Stouffer in action and to work closely with him over the extended period when NORC did the interviewing and coding on its sample, and also during the planning and analysis. It had been five years since my last experience of working intensively with him on the Social Science Research Council investigation of the failure of the presidential pre-election polls of 1948, an important episode in the history of survey research. And it had been ten years since I had known him during the war. From wartime to peacetime, over those ten years, and in his later years when our association continued intermittently until his death in 1960, his style of work remained the same and his rare ability to excite his co-workers never diminished. In chapter 3, I described the whirlwind of activity he set in motion, his passion for survey research which swept contagiously over his colleagues, the exciting ideas he showered on us. But I did not mention his receptiveness to our ideas. Sheatsley and I had been monitoring trends in support for civil liberties long before the 1954 study, going back to a 1943 baseline NORC had established with a battery of questions and even earlier through occasional questions Gallup had asked; we updated those trends by piggybacking the old battery on later NORC surveys or by relevant questions asked at the request of the American Jewish Committee (Hyman and Sheatsley 1953). We reminded Stouffer that the erosion of civil liberties predated McCarthyism. At his request, we summarized those earlier findings. When they were added to the chapters of his 1954 book, they reduced the danger of the findings being attributed solely to the events of the 1950s (1955, pp. 274–277).

This review of research, though incomplete,[26] does show NORC's progress toward its several goals in the early years at Chicago. Surveys for various nonprofit agencies produced many practical, socially useful findings and also methodological and substantive findings of value for the larger scientific community which often, though not always, were disseminated in scholarly publications. And sometimes the surveys served as vehicles for training students. The problems posed often required novel and sophisticated designs which sharpened the staff's skills, and the utility of the findings increased the staff's devotion to survey research.

Understanding of Mental Illness   Another series of surveys in the 1950s, by good fortune and with the support of recently established foundations, coalesced into a major program which produced a large body of findings on and improved methods for studying an important social problem. The work in turn led some of the staff to a new, lifetime commitment to that specialized area of survey research and to the establishment of new specialized centers which trained later cohorts and carried on research on the problem.

The series began in 1950, with a national survey of 3,500 adults on their understanding of mental illness, sponsored by the Commonwealth Fund and the National Institute of Mental Health and directed by Shirley Star.[27] The vignettes describing the behavior of individuals ranging from the severely disturbed to those with mild problems and those exhibiting eccentric but normal patterns were the most innovative feature of the intensive interviewing. These simplified case studies tested respondents' knowledge of and reactions to mental illness. The series continued in 1952 when the newly established Commission on Chronic Illness sponsored a study of such health problems in a rural area in Hunterdon County, New Jersey, which was to be served by a new health center. NORC was invited to conduct the baseline survey on the prevalence of illness and disability and the needs of the population. Hart had to find a study director. Star recommended Jack Elinson, her wartime colleague in Stouffer's unit. That began the collaboration between Elinson and Ray Trussell, the medical director of the Hunterdon County Center, which continued for five years during the successive phases of the study and long after. As Elinson wrote years later, "I really got hooked on things medical when I became study director . . . for the socio part of the sociomedical Hunterdon study" (Elinson and Nurco 1976, p. 13), and he remained hooked for the next thirty years.[28]

The most innovative feature of the Hunterdon survey was the combination of a careful, exhaustive interview with a medical examination. It established the special contribution and limitation of each procedure in assessing various conditions and disabilities and suggested that the ideal, though expensive, method was to apply both procedures in a sample survey. Those methodological findings were reported in various papers by Trussell and Elinson (Trussell, Elinson, and Levin 1956; Elinson and Trussell 1957), and influenced the design of the U.S. National Health Survey, then in the planning stage.

The Elinson-Trussell connection, forged initially by lucky accident at Hunterdon, had many ramifications in later years. Trussell left Hunterdon to become dean of the Columbia School of Public Health, and Elinson left NORC in 1956 at the invitation of Trussell to establish a Division of Sociomedical Sciences at the school. There he taught courses in survey method and for almost thirty years directed a program of survey research on problems of health. For ten years, he operated the Washington Heights Community Master Sample Survey, using that neighborhood as a "natural human population laboratory" where problems of illness, its causes and its care, could be brought under prolonged scrutiny by ongoing surveys.[29] Diverse investigators would have an efficient and economical vehicle available to them, substantive knowledge could be advanced through the merger of data from the various surveys, and methodological findings that would be of service to successive surveyors could also be accumulated (*Milbank Memorial Fund Quarterly* 1969, no. 1, pt. 2). Such were the ramifications and ultimate benefits from only one of the surveys in the series NORC conducted on health.

Costs of Medical Care (1953)   The series continued in 1953, when NORC conducted the first nationwide survey on the costs of medical care based on a probability sample of about 3,000 families, sponsored by the Health Information Foundation and directed by Jacob Feldman. The private foundation had been established in 1950 to support research on social and economic aspects of health. Its research director, Odin Anderson, and officers realized the need for current, accurate, and generalizable information on morbidity and the costs of care. The last and only national health survey had been conducted in 1935–36, during the Depression and before the advent of voluntary health insurance, and had been based on a nonprobability, albeit gigantic, sample of urban households. Studies by the Committee on the Costs of Medical Care in 1928–31 were even more out of date, but they had shown the severity of the problems facing families in meeting medical costs and sensitized Anderson, who had studied with a member of the committee in later years, to the problem. The 1953 NORC study provided a new benchmark to see if the situation had improved with better times and the institution of health insurance. Repeated surveys would establish further changes as the institution of insurance grew and spread.

Changes in Costs of Medical Care (1958)   The 1953 findings were so productive (see Anderson and Feldman 1956) that the foundation, according to plan, sponsored a similar but larger nationwide survey in 1958 to document changes over the five years (Anderson, Collette, and Feldman 1963). Respondents' reports of insurance and hospital admissions were validated in the second survey against records. In the interim the foundation sponsored other studies—for example, a 1955 national survey on attitudes, information, and behavior in health matters, in which samples of the doctors and pharmacists of the respondents were also interviewed, directed by Feldman and Sheatsley (see Feldman 1966). Subsequently the foundation sponsored additional benchmark and other surveys. For example, the health and care and costs of older people were studied in 1961 by a complex design involving national surveys of the old, of the caretakers they mentioned, and of the general population (Shanas 1961).

Feldman's involvement in this special area of survey research,·like Elinson's forged luckily and accidentally in the 1953 survey, led to his long-term commitment. He left NORC in 1964 to become professor of biostatistics at Harvard, and then went on to become a senior member of the National Center for Health Statistics, where he has remained for many years. And NORC's expertise and prominence in this area, established in those early studies, led to a long series of related surveys sponsored by various agencies and foundations—for example, a 1959 nationwide survey of adults, and of teenagers, on knowledge, attitudes, and behavior affecting dental health and care (Kriesberg and Treiman 1960, 1962); a 1956 national survey of medical students (Cahalan, Collette, and Hillmar 1957); and a 1958 survey of Army medical officers that, along with other surveys of interns, doctors, hospital administrators, public health officials, pharmacists, and so on, produced a body of knowledge on health professionals.[30]

From the small beginning in 1950 came this long and large program of surveys on health, which continued into the 1970s (see Allswang and Bova 1964; Sheatsley 1982). But there was one other ramification. By the summer of 1956, NORC had built up enough experience in health surveys, and the scientific value and social importance of such research was sufficiently established, that the Social Science Research Council sponsored a summer training institute for postdoctoral students, Survey Methods in Research on Health Problems, conducted by NORC.[31]

Leaving NORC

I have taken the history of NORC up to the end of the 1950s, when it was already well established at the University of Chicago and had made substantial progress toward its several goals. Clyde Hart, having accomplished his mission, retired as director in 1960 at age 68. In later years, under a series of directors—Peter Rossi, Norman Bradburn, James Davis, and Kenneth Prewitt—NORC expanded greatly and made significant progress toward each of its major goals. Progress was not continuous. There were plateaus and periods of retrenchment, a spurt of wild growth followed by a severe crisis, but NORC survived all such difficulties. Its training program expanded, supported by the National Institute of Mental Health for many years beginning in 1962. Its services to the scholarly community grew, supported for many years in the form of the General Social Survey by the National Science Foundation beginning in 1972.[32] Its growing stature in the university is certainly suggested by the fact that Bradburn, its director from 1967 to 1971 and again from 1979 to 1984 and from 1989 on, became provost of the university in 1984. And when a severe financial crisis occurred in the 1960s, the university saved NORC from bankruptcy, suggesting the strong support that had developed. NORC's applied and basic research also expanded in many directions, annual revenues rising from about $500,000 in 1960 to as high as $7 million in the 1970s.

During the years I spent at NORC, the insulation of the New York office served its organizational goals. It denied me, however, the opportunity to teach on a regular basis, which I had relinquished willingly but missed to some degree. However, under Hart's generous policies, I was granted leaves for interesting teaching and other assignments which periodically provided extra gratification. In November 1948 I took leave for several months to work on the SSRC investigation of the failure of the preelection polls (Mosteller et al. 1949). In effect, Hart almost commanded me to take that assignment, seeing the failure of the commercial polls as affecting the welfare and future of *all* survey research.

Hart granted me another leave, for the academic year 1950–51, to teach survey research methods in Norway and help the infant Oslo Institute of Social Research develop. That foreign assignment, too, came through the wartime network. Krech had had the assignment the year before and passed it to me, who passed it on to Daniel Katz in 1951–52. Thereafter, the chain of influence was extended through Burton Fisher and Angus Campbell and other "old boys."

I intended to return from Norway to my normal, full-time position at NORC, but a cable from Paul Lazarsfeld in the spring of 1951 changed the course of my career. I accepted his offer of a full-time position teaching survey methods in the Columbia graduate Department of Sociology. The offer reflected Lazarsfeld and Merton's tolerant conception of sociology, since I had no official credentials as a "sociologist." I had taken my doctorate in social psychology in the adjacent Department of Psychology at Columbia which, ironically, never offered me a position. But the offer also indicates that survey research had been incorporated into academic sociology by 1950, at least in some places. In September 1951, officially, whimsically, I became a "sociologist," the change in my identity mainly the result of my experience in survey research.[33]

I had attached only one condition to my acceptance, that I would continue my research association with NORC. So I resumed my earlier gratifying career as surveyor-scholar-teacher, again in oscillating fashion by commuting back and forth on the subway between Columbia and downtown New York. I could have simplified life by joining the adjacent, affiliated Bureau of Applied Social Research. My apparently strange behavior deserves analysis. The obligation to complete the NORC work on interviewer effects did not account for my actions. The basic manuscript was completed by 1953, but I continued my official association with NORC until 1957. The major factors were my strong affection for Hart and Sheatsley and my long collaboration with Sheatsley, which had been productive and gratifying. NORC understandably pulled me in its direction, but why did the Bureau not pull me in the other direction? The decision says something about my perception of the Bureau in 1951, and my joining the Bureau as an associate director in 1957 indicates the gradual changes in my perception as I worked there in the interim on ad hoc projects.

Notes

1. The brochure issued at NORC's founding, from which I extract some passages, conveys Field's credo, his populism: "By virtue of its national staff, the Center will be able to determine how people, in all parts of the country, and in all walks of life, feel on questions of current importance." The populist flavor is even stronger in another passage underscored in the original: "The average voter realizes that once he has voted, he, individually, has little more power to influence the men who are elected. This has doubtless resulted in a feeling of impotence among the people and may be responsible for much of their apathy toward political matters." And it comes through in the explanation that the brochure gives for the choice of Denver as the headquarters. "The headquarters of all the well-known national polling organizations are situated along the Atlantic seaboard. It was, therefore, decided to locate the National Opinion Research Center west of the Mississippi, in the belief that interest and familiarity with this new type of research might be extended throughout the country."

2. Cantril claims a strategic role in the negotiations. "I helped my friend, Harry Field, create the National Opinion Research Center by having a number of meetings with Mr. Marshall Field II and his lawyer, Louis Weiss. As a result, Mr. Field put up enough money to establish the first nonprofit survey organization able to do research for organizations working in the public interest" (1967, p. 165). Sheatsley's history (1982) makes no mention of Cantril's meetings.

3. In 1943, another member, Gordon M. Connelly, was added to the senior staff in Denver, recruited from the same basic pool of experienced pollsters. He was the co-organizer of a small independent organization in Portland, Oregon, named the Front Door Ballot Box. That name again strikes the symbolic note of polling as a new political vehicle for expressing the people's views.

4. In his preface to the second edition of *The People's Choice* (1948), Lazarsfeld illustrates the value of continuity in social research in corroborating, specifying, and clarifying earlier findings by citing the findings of the 1944 NORC study. This surely suggests the value of that early study.

5. *Opinion News*, started by Field in 1943, exemplifies the concept. For the first two years it was a six-page mimeographed publication reporting various poll findings from Gallup, NORC, and other sources with a minimum of editorial comment and appearing twenty six times a year. By 1947 it was a sixteen-page printed publication with a board of advisory editors including Allport, Bernard Berelson, Leonard Cantril, and Cottrell and offering "Opinion Briefs," "Notes on Current Research Publications," "News of Research Developments," as well as more extended coverage of a leading issue. Publication was suspended in 1948 and never resumed.

6. In 1937, Cahalan and Meier isolated the major sources of error in the *Literary Digest*'s prediction of the 1936 presidential election by piggybacking a battery of questions on a Gallup survey and by a local survey in Cedar Rapids, Iowa, of a sample on the *Digest* mailing list. For this novel design and fruitful product of the Cahalan-Meier-Gallup collaboration, see Cahalan and Meier 1939.

7. Here one notes the sharp contrast mentioned earlier between the Army, where Stouffer's unit conducted large-scale surveys of soldiers, and the Navy, where the unit focused exclusively on civilian opinion. Cahalan explains the difference in terms of the hostility of the commanders to soliciting the opinions of sailors, that never being undermined as it was in the Army by such a powerful and persuasive figure as General Osborne.

8. The major theme of the conference was public opinion and world peace, but considerable attention was also devoted to problems of sampling, interviewing, validity, and ethical standards. For a summary discussion of the papers and panels presented at the Central City conference, see Converse 1987, pp. 230–232. [Ed.]

9. Hart's staff included Elizabeth Herzog, Harry Alpert, Gabriel Almond, Henry Ehrmann, and Herbert Marcuse.

10. For further details on NORC's move to the University of Chicago, see Converse 1987, pp. 315–318. [Ed.]

11. Increasingly today the necessity and the ethics of withholding such information are being questioned by survey and other researchers, but at that time the need for doing so was taken for granted.

12. In 1946, Jones served as the executive officer of the Allied Commission to supervise the Greek elections, a mission which employed a unique application of sample survey methods to provide a criterion to test whether the election had been bona fide. See Jessen et al. 1947.

13. These reprintings include the following: Swanson, Newcomb, and Hartley 1952; Katz 1954; Maccoby, Newcomb, and Hartley 1958; Schramm 1972; Dunod 1972; and Welch and Comer 1975. Note that the paper referred only to NORC surveys, no mention of the State Department being allowed, although we were given clearance to publish the data by 1948. Another part of the paper, documenting selective exposure to information that was congenial with prior attitudes, was based on State Department surveys in which we had adapted the basic experimental design used earlier in the OWI survey in Corning and Hornell, New York, to test a pamphlet on security of information (see chapter 2).

14. In 1958 fragments of the findings from NORC's surveys for the State Department relating to the UN, along with findings from Gallup and Roper, were used by William A. Scott and Stephen Withey in *The United States and the United Nations: The Public View, 1945–1955* and in 1984 Schuyler Foster made fragmentary use of the NORC materials in *Activism Replaces Isolationism: U.S. Public Attitudes, 1940–1975*. Neither work treats any of the methodological aspects of the surveys. Gabriel Almond synthesized findings from many surveys on foreign affairs conducted by NORC and other polling organizations in his pioneering study, *The American People and Foreign Policy* (1950), but the State Department classified surveys were not included. Jerome Bruner's earlier trailblazing study, *Mandate from the People* (1944), antedated the NORC surveys for the State Department but may have drawn on confidential surveys during the war, since Bruner was associate director of the Princeton Office of Public Opinion Research for some of the war years. Another study drawing on the NORC materials was Alfred O. Hero, Jr., *The Southerner and World Affairs* (1965).

15. Shirley Star was the first NORC staff member to complete the Ph.D. at Chicago, in 1950. Converse 1987, pp. 319, 523n. [Ed.]

16. The National Research Council and natural scientists and engineers were especially interested in surveys of consumer wants, the findings contributing to their work on testing and standardization of products and materials. Representatives of the American Society for Testing Materials and the American Standards Association served on the commit-

tee, as did Walter Shewhart, the distinguished physical scientist from Bell Telephone Laboratories.

17. When Cobb joined NORC he was already regarded by insiders as a sampling expert and an excellent mathematical statistician. His extraordinary biography illustrates in extreme form some larger features of the early development of survey research.

My generation had to learn on the job, but the social science and statistics courses we had taken as undergraduate and graduate students were useful general background. Cobb did not have even that background. He came from a poor family, made even poorer by the Great Depression, and had never gone beyond high school. But then his good fortune was to land a clerical job in the WPA, in the section where Stock and Frankel and other trained mathematicians, statisticians, and social scientists were developing the theory and procedures needed for sample surveys of unemployment. While on that job, everyone learned to some degree, but Cobb learned it *all* the hard way. As his colleagues tell the story, he borrowed some of the mathematics and statistics books on their desks and displayed his virtuosity by learning the lessons in the books almost overnight. With that, so to speak, night school background, helped along by their tutoring, he progressed with the rest of the section to become the first generation of skilled samplers.

18. For the complete list see *Interviewing in Social Research*, Appendix D.

19. Helen Hughes's stimulating paper "The Compleat Antivivisectionist" (1947), based on a miscellany of available materials, will suggest how much could have been learned about the sentiments from the systematic national data of the NORC survey. The early data could have served as a baseline for what has been a continuing social movement which in the 1980s took on a new momentum.

20. In Rossi's presidential address to the American Sociological Association (1980), the survey is used to illustrate the fuzzy boundary between applied and basic research and the way in which applied research often provides opportunities to study basic problems.

21. The book is a fascinating case for sociologists of science interested in the symbolism employed in co-authored publications. The title page lists Field and NORC first and Lazarsfeld and the Bureau second. The spine on the cloth binding lists Lazarsfeld first and Field second. The preface by Lazarsfeld is punctiliously correct in allocating credit to the several parties for their respective roles in the study.

22. The title page of the second book gives prominent credit to NORC for conducting the survey.

23. During the war, the division was directed by Max Horkheimer, and the staff and focus of research were different, reflecting the influence of the Frankfurt Institute of Social Research. The series Studies in Prejudice (1949–50) was concerned with the personality factors that predisposed

individuals to prejudice, the best known being *The Authoritarian Personality* (1950).

24. Since the end of World War II, and through the 1950s, Stember found that "anti-Semitism in all its forms has massively declined in the United States," but between 1938 and 1945, there was

> increasing enmity to Jews. . . . In the bloody cataclysmic days of 1944, these feelings burned more widely and fiercely. Nor do they appear to have been affected at all by the growing realization of what was happening to the Jews of Europe, of the horrors that anti-Semitism had led to. From first to last, the plight of Hitler's favorite victims had little effect on the climate of opinion and feeling about American Jews. [pp. 8–9]

25. For reviews of the many disaster studies, see Barton 1963; Quarantelli and Dynes 1977.

26. For a comprehensive, annotated bibliography of NORC surveys in the early years, see Allswang and Bova 1964.

27. Earlier, under Harry Field's direction, NORC had conducted several surveys on tuberculosis, cancer, and alcoholism, but these predate the move to Chicago. For summaries, see Allswang and Bova 1964. The survey on the use of animals in medical experiments might be included in the series on "health," thus dating the beginning of the program as 1947.

28. While working in Stouffer's unit during the war, Elinson had directed two surveys relating to health: one on the morale of wounded soldiers in Army hospitals and the other on the epidemiology of trench foot. In the postwar unit, he had conducted an epidemiological survey on venereal disease among soldiers. But these were only a few of his many assignments and had in no way created the commitment to the health area which, as he indicated, followed his association with Trussell at Hunterdon.

29. The same strategy was employed by the California Department of Public Health, the staff using Alameda County for its so-called human population laboratory. Here again one notes the small network that was influential in the early development of survey research, some of the members by successive migrations forming the core of the California human laboratory staff, which included Don Cahalan and Dean Manheimer, whose prior locations were already plotted. Josephine Williams Meltzer started with NORC, joined Elinson at Columbia, and then went to California. Joseph Hochstim, the director, started with the Psychological Corporation.

30. The growth of the NORC program in part reflected the broader trend toward research on social and economic aspects of health, especially by survey methods. By 1957, the Health Information Foundation's annual

"inventory" of research listed about 400 studies, over half of which involved sample surveys.

31. The instructors included Elinson, Feldman, Hart, Hyman, Eli Marks, Sheatsley, Star, and Odin Anderson. The thirteen students selected from a larger number of applicants included Seymour Bellin from Syracuse, Warren Breed from Tulane, James A. Davis, then at the Harvard School of Public Health and years later the director of NORC, William Mooney from the California Department of Public Health, Charles Willie, then at the Department of Public Health of the New York College of Medicine.

32. The values of the General Social Survey for teaching and scholarship were reviewed in a symposium by Converse, Cutler, Glenn, and Hyman 1978. The generalizations derived from the more than 600 studies using the data were reviewed by Davis and Smith 1982, who also provide an extensive bibliography. In the 1960s, many scholarly contributions appeared in a series titled Monographs in Social Research.

33. The concept "reference group," which I formulated and explored in my doctoral dissertation, "The Psychology of Status" (1942), may also have led to the invitation, since Merton had brought the work back from obscurity and given it favorable attention in his "Contributions to the Theory of Reference Group Behavior" (Merton and Kitt 1950). Thus my earlier work in social psychology, prior to my entrance into survey research, would have contributed to my acceptance as a "sociologist." However, since Merton's essay itself was stimulated by a reanalysis of the Stouffer wartime surveys (see chapter 3), the source of my invitation and entry into sociology might still be traced back to survey research.

· 6 ·

The Rise and Fall of the Bureau of Applied Social Research

A knowledge of the history of the Bureau of Applied Social Research and of NORC is essential to understanding the various ways survey research became established in major American universities and integrated with the social sciences. Allen Barton, the Bureau's director over its last fifteen years, proposed one model to guide him and other writers.

> The rise and fall of the Bureau of Applied Social Research, and the life of its founder and mentor, Paul Lazarsfeld, should ideally be presented as a drama by Brecht, accompanied by the dissonant and jazzy music of pre-Nazi Central Europe, and its depression-time equivalent in the United States. [1982, p. 171]

Lazarsfeld's life and the early days of the Bureau have the flavor of a picaresque novel. Austrian fascism forced him to become homeless and start a precarious life in a strange country. Without resources, he survived by his quick wits, by making the most of accidental bits of good fortune, by resilience in confronting misfortune, and by prodigious effort and energy. He created a series of research centers, which met with a string of mishaps, which he overcame by brilliant improvisation. Indeed, Barton tells us, "he brought new meaning to the words 'non-profit' as he used one deficit-ridden project to support another, and pyramided his intellectual assets from grant to grant" (p. 18).

Although I lack the talents of a novelist or playwright, I had the advantage of observing and participating in the development of the Bureau over a long period. While I worked only periodically on Bureau projects from 1951 to 1956, I served continuously as an associate director from 1957 to 1969. However, as a member of the sociology department I observed events throughout that important, relatively early stage of the Bureau's development. And I learned about the earliest stage, when the Bureau was still the Office of Radio Research, from my wartime colleagues at OWI who had been members of the Office before 1942[1] and contributors to its classic research—notably Eunice Cooper, Alberta Curtis, Helen Schneider Dinerman, Hazel Gaudet, and Elmo Wilson. NORC, as I noted, collaborated on classic Bureau projects conducted between 1945 and 1948, and my duties at NORC thus involved me in that phase of the Bureau's development.

Moreover, I, like others, can draw on a substantial published literature for the Bureau's history.[2] As noted in earlier chapters, other founders of survey research and their staffs wrote little or nothing about themselves and the centers they created. Apart from *The American Soldier*, even the early major surveys of other pioneering centers, the products and indicators of their histories and testimonials to their achievements, were rarely published. Those who write about the history of survey research and rely on published sources are likely to underrate the contribution of those centers whose achievements were unrecorded and overrate the contribution of the Bureau, whose achievements have been amply documented in print.[3]

In light of my career in the various early centers, I hope to write a balanced account of the Bureau. However, I will omit important contributions of the Bureau that have no relevance to the history of *survey* research. By 1944, when "the research program of the Office of Radio Research had so far transcended the field of radio that its name had become an anachronism" (Twentieth Anniversary Report 1957, p. 4), the new name advisedly and appropriately chosen was the Bureau of Applied Social Research. Clearly, the Bureau did not wish to be identified narrowly and, in fact, was not limited to survey research.

The Bureau's Origins

Paul Lazarsfeld, then age 25, founded a research center in Vienna in 1926, the first of a chain of centers. Their distinctive features were shaped by his character and by circumstances. I begin with the first link in the chain, since so much of the history of the Bureau was foreshadowed in the earliest venture.

The Vienna Center

Politically, Lazarsfeld was a socialist, active and skilled in organizing youth movements. Hans Zeisel, his associate in the Vienna Center and a co-author of its famous study, *The Unemployed of Marienthal* (Jahoda, Lazarsfeld, and Zeisel 1932), stresses that "of all the influences on our lives one was paramount—that of the socialist party of that day" (1979, p. 12). Professionally, Lazarsfeld was a mathematician with a doctorate in applied mathematics, who began his career teaching mathematics and physics in a *Gymnasium*. However, on the appointments of Professors Karl and Charlotte Bühler in 1923 to build a new department or institute of psychology at the university, he became interested in that discipline, took their early seminars, and received a part-time appointment as an assistant, teaching statistics at first, and then social and applied psychology.

In his memoir, Lazarsfeld describes the origins of the research center.

> I got the idea that I would create a division of social psychology at the Institute. This would permit work on paid contracts and from such sources I would get a small but adequate salary. . . . The idea was realized in the form of an independent Research Center . . . of which Karl Bühler was the president. From then on, I directed the applied studies of this Center, and at the same time gave my courses at the University Institute and supervised dissertations. [1968, p. 274]

In organizing the venture, Lazarsfeld showed his entrepreneurial skills:

> In order to provide his new institute with both university prestige and commercial appeal and also to legitimize it vis-à-vis the university and at the time gain access for it to big business firms Lazarsfeld put together a presidium and a board so glamorous that in retrospect one can only marvel how he got them all together . . . members of the presidium were the presidents of the Austrian Chamber of Commerce, of the Vienna Chamber of Labor, the Lower Austria Chamber of Agriculture. Members of the board included several famous university professors and a whole galaxy of presidents or directors general of the biggest commercial firms in Austria. [Neurath 1983, p. 369]

Whatever the original intent, the independent center remained only tenuously connected to the university through the persons of Bühler and Lazarsfeld and their dual membership in both institutions. The university provided no budget, and the *Wirtschaftspsychologische Forschungsstelle* (Center for Psychological Research on Economic and Social Problems) "sustained itself mainly on ideas, all of them more or less Paul's, on the unabated enthusiasm of its members, and on no money worth talking about" (Zeisel 1979, p. 13), the income being derived mainly from market research. However, after the first studies proved profitable for a few clients, "life became easier. . . . After a while we could point to a respectable list of products we had studied: butter and lard, coffee, milk, beer, vinegar, coat hangers, soup, malt, shoes, laundries, rayon, wool" (Zeisel 1979, p. 14).

A center organized by Socialists to advance social psychology and then conducting market research to increase businessmen's profits seems incongruous. Lazarsfeld and his associates resolved the conflict between their principles and their practices in part because they saw such research as a temporary expedient, compelled by necessity, until the time they could redirect the research. When Marie Jahoda, the third author of Marienthal and Lazarsfeld's successor as director of the *Forschungsstelle*, was asked that very question many years later, she answered:

> . . . many of us had no other income . . . we had among our interviewers people with doctorates in law and economics . . . for whom this was their only income. That was in that time, which was so horrible in Austria, especially for young people, so much of a justification that we did not have any time left for having a bad conscience. . . . But the money that we got for it [market research] we used for socio-psychological studies . . . always with the one thought in the back of our minds: how much money can we get toward that which we really wanted to do? [Neurath 1983, pp. 370–371]

Lazarsfeld also saw such applied research as directly serving, not opposing, their intellectual and social goals. He reports: "I certainly never missed the chance to show that even 'trivial' studies, if properly interpreted and integrated, could lead to *important* findings, 'important' implying a higher level of generalization. Thus, I once summarized a number of our consumer studies by carving out the notion of the proletarian consumer" (1968, p. 280). That concept and its implications for purchasing products linked the market research to the staff's intellectual and political interests in social stratification.

To the clients, the consumer studies were a way to increase profits. To Lazarsfeld, gifted with great powers of abstraction, the studies increased knowledge of decision processes, of the social influences, motivations, and other fundamental factors governing choices and actions. Thus, the studies had theoretical as well as practical value if abstracted properly, and Lazarsfeld concluded that "the consumer purchase became a special case of a problem which had great sanctity in the European humanistic tradition: *Handlung*, action" (p. 281). With his vision, he could see "the equivalence of socialist voting and the buying of soap" (p. 279), a study of the latter decision giving clues to how to study the choice of a party and help the Socialists.[4]

The staff would have gratified their scientific interests even if the market research findings had lacked substantive or theoretical significance. The studies also were opportunities to develop and test new research techniques. Like the American pioneers described earlier, the Vienna pioneers learned the methods as they invented and practiced them. Their academic training provided no ready-made solutions to the difficulties they faced, although it gave them a solid intellectual foundation on which to build.[5] The staff, at times, seemed so enthralled by methodology that the embarrassing content or conclusion of a study was lost to sight. A vivid case is the early study Lazarsfeld used to recount to his students to illustrate the center's strategy of seeking the deeper, general explanation underlying diverse findings.

A study for the Habsburg Laundry explored the circumstances leading housewives to use a commercial laundry. These were diverse: a new baby, an illness in the family, or any unexpected event interrupting daily life in the household. This fundamental explanation led the center to give the client the following advice: Find families in disarray, the most significant instance being a death in the family. As a result, the laundry studied the death notices and offered its services to bereaved families with considerable success.

Occasionally, noncommercial clients also sponsored research. For example, the center conducted a study in 1930–31, regarded as the first such survey in Europe, of the Vienna radio audience's preferences, describing the patterns in different social strata. That study adventitiously took on added importance later when Lazarsfeld became involved in radio research in America in 1937. The center also conducted the field work in Austria for a study of authoritarianism by Erich Fromm of the Frankfurt Institute of Social Research. That connection also helped Lazarsfeld's fortunes in America, the institute contributing support to his next center, established in Newark in 1936.

In 1931–32, late in its lifetime, the center conducted a noncommercial study of the social and psychological effects of the pervasive and prolonged unemployment afflicting a small industrial community,

Marienthal, during the Great Depression (Jahoda, Lazarsfeld, and
Zeisel 1933, 1971). The study deservedly became a classic and brought
a chain of good fortune to Lazarsfeld. The Marienthal study led the
Rockefeller Foundation to award him a traveling fellowship in the
United States in September 1933. Then when fascism in Austria
forced him to emigrate and find a permanent position in America,
the study of unemployment in Marienthal was the credential which
led to his employment in 1935 at the University of Newark. Ironically,
his duties were to analyze 10,000 questionnaires on the effects of
unemployment among American youth and to supervise unemployed students on work relief, whom he put to work coding and
tabulating the questionnaires. By 1936, Lazarsfeld had transformed
the project into the Research Center of the University of Newark,
and the position into acting director.

Marienthal created a bond between Lazarsfeld and Robert Lynd,
whom he visited during his traveling fellowship and who was also
studying the effects of unemployment.[6] That association was crucial
to Lazarsfeld's American career. Lynd recommended Lazarsfeld for
the Newark position, later for the directorship of the Radio Research
Project, and then for an appointment at Columbia. Marienthal also
led to Lazarsfeld's first collaboration with Samuel Stouffer, who had
been appointed research director for the Social Science Research
Council's studies on the effects of the Depression, which in turn led
to their lifelong, mutually fruitful association.

The study that brought Lazarsfeld such good fortune was itself an
accident, its conception the product of a chance encounter. Zeisel
tells the story:

> Through an unexpected turn of events, our immersion in the socialist
> movement was to lead to the most important piece of work of those
> years. The Austrian trade unions had just rid themselves of the ten-
> hour working day. Stimulated by American studies, Paul thought that
> we should explore how the workers were using their newly won leisure
> time. At that time we had the privilege of occasionally talking over our
> plans with Otto Bauer, the scholarly, ascetic leader of the socialist
> party. When Paul told him of his plan, Bauer reacted angrily: What a
> mockery to study leisure-time activity in a country that suffered from
> a chronic unemployment rate of around ten percent. *That*, he said, was
> the leisure time to study, the social and psychological effects of lasting
> unemployment. And that is exactly what we did—in Marienthal. [1979,
> p. 13]

The Marienthal study was not a sample survey. All 478 families
in the small community were studied. Some adults did complete a
questionnaire describing the daily time budget, but it was only one

of many instruments in an inquiry using multiple methods. The team obtained detailed life histories from adults and lengthy essays from adolescents, a diary of the families' meals over the course of a week and the lunches the children took to school. They used a variety of existing records from government and other sources, conducted intensive interviews with informants and respondents, reviewed findings from medical and dental examinations, and observed behavior. Then by qualitative and quantitative analysis all this evidence was skillfully blended to produce a comprehensive report on the social and psychological effects of unemployment.

Jahoda, Lazarsfeld, and Zeisel title their work, appropriately, "a sociography"—another apt term would be a "community study." Their strategy "was to find procedures which would combine the use of numerical data with immersion (*sich einleben*) into the situation . . . we have tried to build up a comprehensive picture of life in Marienthal. . . . Every path that could bring us closer to our objective was explored" (1971, pp. 1–2). Lazarsfeld is commonly thought of as a researcher devoted to quantitative methods. But Marienthal provides vivid evidence that he had no early fixation on survey method and quantitative analysis.

"The Vienna Center," as Lazarsfeld states, "was a sequence of improvisations" (1968, p. 287). The obstacles blocking a direct, fast route toward the goal of a university-based social research organization forced him to detour, to create a shaky enterprise marginal to the university. He also had to adopt what Barton calls "the hectic Lazarsfeldian lifestyle—running from lectures to the Research Center, trying to satisfy clients and at the same time experiment with new methods, trying to get research done while training apprentices, and making the whole thing self-supporting in the market-place since it had no university budget" (1982, p. 22).

We shall never know whether Lazarsfeld would have achieved his ultimate goal in Vienna, given enough time. A center staffed by Socialists and Jews was doomed under fascism. Lazarsfeld had to pursue his goal in America, but, by then, he no longer was improvising. He came equipped with the Vienna plan, habituated to the lifestyle it demanded. At the University of Newark, "the different components all concurrently in my mind could be integrated into some kind of institutional plan. Even so, the beginning in America was chaotic" (1968, p. 287).

The Newark Center

Lazarsfeld launched his plan in late 1935, almost upon arrival at the University of Newark to direct the unemployment project. "At the first talk" with Frank Kingdon, the newly installed president of the university, "I suggested that the . . . NYA project should be made the beginning of a 'Research Center of the University of Newark' which I proposed to create at the same time" (p. 288). By May 1936, the trustees had approved and Lazarsfeld received an official one-year appointment as acting director of the new center. Conditions seemed propitious, far better than those in Vienna.

The Newark Center and Lazarsfeld were now within the university, and President Kingdon and Lazarsfeld "got along well with each other from the start" (p. 288). The Depression, sadly, had created, in America as in Vienna, a group of young unemployed intellectuals eager to find employment and willing to work for meager pay. Moreover, Lazarsfeld had a supply of free labor, students on work relief, and funds from the WPA for new field studies of unemployment. But the fundamental economic obstacle had not been removed.

Lazarsfeld had to continue the hectic Vienna lifestyle in Newark: teaching, directing and doing research at the center and training the staff, and selling research to clients—all at the same time—in order to eke out the budget for his and the staff's salaries and keep the center alive. Between times, he managed to publish a series of papers, more amazing since they were written in a foreign language, English, within the first years after settling in the United States. There was the monograph with Stouffer on the family in the Depression (1937), an important methodological paper on market research (1935) with Arthur Kornhauser, and other substantive and methodological papers, notably his classic "The Art of Asking Why" (1935).

Lazarsfeld also published several papers under the pseudonym Elias Smith, which in terms of precise dates belong in the chronicle of the first years of the Office of Radio Research.[7] Nevertheless, they are additional evidence of his juggling many tasks simultaneously, and the perfect illustration of his wild inventiveness and its comic-ironic implications. The Newark staff was tiny, in his words "accidentally assembled" (1968, p. 308), not trained scholars.[8] To inflate the public image of the center, to conceal the fact that it was a one-man show, he invented an additional scholarly staff member, namely, Elias Smith, thus enhancing its—not his—prestige. However, Elias Smith created an unanticipated consequence in the McCarthy period. In connection with a government clearance, Lazarsfeld answered, correctly in terms of its political implications, that he had never used an alias. The agency, knowing he had masqueraded as Elias Smith but not why, regarded him as suspect until, luckily, his innocent intent was established (Lazarsfeld 1968, p. 308n).

The University of Newark could not give any financial support other than free space and Lazarsfeld's meager salary. He had to spend a great deal of time finding clients, and he could not be choosy. Rose Kohn Goldsen, whose long association with the Bureau began in Newark, captured the flavor of those early days in a paper commemorating the twentieth anniversary of the Bureau. The center operated by "the cliff-hanging principle of finance. . . . Paul Lazarsfeld spent his days peddling to potential 'marks' the idea of hiring us to do research for them. Research on anything" (1957, p. 4). When was the scholarship done? "Nights and weekends Paul and I spent together—he dictating; I typing and retyping the manuscripts."

Lazarsfeld's mission to establish a university-based research center—begun but then interrupted in Vienna and continued in Newark—drove him onward and inspired him to bear many burdens. The distinctive origin of Lazarsfeld's mission and ability to pursue it over a grueling course are revealed by poignant passages in his memoir.

In Vienna even before the rise of fascism, Lazarsfeld recognized that "under the adverse economic circumstances in Austria and the strong current of incipient anti-Semitism, a regular academic career would have been almost impossible" (p. 302). When he needed to continue his career in America, "only a position connected with a university was conceivable" (p. 298), but being both foreign and Jewish now doubled the obstacles. "I did experience the proverbial transition from a distinguished foreigner to an undesirable alien" (p. 303). . . . But, even so I was not seriously hampered, because it never occurred to me to aspire to a major university job. I took it for granted that I would have to make some move similar to the creation of the Vienna Research Center if I wanted to find a place for myself in the United States" (p. 301).

In order to achieve his goal, he adopted a "latent strategy" requiring "an underlying vigilance which connects accidental situations to a latent goal" (p. 299). To be vigilant enough to sense every danger, to see every opportunity and exploit it, would strain many people, but involved for Lazarsfeld "a kind of 'libidinal' element which makes all these things pleasurable within their own right" (p. 299). In observing and working with him over many years, I sensed that he found pleasure in devising strategies for the Bureau, schemes to advance it, defeat its adversaries, or placate clients, solutions to turn a failing project into a success, ways to exploit some stroke of good fortune or overcome some misfortune. Brinksmanship seemed to exhilarate, not scare, him.

Just as his sense of mission inspired the early staff, so, too, his exuberant spirits and pleasurable outlook were contagious. Twenty years later, Goldsen recalled: "One of the first things that comes to my mind when I think back to the early days . . . is that everything seemed so funny. Laughter was very much a part of our atmosphere then" (1957, p. 1). The wild escapades involving the Newark staff were funny for those who had strong nerves and a sense of humor. "If Paul was due at a meeting and the manuscript which he had not quite finished dictating before dashing for his cab was still untranscribed, we would line up a string of taxis, send the pages in relays as they came out of the typewriter, he improvising the paragraphs while he stalled for time at the conference table" (p. 6).

Lazarsfeld's incredible energy helped carry him along on his mission and lighten his burdens. "A visit by Paul," his son-in-law Bernard Bailyn recalls, "was like some wonderfully benign hurricane" (1979, pp. 16–17). Lazarsfeld's energy charged the atmosphere of the Newark Center, and Goldsen and other early staff recall the intensity with which they worked, their own high energy level, and the many duties they managed to juggle. Of course, it is one thing to be visited by a hurricane occasionally; it is another thing to face hurricanes—even benign ones—every day of the week. However, the early staff were rugged pioneers and do not report being shattered.

The Newark staff were "young, enthusiastic, and energetic . . . deeply involved with . . . work . . . and with each other" (Goldsen 1957, p. 1), inspired by the mission, and entertained by the escapades into which they were drawn. They did suffer financial insecurity and austerity. "We were quartered not exactly in the men's room, but in what formerly had been the men's lounge" (p. 2). But they coped. They knew they were better off than the millions on the breadlines.

Lacking the advanced academic training which would have helped the research and scholarship of the center, the Newark staff learned on the job. And they were apprenticed to an unusually creative and demanding master. Lazarsfeld's effective teaching and their abilities are documented by their later accomplishments.[9] Goldsen describes his style of training and the tension it generated.

> There was . . . the feeling that you were constantly being tested, constantly being tried, constantly being asked to live up to standards which were always a little vague and always a little beyond your ability to achieve. . . . Paul never told us what to do. He gave us instead a very general conception of what he thought the end product ought to approximate. I think now that he didn't even know what had to be done, in specific terms, but could give us only a tenuous and elusive image. We tried to fill it in, to the best of our abilities. . . . Many times I was irritated. Many times I was crushed. But this is unimportant. For

me, it was a thoroughly exhilarating experience. . . . There was . . . the excitement of rising to the occasion, using yourself to your greatest capacity—even beyond your own limitations. [1957, pp. 1, 5–6]

Helen Kaufman did not join the staff of the Office of Radio Research until 1940. The name and the place had changed, but the style had remained the same.

Paul was demanding, impatient, critical. *Now* I think inspired. Whatever the hell you gave him, he wasn't satisfied. . . . You didn't know how to do a better job and you didn't know when you had done it . . . but it was task anxiety, not job insecurity—He didn't fire people. . . . It's a training no one will ever get again. I'm very grateful that I was part of it. It brought out the best. [personal interview, February 27, 1984]

To satisfy a high standard is hard work; to satisfy a high standard that is only vaguely defined is harder yet; to face that task when one is young, without prior training to help or past achievement to bolster self-regard, and when one cares for the work and the teacher, is an awesome experience that can make or break an apprentice. Goldsen and Kaufman were made by it. However, the delicate balance sometimes tilted in the wrong direction in the later history of the Bureau. Albert Gollin, who worked at the Bureau from 1958 to 1963, described the problem metaphorically. He talked of the "burn out cases—too close to the bright light" (interview, February 1984).

The Newark staff worked hard and effectively and Lazarsfeld labored day and night, selling and doing research. But their combined efforts could not have saved the center. The bankruptcy of the University of Newark in 1938 would have doomed it. Lazarsfeld averted that fate (not that he could foresee it) by grasping an opportunity presented in 1937 just when the center was completing its first-year trial period and facing an uncertain future. That opportunity was the Princeton Radio Research Project, about to be started in 1937 under a grant from the Rockefeller Foundation to support a proposal by Hadley Cantril of that faculty. He needed a full-time research director and offered the post to Lazarsfeld, who accepted and worked some magic that might be titled "The Disappearing and Reappearing Project."

Lazarsfeld had converted the unemployment project into the Newark Center. Now he converted the Princeton Project into the Office of Radio Research and located it in Newark for a short while although it appeared to be in Princeton. In 1938 when the Newark Center was shut down, the "Princeton" office magically moved to Union Square in New York City. In 1940 Lazarsfeld liberated it administratively from Princeton University and transported it to Columbia, where it later became the Bureau of Applied Social Research. The origins of the radio project and its transformation will be described,[10] although Lazarsfeld's magic, like that of any good magician, has an aura of mystery. The important fact, as Barton states, is that "Lazarsfeld's third research center had emerged from the ashes of the second" (1982, p. 25).

The Office of Radio Research: The Pre-Columbia Phase

In 1934 the Rockefeller Foundation had become interested in radio, then a new medium. Subsequently, John Marshall, the foundation officer in charge, was so impressed by Cantril and Allport's *The Psychology of Radio* (1935) that he approached Cantril and suggested he undertake new research. Cantril, aided by Frank Stanton, also a psychologist then in the research department at CBS, submitted a proposal in 1937 which was promptly funded for two years by a grant to Princeton University in the amount of $67,000, with intimations that it could be extended.[11] Lazarsfeld had heard of the project and saw it as a target of opportunity, but his associations with Cantril and Stanton were too slight for him to approach them directly. Good luck came his way. Stanton had been slated to direct the project but declined. He had just become director of the CBS research department and was on his way to becoming president of the company. Cantril did not want the full-time responsibility. He had too many other interests and plans, including the Office of Public Opinion Research, which he established in 1939, and the *Public Opinion Quarterly*, which he helped found at Princeton in 1937.

Cantril asked Robert Lynd to suggest candidates. Lynd recommended Lazarsfeld. Cantril cabled Lazarsfeld (who was vacationing in Austria in August 1937) offering him the appointment in Princeton at an annual salary of $7,000 for two years and the prospect of two more to follow. Compared with Lazarsfeld's salary of $4,800—only half of which was secure—that was a magnificent figure, and Cantril added the inducement of a stipend for Herta Herzog, Lazarsfeld's wife at the time and research associate.

Cantril's follow-up letter added another inducement: "The project we outlined was essentially vague, general, and able now to be put into anything you would really like. Our idea was to try to determine eventually the role of radio in the lives of different types of listeners, the value of radio to people psychologically, and the various reasons why they like it" (Cantril to Lazarsfeld, August 9, 1937).

Lazarsfeld nevertheless did not seal the bargain. The issue was the Princeton Project versus the Newark Center. His letter to Cantril reveals his concern about moving to Princeton and the personal significance he attached to a research center with which he could identify:

> . . . I am somewhat worried in regard to [moving to Princeton] . . . it should be possible to work out a procedure which permits somehow not to interrupt too badly what I have started in Newark, I feel strongly that I don't want to [go] ahead alone, that I want to stand for an institution and I try to build up an institution which is able willing to stand for me. Of course, I will have to do very different things, less glorious but about the same way as you are a Professor in Harvard, then in Columbia, then in Princeton. But as my poise and my past and my name cannot compare with yours, I try to identify whatever I do with an institution which might after some time acquire the dignity which I myself for reason of destiny can hardly aspire at. [August 8, 1937]

Lazarsfeld intimated delicately that the Princeton Project be handled by the Newark Center and proposed most diplomatically that they continue negotiations. Cantril's August 9, 1937, letter offered various inducements, mentioned Lazarsfeld's new title, research associate in the School of Public and International Affairs at Princeton University, with the added jocular remark, "Doesn't that appeal to your bourgeois soul!" but was firm on the crucial issue: "Your suggestion about a tie-up with the Newark Research Center is, I fear, out . . . it would be impossible to have the work carried on elsewhere."

In September, out of Cantril's need for a director and Lazarsfeld's talent at negotiations, a compromise emerged. Lazarsfeld became the director with working headquarters at Newark, but a titular office was established at Princeton University, which was officially entrusted with the funds. Cantril and Stanton became associate directors, which was stipulated by the foundation. Lazarsfeld was responsible to them, but had substantial freedom in designing and directing the research. Their authority in no way hampered Lazarsfeld and their contributions, as we shall see, were exceedingly valuable. Lazarsfeld had hit a lucky streak. He wrote Lynd privately: "The entire arrangement is so favorable that somehow I cannot yet believe that it is true."

"In practical terms, the whole arrangement," as he explained to Lynd, "therefore means that the Research Center has a huge new job" (September 9, 1937), the Radio Research Project budget amounting to more than three times the total budget for the Newark Center. Now Lazarsfeld could expand his tiny staff and no longer needed to search for clients to support the center—not that he stopped. But this understates the benefits from the Radio Research Project. In 1938, the foundation granted additional funds for fellowships attached to the project, in effect providing additional staff and fulfilling Lazarsfeld's goal of training students in empirical research. And in 1939, the foundation renewed the grant, extending it ultimately for four years, thus ensuring continuity for the project and the Office of Radio Research.

The imposition of Cantril and Stanton as associate directors benefited the project and the center greatly, in effect adding two senior staff members who brought a variety of resources to the work. Cantril was a creative and versatile social psychologist, whose very early interest in public opinion research and favored location at Princeton cemented his relationship with George Gallup. Through Cantril, the Gallup poll became the efficient vehicle for some of the radio research. Cantril was ahead of his time in recognizing the value of secondary analysis of public opinion data and created in 1940 probably the first such data bank through the generosity of Gallup and support from the Rockefeller Foundation. Lazarsfeld's use of secondary analysis as a favorite and essential strategy in the early stages of the radio project may have been aided by Cantril's own interest in such a strategy.

Clearly, Cantril contributed in other ways to the methods developed. Lazarsfeld reports: "Cantril introduced an important type of procedure into the activities of the project. He suggested that a small number of open-ended interviews be conducted with listeners who were fans of typical radio programs. His suggestion was taken up by Herta Herzog. . . . The first and most widely quoted result of this approach was her discussion of the then popular Professor Quiz program. She later made a similar study of listeners to daytime serials" (1968, p. 312). Thus began what is now a venerable theoretical and methodological tradition in communication research: studying the audience's uses of and gratification from the media.

Cantril also co-authored one of the first monographs of the project and one of the earliest examples of "firehouse" research, a study of the panic following Orson Welles's 1938 broadcast "The War of the Worlds" (Cantril, Gaudet, and Herzog 1940). Intensive interviews of panic-stricken listeners, designed by Herzog, and quantitative findings from one survey by Gallup and two commissioned by CBS, designed by Stanton, yielded a multimethod quantitative and qualitative study of the unanticipated, disastrous consequences of a radio broadcast.

In addition to his intellectual abilities, Cantril was especially gifted in getting the rich and the powerful to sponsor research. The foundation grant he obtained to study the Welles broadcast is one more example of his fund-raising ability. However, when the Rockefeller grant came up for renewal in 1939 and the Office of Radio Research soon thereafter moved to Columbia, Cantril's connection was broken and his contributions to the research and the office ceased.

Stanton also had many talents, and his substantial contributions to the research and the growth of the center, in contrast to Cantril's, continued over many years. Stanton added not only general skills and training in applied psychology, but rare and valuable experience in audience research conducted at CBS, where he organized the research department in 1935.[12]

That preparation enabled him and Lazarsfeld to develop an electronic instrument, the "Lazarsfeld-Stanton program analyzer," by which each member of a small studio audience experimentally exposed to a radio program (or movie) could instantaneously register liking or disliking for specific elements of the presentation.[13] Stanton's intellectual contributions to the work of the office were not limited to the program analyzer. He and Lazarsfeld co-edited a series of books reporting the studies of radio and other media made by the office and later by the Bureau (Lazarsfeld and Stanton 1941, 1944, 1949). And his contributions to the work were not simply intellectual. Just as Cantril was the avenue to foundation grants, Stanton, in his position as director of CBS research (as vice president after 1944 and president after 1946), was the gatekeeper to corporate funds for the research of the office.

The Orson Welles broadcast in 1938 had provided a rare, strategic opportunity to study extreme negative effects of radio which the Office of Radio Research could not have exploited without special funds. Through Cantril, the Rockefeller Foundation was one source. Through Stanton, CBS was the source of funds for two of the surveys and for the firehouse research. Lazarsfeld "phoned Stanton the morning after the event and he provided money from his CBS research budget for immediate preliminary work" (Lazarsfeld 1968, p. 313). Then in 1943, Kate Smith's eighteen-hour broadcast, in which her appeals to Americans to purchase war bonds netted $39 million in pledges, provided another rare, strategic opportunity for firehouse research on extreme persuasive effects of radio. Again, special funds were needed. Again, Lazarsfeld phoned Stanton the next morning and the funds were provided (1968, p. 313). Merton, Fiske, and Curtis then conducted their classic study of mass persuasion (1946), combining a content analysis of the broadcast, intensive focused interviews of a small sample, and a large-scale sample survey into a multimethod qualitative and quantitative study.

Although the original grant for the Radio Research Project was lavish compared with the Newark Center's budget, and additional foundation and commercial support occasionally financed large-scale special studies, normally the Office of Radio Research could not afford to conduct major primary surveys. Lazarsfeld's ingenuity and amiability toward commercial research aided him. "Almost by necessity much of the early work was based on what I later called secondary analysis" (1968, p. 311). Findings on reading and radio listening from Gallup polls were analyzed, the flow of data facilitated by Cantril. Commercial surveys by the networks or by the regular rating services to measure size of audience and popularity of stations and programs were subjected to deeper secondary analyses, the knowledge of and access to such data facilitated by Stanton. The fruitfulness of the general strategy, of course, depended on Lazarsfeld's powers of abstraction, and this specific application reflected his substantive and political interest in social stratification.[14] That turn of mind and theme recalls his Viennese period.

The pattern of work at the office, during the years of the Rockefeller grants, recalls the Vienna period in one other important respect. A variety of small-scale market research studies were conducted for commercial clients, of little or no relevance to the Radio Research Project and seemingly too trivial to have any scientific significance. In Vienna it was necessary; in Newark and New York between 1937 and 1943 the grants relieved Lazarsfeld from selling and accepting such studies. Yet the complete *Guide to the Bureau* (Judith Barton 1984) has a string of entries such as "Should Bloomingdale's Maintain Its Restaurant" (1940), "Preliminary Test of Six Kolynos Commercials" (1942), "Test on Bisodol Commercials" (1942), "Exploratory Study of the Psychology of Refrigerator Purchasers" (1941), "The Buying of Vitamin Preparations" (1942), and "Test of Golden Wedding [whiskey] Trademarks" (1943).

Lazarsfeld never knew whether and for how long the Rockefeller grant would continue. Indeed, in 1938, at the end of the first year of work, dissatisfaction with the progress had been expressed and in 1939, at the end of the first grant, its continuation under his direction was questioned. Although the office survived both those crises, they may have compounded the deeper insecurity he felt from having been uprooted and having two centers doomed. Prudence dictated accepting clients and funds wherever he could find them in order to ensure the future of the office. And Lazarsfeld wanted the center not only to survive, but to grow.

Helen Kaufman told us that Lazarsfeld "didn't fire people." Moreover, out of compassionate concern for other refugee scholars, he hired them and gave them a haven at his American centers. Thus he often assumed a responsibility to provide for staff who could not be supported by the Radio Research Project's budget, and then needed to find commercial clients. Sometimes he was rewarded for his virtue by the classic studies such European scholars produced. Leo Lowenthal's content analysis of biographies in popular magazines (1944), Rudolf Arnheim's content analysis of radio soap operas (1944), and Katherine Wolf's intensive interviews of children on the gratifications and conflicts experienced in reading comic books, in collaboration with Marjorie Fiske (1949), are examples. Occasionally, Lazarsfeld's financial burdens were compounded by the tempest a staff member created. The extreme case was Theodor Adorno, who offended the Rockefeller Foundation officer who made the grant and the networks whose cooperation was needed (Morrison 1978b).[15]

Another financial pressure led Lazarsfeld to seek commercial clients. He reports candidly: "I often exceeded the Princeton [radio research] budget, sure that I would cover the deficit with additional income from some other source" (1968, p. 310). This pattern of management characterized him in later periods also. Lazarsfeld recognized the risks involved: "As long as I handled situations myself I was somehow always able to balance the budget, though often I came in by the skin of my teeth. But in situations where I could not go on juggling or raising additional funds, the matter became more complicated" (p. 310). Despite the risk, the pattern continued.

Panel Surveys The Office of Radio Research, as shown by the studies cited, used a variety of methods. It was ahead of the times in exploiting available survey data by secondary analysis, but rarely conducted its own sample surveys. In those rare instances, it set a good example by combining other procedures into a multimethod study and by using qualitative and quantitative analysis. However, its most notable contribution to survey research was the use of a panel, a sample whose members are measured more than once over some interval of time in a series of surveys.

In some circles, Lazarsfeld is thought of as the inventor of panel surveys, but this view ignores or distorts history. To begin with, the before-and-after experimental designs traditionally used by social psychologists to measure changes in attitude produced by some experimentally introduced stimuli or by some natural experience may, of course, also be regarded as panels, generally involving two waves of measurement over a short interval, but sometimes operated over more waves and a longer interval.[16] Academic social scientists—Stuart Rice in the 1920s, for example—also preceded Lazarsfeld in measuring a group of individuals repeatedly in order to study processes and causes of change (1928). To be sure, the subjects in these early academic studies were almost always students or schoolchildren, not adults, and the mode of analysis usually involved the change in the average score of the total group or of subgroups. By contrast, panel analysis examines "turnover" or *individual* changes of various types and then pursues the sources of such change. In the 1930s, market and media researchers had also begun to organize, and maintain over long periods by various incentives, different kinds of panels—for example, readers of a particular magazine, regular listeners to a particular type of radio program, farm families or other types of consumers, drug stores or grocery stores or other suppliers to consumers.[17]

Through his involvement with commercial research and especially his association with Stanton, Lazarsfeld learned of these panels. In his first publication on panel methods (Lazarsfeld and Fiske 1938), the *Woman's Home Companion* panel of readers, organized in 1935, was reviewed in detail. In an earlier memorandum to Stanton on November 10, 1937, he expressed interest in the BBC listener panels and asked Stanton for more information on that operation. However, the media researchers had used the method mainly as a practical and efficient way to obtain rich, detailed, and qualitative information on audience reactions to various kinds of content or to an extended series of presentations, the panel members being selected from regular readers or listeners with strong and continuing interest in certain types of programming—for example, serious music, talk shows—and/or those who agree to participate for an extended period.[18]

By contrast, Lazarsfeld with his usual quickness of mind and vigilance about opportunities, realized the panel's great potential for studying effects of and changes produced by radio. He soon began a systematic analysis of the properties of the method. Later he and a group of collaborators conducted a series of methodological tests of panels, applied the method initially to the study of radio and then to politics, codified modes of panel analysis with special attention to causal analysis, and promoted the use of panels in a series of persuasive publications.[19]

The Radio Research Project could afford very few large-scale single surveys; it certainly could not afford repeated surveys of a panel. Initially, Lazarsfeld stretched the funds by hitching panels onto other people's surveys. The Psychological Corporation had conducted a survey in New Jersey in the spring of 1939, two weeks before a vote on a referendum. By interviewing a subsample after the election, the office created a two-wave panel at little cost and was able to measure changes in opinion and the effects of the campaign. The same strategy was applied in New York State in 1938 around the Dewey-Lehman campaign for governor by hitching onto a Gallup preelection poll with intent to examine campaign effects and revealed serious difficulty in tracking down and reinterviewing those panel members. Given the focus of the project, however, the early panel studies were mainly on the effects of prolonged exposure to various series of radio programs done, in the fashion of the period, at little cost by mailings to groups who had agreed to listen and return the repeated questionnaires. Those panels revealed the problem of differential mortality (Lazarsfeld 1940).

The People's Choice   In 1940, the request for the renewal of the radio research grant "proposed, by utilizing the panel technique developed in the first two years of the project, to locate those individuals who do change their habits in response to a continuous sequence of broadcasts; and then to study in detail the circumstances surrounding the listening and subsequent changes in these individuals" (Lazarsfeld 1968, pp. 329–330). The three-year grant beginning in March 1940 was to support the panel studies of radio that were envisioned, but for reasons we shall never know the plan changed. Lazarsfeld reports, "I do not remember how this proposal was altered so that the November 1940 election became the focus of the first panel study" (p. 330), and in May 1940 in Erie County, Ohio, the first wave of interviewing was conducted.

Whatever the reasons for the switch in plans, clearly improvised at short notice, it had fortunate consequences. It led to *The People's Choice* (Lazarsfeld, Berelson, and Gaudet 1944), the first large-scale panel survey among a cross-section of adults measuring stability or change in political behavior during a presidential election campaign and its causes. That, in turn, led to the widespread use of panel methods in the study of political behavior and to the cumulation and replication of findings. The Bureau conducted a second major panel study during the 1948 election (Berelson, Lazarsfeld, and McPhee 1954), and other investigators and organizations conducted panel surveys on elections in the United States and elsewhere.[20] And the unexpected findings of *The People's Choice* that radio's influence during the campaign had been modest, that interpersonal communication was important, and that opinion leaders mediated the flow of influence from the mass media—ironic when one recalls the original plan and the auspices—led the office (or the Bureau) to conduct further studies of opinion leadership (Merton 1949; Katz and Lazarsfeld 1955). Others here and abroad were also stimulated to study opinion leadership.

Although the Rockefeller grant would have covered the cost of the listener panel studies originally planned, it could not cover the costs of the Erie County panel survey involving seven waves of personal interviewing conducted under difficult field conditions with much larger samples. Lazarsfeld used his entrepreneurial ability to find backers for so big a venture. Elmo Roper co-sponsored the study and contributed funds. *Life* and *Fortune* magazines also made a contribution through Roper's intervention in return for the privilege of publishing several feature stories about the findings in Erie County.

Roper also provided essential staff to help in the sampling and questionnaire design and assigned Elmo Wilson to supervise the six months of field work. Roper's importance for the growth of survey research is again revealed here. His support of the panel survey reflected both his generosity and enlightened self-interest. He realized that the "confidence with which the public watched the election surveys" (1941), created by the successful predictions in 1936, could easily be undermined if the 1940 preelection polls failed. One hazard was a shift after the last poll had been conducted. From the Erie County study, "a general estimate could be had of the importance of different circumstances and events, and an idea of what sort of change in opinion to expect in the case of future events" (Roper 1941, p. 87). Roper was also one of the contributors to the 1948 panel study.

Lazarsfeld had been fortunate in having as associate directors of the Radio Research Project men so gifted and close to seats of power and wealth as Cantril and Stanton. And he was fortunate to have Berelson as a co-author of the 1940 and 1948 panel studies. His style of work, as Sills documents, was "organized and goal directed. . . . Each day he carried in his pocket a little list of things that had to be—and usually were—done that day" (1981, p. 309). That style counterbalanced Lazarsfeld's style of improvisation and helped bring to completion long-awaited monographs from the panel studies.

The several panel studies and these other developments in survey research take us ahead to the time when the Bureau was already established at Columbia. Therefore, I turn back to those earlier times to describe how it came to Columbia, became established, and began to integrate its survey research with the educational activities of the university.

The Establishment of the Bureau at Columbia

When the Newark Center was shut down and the Radio Research Project needed new quarters, Lazarsfeld reports: "It never occurred to us to move to Princeton; so many of our research contacts had been established in New York City. . . . In the fall of 1938 the Princeton Office of Radio Research moved to 14 Union Square where we rented a few rooms" (1968, p. 309). That Lazarsfeld did not consolidate the physical and nominal headquarters in Princeton and in the bargain save the rent money suggests that a conflict with Cantril was already incipient.[21] By 1939, when the first grant was expiring and its renewal under consideration, they could not be reconciled. "It became clear that an administrative decision had to be made. Either the project would stay at Princeton with Cantril as the main figure but with a new director, or, if I were to remain, the project would have to look for another institutional base" (1968, p. 329).

Despite the fact that the foundation expressed concern about the progress made in the first two years, Lazarsfeld received a short-term grant to prepare a new long-term proposal, which was then supported by a three-year grant in 1940. In 1940 the Office of Radio Research was transferred from Princeton to Columbia, where Lazarsfeld received a nominal appointment as visiting lecturer in what was then called the Department of Social Science. Lynd and Stanton had helped him work that magic. Lynd wrote a strong letter to the foundation supporting Lazarsfeld and prevailed upon President Dodd (his Princeton contemporary in 1914) to release the project. Stanton sided with Lazarsfeld rather than Cantril in discussions with the foundation.

It might appear that Lazarsfeld finally had fulfilled his mission of securely establishing a research center in a major university, properly structured to achieve his goals, but that is illusory. In a monograph on the history of the Bureau, Phyllis Sheridan, its administrator over its last ten years, aptly describes the office on its rebirth at Columbia as a "foundling." It was "an unsought project . . . dumped onto the administrators of the University." There is "no evidence that it was accorded any initial significant campus role by them at all" (1979, pp. 15–18). Indeed, no document has been found that recorded its official establishment or existence at Columbia in 1940, and not until 1947 were the university statutes changed to give it formal recognition.

Columbia paid Lazarsfeld no salary as director, nor did it support the office itself. To give Columbia its due, the foundling was sheltered, "in a condemned building, the former site of the medical school on 59th Street and Amsterdam Avenue—a neighborhood then called 'Hell's Kitchen' " (Lazarsfeld 1968, p. 330). The name was deserved, and the building, though usable, deserved to be condemned. One stood the risk of breaking a leg or being bitten by a rat in going through the surgical amphitheater to reach an office.

The office was three miles off the Columbia campus, out of sight of the general university community and out of the minds of the central administration, which had not invited it to the campus in the first place. "The financial core was the Rockefeller grant . . . supplemented by commercial contracts. Often the fees were paid in checks made out to me personally, which were then redistributed as staff salaries" (Lazarsfeld 1968, p. 330). The only thread of an organizational connection was a supervisory committee appointed by the Columbia Council on Research in the Social Sciences composed of Lynd as chairman, Stanton and Stouffer, Lyman Bryson of Teachers College and also CBS, and Herbert Brucker of the journalism school. Its function and powers were not defined and, given its composition, it clearly would be a gentle overseer.

From the vantage point of the 1980s—or even the 1950s—the indifference and lack of support of the Columbia authorities may seem foolish. Remember that it was 1940. The authorities could not foresee the golden future of their foundling. The first monographs of the Office of Radio Research had not yet been published. Lazarsfeld had not yet risen to a position of eminence in the social sciences. The market and media research that the office was conducting blemished its scholarly image, and survey research even on noncommercial topics had not yet achieved prestige in the social sciences. Survey research did not gain many adherents among social scientists or dramatically demonstrate its value in basic and applied social research until World War II. The behavior of the Columbia authorities in 1940 was not peculiar.[22] That they continued to be indifferent and only gave meager support to the Bureau beginning in 1946 and for a long period thereafter was peculiar.

The office (later the Bureau) nevertheless expanded and gradually and informally became integrated with the educational activities of the sociology department. In 1941, Lazarsfeld received a regular professorial appointment in the newly named Department of Sociology, recruited for his experience and skills in empirical social research. Although the office had no official connection to the department (it was not mentioned in the bulletin until 1946–47), from the start Lazarsfeld's courses mirrored the office's research. He taught a year sequence on methods for the empirical study of action, a course on "the new and rapidly developing field of communication research," and one on research in public opinion management. Later courses incorporated other developments at the Bureau. The first master's thesis on office topics and data was completed as early as 1942 and the first doctoral dissertation by 1946.

In the first years at Columbia Lazarsfeld carried a full teaching load; supervised graduate students; directed the office; conducted, consolidated, and edited with Stanton the studies of the Radio Research Project; and analyzed the ambitious 1940 panel study. With no financial support from Columbia, with the Rockefeller grant drawing to a close, and for all the other reasons noted earlier, he was, as usual, also seeking commercial clients and conducting market research by small-scale, nonsurvey studies which, apart from training staff and bringing in income, were of trivial social and scientific significance. Things would have continued in this hectic and precarious fashion if World War II had not intervened.

Wartime Developments

The war, crucial for the development of survey research in all the ways previously described, radically changed the work and greatly improved the situation of the office. Lazarsfeld became a consultant to the OWI Surveys Division directed by Wilson, his former associate in the Erie County panel study, and a consultant to the Research Branch of the War Department directed by Stouffer, his longtime associate. He used the consultant fees not for personal profit but to sustain his cherished center. In working for Stouffer, he first developed latent structure analysis, a theory and method for constructing scales of measurement for surveys, and developed it further in a postwar program at the Bureau. (For his first publications on the method see Stouffer 1949–50, vol. 4, pp. 362–412; for the postwar publications, see Lazarsfeld 1954; Lazarsfeld and Henry 1968). The office also obtained contracts from another branch of OWI and Stouffer's branch to conduct program analyzer tests of films and broadcasts to heighten the morale of civilians and the morale and training of soldiers. Working on these contracts not only brought Lazarsfeld into close contact with Stouffer's group, but it brought him unwittingly and briefly to the admiring attention of a Hollywood director, and it gave him the opportunity to bring Merton into the office. Both stories—one inconsequential and the other not—are worth reporting.

Frank Capra, the famous movie director, commissioned as a colonel to make films for the Army, was housed in a Washington office separated from Stouffer's only by a glass partition. According to Dean Manheimer, who was working in a nearby office, Capra had occasion to observe Lazarsfeld in the process of consulting with Stouffer:

> Capra was watching with great interest Lazarsfeld's antics. Lazarsfeld, of course, is pacing up and down and grunting and looking at the tabulations, and smoking his big black cigar. So periodically I'd go back to the office and get some papers and at one point Capra called me over and said to me, "Dean, who is that guy?" And I said, "That's Paul Lazarsfeld." "Who's Paul Lazarsfeld?" "He's a psychologist." "Where did he teach?" "Columbia." "What do you think he makes a year?" I said, "Well, I don't know, maybe $12,000 a year." He said, "$12,000 a year, my God, that's nothing. That guy is fantastic. I could use him as he is right now and put him in one of our movies and he'd be a natural comic. Do you think he would be insulted if I approached him?" I said, "Yes, I think he would be."

Capra did not tender an offer and Lazarsfeld's movie career was aborted.

Merton had also joined the sociology department in 1941, his appointment as a social theorist counterbalancing Lazarsfeld's appointment in empirical research and the two together satisfying the opposed factions in the department. The ironic result was that Merton and Lazarsfeld joined forces, jointly strengthened the Bureau, shared its burdens, and integrated it with the department.

The merger began one night in November 1941 when Lazarsfeld had invited the Mertons to dinner. In the afternoon, Lazarsfeld received an urgent call to test one of the OWI radio programs that night with the program analyzer. When the guests arrived, Lazarsfeld hustled Merton off to the studio leaving the wives to dine alone at home. After Merton observed a first group of subjects being tested, Lazarsfeld asked him to conduct the "focussed interviewing" of a second group, then remarked: "Marvelous job, we must talk it all over. Let's phone the ladies and let them know we're still tied up." His "purpose was to recruit Merton's collaboration," and he succeeded (Lazarsfeld 1975, p. 36). By March 1942 Merton already was "spending six and eight hours a day on a 'project' to 'test' the effectiveness of the morale program, This Is War, which is broadcast over all four networks Saturday nights." And he was "getting home at one and two A.M., times without end." By 1943 Merton was the associate director of the office, and Lazarsfeld had insidiously lured him into another lifestyle. Lazarsfeld tells the shameless but comic story: "In the beginning . . .

Merton worked conscientiously in his office from 9 to 5. At 5 o'clock he left. I badly wanted to discuss with Merton events of the day and plans for the next day, but only after 5 o'clock did I have time for exchanging ideas. So I invented a special strategy. About 4:45 I would come to his office with a problem I thought would interest him. The ensuing discussions gradually lasted longer and longer until, finally, the time between, say, 5 and 8 o'clock was rather regularly devoted to the scheming sessions" (Lazarsfeld 1975, p. 37).

Integration of the Bureau and the Department

Earlier, Lazarsfeld had been fortunate in having such gifted associate directors as Cantril and Stanton. Now, by good luck plus vigilance, he had found in Merton a new associate director who was exceedingly gifted, devoted to the organization, and a voting member of the department which Lazarsfeld hoped would incorporate the office. Surprisingly, the social theorist—no armchair type—was interested and skilled in applied social research as shown initially in the program analyzer studies for the wartime agencies. Like Lazarsfeld, Merton had the powers of abstraction to make applied research yield scientific by-products. The interviewing procedures developed in those studies were codified to produce a manual for Stouffer's staff, and then expanded into a published methodological contribution (Merton, Fiske, and Kendall 1956).

In 1943, Merton showed his versatility in applied research by directing the multimethod firehouse study, described earlier, of Kate Smith's war bond drive. From that project, Merton and his collaborators extracted a substantive scientific contribution on the social psychology of mass persuasion (Merton, Fiske, and Curtis 1946), a study of the social and moral sentiments.

In 1943, Merton also directed another project which showed his varied skills in applied research and in extracting the scientific by-products. The 1940 panel study had suggested the importance of "opinion leaders," "the two-step flow of communications" in which "ideas often flow from radio and print to the opinion leaders and from them to the less active sections of the population" (Lazarsfeld, Berelson, and Gaudet 1944, p. 151). Since the findings were unexpected, the process had not been adequately traced and needed further study, for which funds had to be found. An exploratory study in 1943 was financed by *Time* magazine, happy to invest for a hoped for payoff in finding that *Time* readers were opinion leaders.

Merton supervised that study in Dover, New Jersey (labeled "Rovere" in publications). A small sample was intensively interviewed and identified others in the community who had influenced them in various ways, the influentials with the widest circle of followers in turn being interviewed. The main scientific by-product Merton extracted from this practical project was a theory of patterns of influence (1949) derived from the unexpected discovery of two types of influentials in the social structure of the community: "locals" and "cosmopolitans." The study also yielded a methodological by-product, the procedure later named "snowball sampling," for locating samples of influentials from the nominations made by prior samples, the sampling being carried through one or more stages. The Bureau of Applied Social Research (as the office was renamed in 1944) applied the procedure and elaborated the theory in a large-scale survey in Decatur, Illinois, in 1945, financed by McFadden Magazines in the hope that many influentials would be found among their readers. That ultimately yielded a scientific by-product, the monograph *Personal Influence* (Katz and Lazarsfeld 1955).

Merton had extracted scientific by-products from specific studies, demonstrating only, although persuasively, that particular applied research projects could also have scientific value. However, in 1948 he published the first of a series of essays making an eloquent general argument for the value of applied research in the development of sociological theory, documenting it with examples from Bureau projects and other learned references. A revised version appeared in his *Social Theory and Social Structure* (1949, 1957, 1968), the message thus being disseminated over the years in the English and many foreign-language editions of his famous text.

In these scholarly ways, Merton helped the Bureau toward its ultimate scientific goals. But he also contributed directly to Lazarsfeld's immediate goal of integrating the Bureau with the sociology department. When they joined forces they became a big weight in what then was a very small graduate department. As they rose in rank and power, they exerted their joint heavier weight to integrate the Bureau. When Lynd supported them, they were an even weightier force, indeed the majority of the senior members in the late 1940s. In 1946–47, the Bureau was listed for the first time in the printed bulletin as "an adjunct of the Department."

In that same year, Merton and Lazarsfeld taught a joint seminar on the theory of propaganda, reflecting research of the Bureau on mass media and mass persuasion. In later years, they taught other joint seminars—for example, on the "relations between sociological theory and methods of research." Merton's own courses sometimes focused on Bureau studies. For example, "Social Organization of Housing Communities," offered for several years after 1945, was congruent with a Bureau study of such a community under his direction. Thus, two members of the department implicitly were advertising the Bureau through their courses. Students eager to work with them automatically were drawn into the Bureau orbit. In this natural and informal fashion, training in the Bureau and study in the department became linked.

In the postwar period—with the increasing popularity and possibility of graduate study in the field and the rising reputation of the Columbia sociology department—many students of high ability enrolled in the department. Some with great promise were drawn into the Bureau, received further training and diffused and multiplied its effects through various channels in their own later important careers.

Between 1949 and 1964 Lazarsfeld and Merton also integrated the Bureau and the sociology department by means other than teaching. In appointments of new faculty, the welfare of the Bureau and the value they attached to empirical social research understandably influenced their planning when one or the other was executive officer.

In 1948, Kingsley Davis was appointed to develop the curriculum in demography and the family, and with the Bureau in mind. He became its director in 1949, when Lazarsfeld took on the responsibilities of chairing the department. However, both continued their dual roles, Davis teaching full-time and Lazarsfeld remaining an associate director. Davis also directed a new program of research at the Bureau on problems of manpower, population, and urbanization. By 1950, these three senior faculty were linking the Bureau and the sociology department closely, organically, and integrating student training at the Bureau with graduate study in courses. Thus in the 1940s, Lazarsfeld had progressed steadily toward one of his original goals, and his mission at Columbia in that respect was being fulfilled. That progress is clearly conveyed by one indicator: The first master's thesis on Bureau materials had been completed in 1943; by 1950 the number totaled seventeen. The first such doctoral dissertation had been completed by 1946; by 1950 the number was six and by 1955 it was ten. The numbers increased more rapidly in later years (Judith Barton 1984, pp. 134–148).

In the 1940s, the Bureau also made steady progress in other respects, which continued in the next decades. The burdens of management—directing research projects, training staff, finding new sources of funds in the absence of university support, which Lazarsfeld had carried all alone until 1943—were now being shared. That was bound to bring some order out of chaos and new money into the enterprise, although the three directors never could devote sufficient time to the Bureau given their teaching and other departmental duties. Their tasks were eased by Charles Glock, who served from 1945 to 1950 as the full-time executive officer in charge of day-to-day management and finances and was aided by a full-time administrative officer.

In 1951, Glock became the director, and Davis joined his two colleagues as the third associate director. This new board of directors, composed of the full-time director and administrative officer and associate directors from the sociology faculty, administered the Bureau effectively throughout the 1950s and 1960s, promoted financial growth, modified and enlarged the research program, and increased the integration of the Bureau and the department as other sociology faculty were added as associate directors. Glock, David Sills, and then Allen Barton, aided by a series of administrative officers—Yorke Lucci, Clara Shapiro, and then Phyllis Sheridan—provided capable management. However, all three directors had been students in the department, and Glock and Barton had been Lazarsfeld's protégés, at times making it difficult for them to impose necessary authority.

A few indicators will convey the progress in those years. Prior to 1950, the total annual revenue of the Bureau never reached $190,000 and the median figure was about $100,000, coming largely from business contracts and some foundation grants. In the 1950s, revenues multiplied, ranging between $380,000 and $590,000, with a median around $500,000, and the mix had changed radically. Government grants and contracts became a major source, business contracts declined, and foundation grants increased. In the 1960s revenues multiplied again, never dropping below $1 million after 1965, government funds providing almost all that income. In the late 1950s and early 1960s, research for nonprofit organizations accounted for about 25 percent of the income whereas earlier it had provided about 10 percent of the total. (For more detailed figures, see Barton 1982, pp. 27–30.) Some of this substantial growth reflects the rising prestige and support of social research by government, nonprofit agencies, and foundations from which university centers generally—not only the Bureau—benefited. But the sponsors could have turned elsewhere. The Bureau's reputation and the effectiveness of the directors accounts for much of the growth.

The changing composition of the research increased the discovery of findings of social and scientific significance. Scholarly publications, as a result, increased markedly. So did the number of authors involved, reflecting the progress in integrating more faculty, recruiting and training extraordinarily good graduate students, and a larger professional staff. In the 1940s, eleven books based on Bureau projects were published. If we omit Cantril and Stanton, Lazarsfeld and

Merton were authors or editors of nine of the eleven, and six staff members (none of them faculty and only one a student) were co-authors. Hans Zeisel and C. Wright Mills wrote the other two. In the 1950s, thirty-one books based on Bureau projects were published: Lazarsfeld and Merton authored or co-authored eleven of them, and nine other faculty members authored or co-authored eleven. The co-authors of the thirty-one books included thirty-two staff members or students, of whom at least eleven had been graduate students in the sociology department. (Students often became staff members and so the line between the two categories is fuzzy.) Scholarly articles show the same trends from the 1940s to the 1950s. And in the 1960s, publications again increased in number and showed the same trends (Barton 1982). What had once been a one-man show, then a two-man show, later involved a large star-studded cast.[23]

Integration of the Bureau and the University

The Bureau had become quickly and fully integrated into the sociology department, where the directors exercised personal influence and authority. Beyond the department, the Bureau was at the mercy of the higher university authorities who were indifferent, stingy, perhaps hostile. The organizational history of the Bureau might be described as a long uphill battle by the directors for thorough support from the university in which they made slow and small gains.[24] All of Lazarsfeld's vigilance, Merton's diplomacy, their "scheming sessions," Davis's muscle, their combined formidable professional stature, and Glock's effective management never brought total victory. That outcome is more surprising when one recalls that Edmund deSchweinitz Brunner—often forgotten in writings about the Bureau—also became an associate director and invested his special and great resources in the battle. Even he could not ensure victory.

Brunner was professor of education and sociology at Teachers College and in the graduate department at Columbia. He was ordained in the ministry of the Moravian church and assigned to rural church work in 1911. A founder of rural sociology, he directed nationwide rural surveys from 1919 to 1933, first for the Interchurch World Movement and then for the Institute of Social and Religious Research, established in 1921 by a grant from John D. Rockefeller, Jr.

In 1944, the sociology department replaced the original "supervisory committee" with a Governing Committee on which Brunner served until 1951. Then the university finally took formal action to legitimate the Bureau and integrate it with the university at large. The president appointed a large board of governors composed of senior faculty from many departments and installed Brunner as chairman of the board to "integrate the Bureau's activities further into the general university program in the social sciences." Brunner simultaneously became an associate director. In these capacities from 1944 to 1963, until his second retirement, he dedicated himself to the Bureau's advancement. His age, lineage, distinguished career, impeccable character, and knowledge of and belief in social research made him an ideal representative of the Bureau. When he fought with the university authorities, he had God on his side. Indeed he looked the part: six-foot-four with flowing white hair and Lincolnesque features.

Brunner and the directors did win concessions from the university. In 1949, the Bureau was brought from exile to a university building on the edge of the campus, making it more visible and accessible to the students and faculty. However, in 1951, the Bureau was informed that it owed the university $18,000 from past years partly for rent, utilities, and maintenance and for deficits incurred on projects—this despite the fact that the university had received $27,000 in the year 1950–51 from overhead on Bureau projects for the government. After negotiations, and in light of the telling fact, the debt was canceled.

In later years the university gave the Bureau funds for general expenses. It provided some funds for student training, never more than $10,000 in any year and generally $5,000; and beginning in 1951 the associate directors received annual stipends of $2,500, thus recognizing and rewarding their service to the university. But this level of support must be put in context. It was given with the understanding that it would come from overhead that the Bureau produced. Between 1951 and 1976 (the Bureau closed in 1977), the university received over $83 million in overhead and gave back to the Bureau about $1 million in support. In that last year, it received $177,000 and allocated to the Bureau $36,000 counting maintenance costs (Barton 1982, Table 1).

My brief summary should demonstrate that the university did not provide adequate or generous support for the Bureau. It needed to find clients to support itself. In hard times and in between projects, it lacked the funds to invest in methodological research and scholarship by the staff and large-scale training of students. Fortunately, in the postwar period, with rising foundation and government support for survey research and graduate training, the Bureau was able to enlarge those activities. In 1961, a long-term training program supported by the Office of Education and NIMH was instituted.

In 1956, Brunner won an important concession from the president and provost over their initial objections. They agreed that the Bureau's full-time director, then Glock, deserved professorial status.

The director personified the Bureau, and their action symbolized its acceptance and elevation in the academic structure of the university. However, before Glock's appointment was approved by the trustees, he resigned to establish the Survey Research Center at the University of California (Brunner's letter to Hyman, November 25, 1965).

Another action symbolized the foundling's acceptance and integration into the wider university. Merton described it succinctly: "The Bureau after almost ten years of vicissitudes owing to institutional resistance and neglect, became officially adopted as a Research Unit of the Graduate Faculty of Political Science of Columbia University" (1979, p. 21).

Postwar Surveys

During and before the war, the Bureau rarely conducted large sample surveys. However, in the postwar period—sometimes to serve the practical interests of commercial clients, more commonly for the government, nonprofit organizations, and foundations—the Bureau often conducted major surveys of social and scientific significance. The nationwide trend surveys of public attitudes toward the institution of commercial broadcasting, done in collaboration with NORC and inspired by Stanton, have already been mentioned. The panel surveys begun before the war and continued afterward have also been mentioned. I present here a very brief summary of a few other valuable postwar surveys.

In 1950–51, the Bureau conducted surveys in seven Middle Eastern countries and Greece sponsored by the Voice of America, to describe the audiences, their responses and evaluations of the broadcasts, and the effects of exposure. Again, note the importance of small networks for the development of survey research. Helen Kaufman, Joseph Klapper, Marjorie Fiske Lissance, and Leo Lowenthal, all former members of the Bureau, held important research posts at the Voice of America. From those connections, the Bureau benefited greatly. The surveys intended for purely practical purposes of guiding such political broadcasts produced a rich scientific harvest.

Earlier, I alluded to the 1954 national survey sponsored by the Fund for the Republic, directed by Stouffer, to study whether the threat of communism raised by the cold war and McCarthyism had undermined the general public's support for civil liberties. In 1955, the fund sponsored a second survey on the possible chilling effects of McCarthyism on a strategic group: college social science teachers.

This time, the fund commissioned the Bureau, and the nationwide study was directed by Lazarsfeld and Thielens and reported in *The Academic Mind* (1958).

The substantive findings illuminated an important social, political, and educational problem and theoretical issues in social psychology and sociology. However, the survey also was important methodologically. One notable contribution was a method for testing the validity of teachers' reports of repressive incidents (pp. 415–422). Another was a large-scale test of interviewer effects, of the type that in recent years has come to be called "house effects," and here there is a parallel with the Stouffer study. Stouffer did not have his own survey organization; the sampling, interviewing, and processing of data, therefore, had to be done by other organizations, and Stouffer had the good judgment to have two equivalent surveys conducted by NORC and Gallup. That provided the first large-scale rigorous test of house effects, analyzed briefly by Stouffer and then more elaborately by Stember, as noted earlier.

In the 1950s, the Bureau conducted various surveys, each of which made some distinctive contribution and all of which applied what the Bureau later called contextual designs and modes of analysis. *The Academic Mind* was a fine example. The influence of some feature of an individual's locality, work place, or organization on his attitudes or behavior or on the interrelations between such individual characteristics was analyzed. The contextual variable might be an institutional, legal, or other global feature of the setting; a demographic or ecological feature such as the density of Catholics in the community; or the distribution of attitudes among the surrounding people as measured by surveying clusters of respondents in the specified social contexts. The analysis of such distributions has been described as the study of "social climates," "structural" or "compositional" effects (Sills 1961). These contextual studies included surveys of physicians and their patients, ministers and their parishioners, printers and their union, voters in congressional elections, and, as noted, social scientists in diverse colleges. The Bureau continued to use contextual designs and analyses in other surveys throughout the 1960s (see Barton 1982, pp. 50–51).

Barton, who had firsthand knowledge of these early Bureau surveys but had no knowledge of the earlier wartime surveys, most of which were never published, wrote, "Lazarsfeld . . . was the inventor or major developer of . . . the contextual survey" (1982, p. 19). Developer with other Bureau staff, yes; inventor, no. The OWI surveys described in chapter 2, which Daniel Katz and I directed in 1942–43 on resistances to taking jobs in war industry, morale of shipyard workers, and absenteeism from war plants, clearly were designed to evaluate the contextual effects of community and working conditions and sampled large clusters in contrasted settings. No doubt other early, but buried, contextual surveys exist. Sills traces contextual designs back to the procedures Durkheim employed in his study *Suicide* (1897). That heritage surely was shared by many survey researchers including Tingsten, whose studies of Scandinavian election statistics (1937) pointed to the class composition of a neighborhood as a powerful context.

In the instance of contextual surveys, as in panel surveys, various innovations in survey research were invented independently by more than one thoughtful investigator. When they confronted similar tasks, had a common scholarly and scientific heritage, were applying the same basic method with its inherent limits and potentialities, and had the common goal of deeper and more comprehensive explanation of phenomena, they ended up, at least some of the time, with the same invention.

Codifications of Survey Research

As noted in previous chapters, the methodological and other scientific by-products of the wartime contextual surveys were rarely diffused in scholarly publications. Lazarsfeld was the great codifier and communicator of survey procedures and organized such activities in the postwar period on a large scale. He used his salesmanship to get financial backers for these ventures and to recruit and mobilize the staff needed to do collectively what he could not do alone. Some, though not all, of the ventures in codification and communication succeeded and contributed to the postwar expansion of survey research and the better training of its practitioners. One of the later ventures brought me into the Bureau.

The publication of Hans Zeisel's *Say It with Figures* in 1947 was, as Lazarsfeld stated in the introduction, "a first step in the direction of codification" (p. xiii), and it was a giant step. Zeisel provided a compact but comprehensive treatment of the procedures of survey analysis with many concrete illustrations often drawn from market research. In the section on causal analysis, two chapters showed the way multivariate cross-tabulation "refines," "explains," and reveals "spurious" explanations; and a third chapter reviewed the uses, problems, and analysis of panels. The quality and utility of Zeisel's codification is suggested by the fact the book continued its life through five editions and was still in print in 1987.

A second major step in codifying survey methods was the completion in 1948 of several mimeographed Bureau "training guides," including one by Arthur Kornhauser on constructing questionnaires and interview schedules. In the original mimeographed form, the guides were used extensively at Columbia but had a limited circulation elsewhere. However, Kornhauser's guide was included in the first edition of Jahoda, Deutsch, and Cook's widely used text, *Research Methods in Social Relations* (1951), and reprinted in a later edition (Selltiz 1959), thus reaching a large audience.

A third major step—as it turned out more in the direction of the testing and refinement of methods than in their codification and communication—was taken in 1947. The Bureau received a grant from the Social Science Research Council Committee on Measurement of Opinion, Attitudes, and Consumer Wants "to analyze, codify, and improve the techniques of panel surveys." This was the companion project to the NORC project on interviewer effects and Stephan's project on sampling described earlier. A series of special studies (unpublished dissertations) were completed, and a few discrete papers (Glock 1951; Anderson 1954) and a brief manual of procedures (Rosenberg, Thielens, and Lazarsfeld 1951) were published. But, unfortunately, a comprehensive codification "for a variety of reasons . . . never materialized" (Lazarsfeld's letter to Hyman, March 12, 1974).

A fourth major step was completed in 1950 with the publication of the Merton-Lazarsfeld *Studies in the Scope and Method of "The American Soldier."* As noted in chapter 3, the Merton and Kitt essay codified many scattered findings of those wartime surveys bearing on "the theory of reference group behavior" and provided another powerful demonstration of the theoretical value of applied survey research. The essay was reprinted and expanded in various editions of Merton's *Social Theory and Social Structure*, spreading that message widely, giving prominence to what had been a neglected concept, and guiding research on the topic. The essay by Kendall and Lazarsfeld (1950) explicated and codified the procedures of survey analysis that had been implicit in the original analyses of the many wartime surveys scattered and buried in the lengthy text of *The American Soldier.* They named the procedures, made a fuss over them in print, clarified and codified the method, and provided a formal model for the "elaboration" of survey analysis[25] easily followed by survey researchers. The model, modified in various ways, was promoted by later writers (Glock 1967; Hyman 1955; Rosenberg 1968), thus diffusing and multiplying its effects on the field.

The fifth step in codifying, communicating, and improving the training of survey researchers began in 1950 when Lazarsfeld and Merton proposed to the university authorities that Columbia establish a professional school for training skilled practitioners of social research. Training would proceed partly by traditional methods —courses and seminars, apprenticeships, internships, and externships—but mainly by the creation of a new curriculum based on a series of case books. Each would be specially designed to impart a body of skills by codifying and exemplifying the problems and procedures and presenting the whole with such exquisite cases and in such an effective pedagogical way that a student would learn what otherwise would take long practice in the profession. (For the detailed proposal, see Lazarsfeld and Merton 1972, pp. 361–391.)

Columbia, after careful consideration, rejected the proposal. However, Berelson, director for behavioral sciences of the Ford Foundation, made a substantial grant to Columbia in 1952, matched by an equal grant from the Rockefeller Foundation for a two-year Planning Project for Advanced Training in Social Research, and Lazarsfeld began the collective enterprise of producing the texts to inculcate the skills. It was the beginning of my gradual involvement with the Bureau. Lazarsfeld suggested that I prepare a text on survey analysis embodying the novel and desirable features vaguely outlined in the original proposal. The idea was so exciting that I agreed without pausing to think how it would be accomplished. However, I made only an ad hoc arrangement, stipulating again that I would continue my official association with NORC.

My Relation to the Bureau

As I noted earlier, my loyalty and affection for Hart and Sheatsley pulled me strongly in that direction, and for reasons important enough to be reviewed before I discuss my work on the planning project the Bureau did not pull me in its direction.

By the time I joined the Columbia department, my years of experience had made me into a confirmed survey researcher, indeed an addict of the method, which had led to my original appointment in the department and to Lazarsfeld's new proposal. Although the Bureau conducted surveys periodically, it was not a survey research organization with the specialized facilities and structural arrangements to suit my needs and gratify my addiction. It was, as its name and record shows, a general facility for many kinds of applied social research, often small in scale and local in extent. It had no permanent field staff, sampling section, or coding section. As Glock notes (1979), such expensive permanent facilities would have reduced the flexibility of the Bureau to use a variety of methods, to choose the one best suited to a problem, and required a continuing search for survey contracts to support the facilities.

What seemed desirable to Lazarsfeld and Glock seemed to me a deficiency. High-quality, in-house facilities immediately available for survey research were an asset for me, and such facilities on a nationwide scale seemed a gilt-edged asset. I came from the early cohort of social psychologists whose research had been limited to college students. The sweeping generalizability of national surveys was my new treasure and continued affiliation with NORC ensured it.

In addition, the Bureau was not in the exclusive business of producing surveys. It was also training students, a desirable but conflicting activity that reduced the efficiency with which surveys were done. Every advance in integrating the department and the Bureau ironically increased that conflict. The same conflicting goals governed NORC, but the structural arrangement of a separate New York office meant that Sheatsley and I were insulated and worked on surveys free from the distraction of students. I, too, wanted to train students and that had motivated me to join the department. However, by teaching in the department and doing my survey research at NORC, I kept the two functions separate and out of conflict.

I taught the required graduate course in survey methods that Lazarsfeld and/or Kendall had previously offered, aided by a series of fine teaching assistants who in turn made later contributions to survey research and the training of students, most notably Charles Wright and John S. Reed. Beginning in 1952, I taught a seminar and workshop in methods and applications of secondary analysis, having become impressed by its potentialities during my earlier survey research at NORC and the war agencies. Although convenient data banks did not yet exist, the seminar soon produced some scientific by-products (Greenblum and Pearlin 1953; Williams and Wright 1955; Hyman 1953) and long afterward led to my codification and text on the method (1972) and to a series of collaborative studies (Hyman and Reed 1969; Hyman, Wright, and Reed 1975; Hyman and Wright 1979). Gradually, other departments and schools of the university began sending students into these courses, and thus survey research training began spreading widely at Columbia into public health, political science, social psychology, social work, and community psychiatry. So from 1951 onward I was serving the Bureau's worthy goal of incorporating such training into the educational activities of the university, although I did not serve the Bureau directly for a time.

One other structural arrangement deterred me from joining the Bureau initially. The integration of the department and the Bureau, created by Lazarsfeld and Merton serving simultaneously as directors and professors and chairmen of the department, was too close for my comfort as a junior faculty member: I would have had the same bosses in both places. That seemed to me to create feedback and complicate my career and independence in directing survey research. The Bureau did provide a valuable, convenient vehicle for the research of other faculty but I had my own private, comfortable vehicle at NORC. To put matters in proper perspective, Lazarsfeld and Merton were good friends and colleagues, behaved fastidiously, and never used their departmental powers to muster me into Bureau service. And Glock, who had become a close friend when we were both at Berkeley in 1950, and Brunner, who had been a close friend of my family for years, were directors of the Bureau without a structural tie to the department. Nevertheless, the tight integration with the department via Lazarsfeld and Merton, although highly desirable from a broader point of view, did not seem desirable from my narrow perspective as a junior faculty member. However, Lazarsfeld's proposal in 1952 that I write a text on survey analysis, serving the exciting goals of the Planning Project for Advanced Training and applying the novel and imaginative principles of the plan, was irresistible. It did not involve me in any permanent Bureau commitment, and he presented it with his usual powers of persuasion.

By then I had long experience conducting all kinds of surveys during wartime and peacetime in Germany, Austria, and the United States, and had trained students and designed survey research in Japan, Norway, and the United States. I was ready and eager to distill and codify that experience. Yet I feel sure that my book would have been delayed by years, perhaps never written, if Lazarsfeld had not promoted the venture and galvanized me into action. He had those rare and great talents.

Lazarsfeld had inspired me with a vision: a book that would codify the principles and procedures of survey analysis, presented so artfully that the student would learn the principles and develop some judgment and skill in their application. My task was to create that finished book and, since it was his vision and project, to satisfy him that the creation had been achieved. I quoted earlier Goldsen's and Kaufman's descriptions of their work situation long before my time. It conveyed perfectly my frustrating situation years later. Goldsen had said about Lazarsfeld, "I think now that he didn't even know what had to be done, in specific terms, but could give us only a tenuous and elusive image"; and Kaufman said, "Whatever the hell you gave him, he wasn't satisfied." In such fashion, I labored at my difficult task, made harder by his high, but ineffable, standards and the need to squeeze our conferences into his hectic agenda. Miraculously, I managed to translate the "elusive image" into *Survey Design and Analysis* (1955), drawing cases and useful procedures out of my varied past and using, out of the distant past, Durkheim's *Suicide* "as an illustration of certain methodological problems of primary and secondary analysis" (pp. 5–6).

We had fought long and hard but remained friends. That his vision was farsighted and that the book had realized it, at least to some extent, is indicated by the nine printings, the Italian, Portuguese, and Spanish translations, and Sibley's finding in a 1960 survey of graduate departments of sociology that it was the most frequently required text on methods (1963, p. 120).

That the grand but vague conception of the project eluded most of the participants is suggested by the fact that only two of the many other commissioned books were published—Lazarsfeld and Rosenberg's *Language of Social Research* (1955) and Komarovsky's *Common Frontiers of the Social Sciences* (1957)—both of these admirable collections of papers, but not integrated texts codifying a particular method.

In 1955 I was exhausted but exhilarated and accepted Glock and Brunner's proposal to start a new exciting Bureau project. The Encampment for Citizenship had requested an evaluation of the effects of a summer training program for youth leaders from various ethnic and racial groups. It provided an opportunity to design and codify methods that had only begun to be developed, to explore substantive problems of interest to social psychologists and sociologists, and to contribute to social action programs for good causes. Wright joined me immediately as co-director, and Terence Hopkins joined us in the later phases of the study, which continued through several replications and waves of panel surveys until 1959. The monograph presenting the findings (Hyman, Wright, and Hopkins 1962) was introduced with a long essay, "Principles of Evaluation," our first attempt at a codification which we enlarged in later publications (Wright and Hyman 1964; Hyman and Wright 1967). In typical Bureau fashion, the work then entered the curriculum of the department, by a seminar on evaluation methods I offered from 1956 onward.

By 1957, I had become deeply involved with the Bureau and my earlier concerns had been allayed by my promotion to full professor. So I accepted happily an invitation to become an associate director. For the next twelve years, I conducted or guided a variety of surveys, too many to be summarized here. One project in which I participated in the 1950s, because of its unusual character, connection with other

Bureau and personal developments, and fruitfulness, deserves special attention.

While Berelson was at the Ford Foundation, grants were given to a number of institutions for "propositional inventories" or systematizations of knowledge in various problem areas, the one to the Bureau on political behavior to be very broadly based on knowledge accumulated by the disciplines of history, political science, sociology, and social psychology. The continuity with the Bureau's and Berelson's previous panel studies, and especially with the appendix in *Voting* (pp. 327–347) charting the findings of major panel studies through 1952, is clear. The substantive inventory is clearly parallel to the methodological codification. An interdisciplinary committee was organized to conduct the inventory: S. M. Lipset, chairman; Richard Hofstadter; William Kornhauser; David Truman; and I; with Juan Linz, then a student, as research assistant.

My assignment was to systematize the knowledge of political behavior derived from psychology. Finally, I focused on political socialization (1959), my attempt to systematize what was known about the learning of politics, in terms of a model of socialization. I gathered the evidence in support of that model mainly from secondary analysis of political surveys. The concept and the book stimulated a great deal of research and the development of a new subfield. The book was widely used, translated, reprinted, and was still in print twenty-five years later. Other publications of the project were Kornhauser (1959) and Lipset (1963).

The Bureau's upward course, sketched earlier, continued long after I resigned in 1970 to join Wesleyan University. Lazarsfeld was honored in that same year for his personal achievements and for founding the Bureau by elevation to a chair as Quetelet Professor of Social Science, named for a precursor of empirical methods and one of his idols. But the Bureau was never honored. In 1977, a year after his death and when he no longer could witness its fall, "the Bureau was demolished and hauled away to make room for a parking lot . . . and a Center for the Social Sciences" (Barton 1982, p. 18).

Sheridan's sad ending to the history reads: "Thus, Columbia University's Bureau of Applied Social Research, one of the first university social science bureaus in America devoted to large scale or team research, was closed after forty years, never having received full acceptance from its university. It began as a marginal organization . . . that was never made an integral part of the University, and was brought to a close by the decision of the University administrators" (pp. 57–58). Its good works, however, were carried on by the many teachers and practitioners of social research it produced, by the new centers its alumni established, and through the lasting writings of its founder, its directors, and staff.

Notes

1. Various sources date events in Lazarsfeld's history and the Bureau's history differently, the discrepancies never varying by more than one year. My datings were derived from careful examination of whatever old records remain and from informants.

2. See, for example, Bailyn 1979; Barton 1982; Coleman 1978, 1980; Glock 1979; Goldsen 1957; Jahoda 1979; Lazarsfeld 1968; Merton 1979; Morrison 1978a; Neurath 1983; Sheridan 1979; Sills 1979a, 1979b; Zeisel 1968, 1979.
   See also Converse 1987, chap. 9. [Ed.]

3. Judith Barton's *Guide to the Bureau* is the most comprehensive listing and includes Lazarsfeld's unpublished writings and the unpublished writings of Bureau staff and students and unpublished Bureau reports. For Lazarsfeld's complete bibliography see Neurath 1979, and for writings about Lazarsfeld, see Sills 1979b.

4. By exercising such powers of abstraction, one conveniently ignores the many ways in which consumer behavior is *not* equivalent to voting behavior. That Lazarsfeld was aware that his assertion was shaky is suggested by his and his co-authors' statement in *Voting* (Berelson, Lazarsfeld, and McPhee 1954): "the usual analogy between the voting 'decision' and the more or less carefully calculated decisions of consumers . . . may be quite incorrect" (p. 311), which they then document. For a more incisive statement of the differences between the two realms, see Roshwalb 1959, pp. 151–152.

5. In his memoir (1968) Lazarsfeld describes the intellectual sources of his later work as the tradition of "clarification" in the Vienna circle of philosophy and Karl Bühler's urging a variety of research methods rather than one exclusive approach, and he traces his use of research teams and interest in problems of stratification to his Socialist background and experience in organizing youth groups. Zeisel (1979) traces the Vienna Center's motivation research back to the traditions of psychoanalysis and "depth psychology" and stresses the formative influence of Charlotte Bühler, especially her emphasis on empirical study and on developmental processes.

6. Zeisel (1979) notes that reading Lynd's *Middletown* influenced their study of Marienthal, and Lynd makes frequent reference to and effective

comparative use of the Marienthal findings in *Middletown in Transition* (1937).

7. Lazarsfeld published three papers under the name of Elias Smith, two of which were co-authored with Edward Suchman and Francis Ollry, respectively. They appeared in the *Journal of Applied Psychology* in 1939 (23; 8–18, 57–60; 24: 673–684). [Ed.]

8. A case in point is Jeannette Green, who was an important member of the staff for many years, distinguished for her expertise in intensive interviewing and qualitative and deviant case analysis. Her contributions, for example, are noted in *The Invasion from Mars* (1940) and *The Academic Mind* (1958), and she and Wright Mills did much of the field work in Decatur for *Personal Influence* (1955). She was trained as a lawyer and learned about the Newark Center from a law clerk in her husband's law office, thought the work "sounded fascinating," and offered her services to Lazarsfeld who said "they had no money." She volunteered anyway, began doing intensive interviews on the Radio Research Project, where her skills were quickly recognized, and subsequently became a member of the professional staff (Green's letter to Hyman, February 12, 1985).

9. Eunice Cooper and Rose (Kohn) Goldsen started as secretaries in Newark with no previous graduate training and went on to become well-known survey researchers. Hazel Gaudet started in a professional post with a master's degree as background, and her co-authorship of *The Invasion from Mars* and *The People's Choice* are only some of her later accomplishments. Mirra Komarovsky also had a master's degree at the time she started working in Newark under the joint auspices of the Frankfurt Institute and the center; her *The Unemployed Man and His Family* (1940, 1971) is only one of her many later accomplishments. In 1937, Edward Suchman had a master's degree and joined the Radio Research Project as a "research assistant." Later he became a senior member of Stouffer's wartime staff and co-author of *The American Soldier* and made many other contributions.

10. In his memoir, Lazarsfeld provides a detailed account (1968, pp. 304–330). Morrison (1978a) provides additional details. Complete copies of letters between Lazarsfeld and other parties involved in the Radio Research Project, from which extracts are quoted in the memoir and in Morrison, were especially valuable to me, and I thank Patricia Kendall Lazarsfeld for generously providing them to me.

11. In a previous paper, "The Social Psychology of Everyday Life" (1934, pp. 316–317), Cantril had proposed a long series of investigations on the psychology of radio, and he and Allport had already published several studies (1933; Allport and Cantril 1934) under the auspices of the Radio Cooperative Group, Bureau of Educational Research, Ohio State University, where Stanton had also done his studies and disserta-

tion. One of the Allport-Cantril investigations (1934) was similar to a study done independently in Austria by Herta Herzog (1933), of the Vienna Center and later the Office of Radio Research.

12. A brief account of Stanton's early research career is included in a series of interviews, "The Founding Fathers of Advertising Research," published in the *Journal of Advertising Research,* June 1977. In the foreword to *Radio and the Printed Page* (1940), Lazarsfeld remarks that Stanton guided him "in his first orientation in the field of American broadcasting. Many an invaluable source of material was tapped, and many a research idea initiated through Dr. Stanton's advice" (p. viii).

13. The composition of the audience was arranged to suit the investigator's purposes, and by coupling the experiment with a questionnaire and a group interview, the reasons for and causes of the reactions could be determined. The instrument and the experimental design were used extensively in early Radio Research Project studies (see Hollonquist and Suchman 1944; Sturmthal and Curtis 1944), during the war for research the office did under contract with Stouffer and Hovland to test indoctrination movies shown to soldiers (Hovland 1949, pp. 104–107) and under contracts with other wartime agencies preparing morale-building radio programs for civilian audiences.

14. For example, H. M. Beville, Jr., the director of research at NBC, analyzed class differences in listening habits (1939, 1940) for the office. Class differences are also a major theme in *Radio and the Printed Page* (1940a), one of the monographic publications of the Radio Research Project.

15. For Adorno's version of the source of his difficulties with the Radio Research Project, see his "Scientific Experiences of a European Scholar in America" in Fleming and Bailyn 1969, especially pp. 347–350. [Ed.]

16. For the multitude of such studies in the early 1930s, see Murphy, Murphy, and Newcomb 1937, pp. 946ff.

17. Because of the incentives used to maintain commercial panels and the judgmental nature of some of the assigned tasks, in the 1930s the method sometimes was called the "paid jury" technique. In a paper reporting findings on a 1937 panel study of a radio program, Longstaff (1939) remarks that the jury technique was "now in use rather widely" and refers to Henry Link's criticism of the method, published in 1932, which clearly indicates how early the method had been used in market research.

18. Silvey's review of the early panel studies by the BBC (1944) shows that they were used to obtain reactions to programming and not to measure change. He also describes panels of "correspondents" who functioned as informants for BBC, reporting periodically on the reactions of other listeners. Such "correspondent panels" were used in England from 1937 on by Mass Observation and during World War II in the United States in

a program of research at OWI directed by the anthropologist Elizabeth Herzog.

19. The prewar methodological papers on panels by the Office of Radio Research were Lazarsfeld and Fiske 1938; Lazarsfeld 1940a; Lazarsfeld and Durant 1942; Fleiss 1940, based on a CBS panel organized by Stanton; Gaudet's study, conducted in 1939 but not published until 1955. *The People's Choice* (1944) was based on the Erie County panel operated in 1940. Postwar published studies were Zeisel 1947; Lazarsfeld 1948; Glock 1951; Rosenberg, Thielens, and Lazarsfeld 1951; Kendall 1954; Anderson 1954; and Levenson 1968. The Elmira panel study was conducted in 1948 (Berelson, Lazarsfeld, and McPhee 1954).

20. These are listed and described in Berelson, Lazarsfeld, and McPhee 1954, pp. 331–332.

21. The differences between Lazarsfeld and Cantril over financial and intellectual matters were far greater than Hyman's otherwise accurate account would suggest. For more specific details about the content and severity of their disagreements, see Converse 1987, pp. 149–151. [Ed.]

22. For a thoughtful analysis of the difficulties encountered by universities in absorbing survey research centers, see Converse 1987, pp. 244–257. [Ed.]

23. That cast, however, was recruited almost exclusively from the sociology department. Although twenty-two faculty members wrote articles based on Bureau projects, only three were not in the department (Barton 1982, p. 34), which indicates its high level of integration but narrow confinement in the university.

24. By the early 1940s Columbia had established a Council for Research in the Social Sciences that provided the Bureau with a small subsidy. In August 1944 the council formed a special committee to supervise the Bureau, and in October of that year it recommended, among other things, that commercial contracts should not be considered inconsistent with the Bureau's emphasis on research and training. While Lazarsfeld believed that this marked "a real turning point in the history of American universities," he protested because the committee's recommendations still did not assert the university's obligation to integrate training in empirical research into its educational program. The council then appointed another special committee, chaired by Elliot Cheatham of the law school, to examine the role of the Bureau within the university. In May 1945 the Cheatham Committee recommended that the Bureau be officially designated a research unit of Columbia University. For further details, see Lazarsfeld 1968, pp. 331–334, and Converse 1987, pp. 274–275. [Ed.]

25. Lazarsfeld had presented an earlier brief version of the "elaboration model" at the convention of the American Sociological Association in 1946, but this formulation was not published until 1955 in *The Language*

of Social Research (pp. 115–125). Apropos the common interest in causation and the common use of some form of multivariate analysis in earlier times, Lazarsfeld and Rosenberg included in *The Language of Social Research* a brief excerpt from Otto Klineberg's 1935 classic *Negro Intelligence and Selective Migration*. They remark that he used "an intricate multivariate analysis" (p. 113).

References

Adorno, Theodor W. 1969. "Scientific Experiences of a European Scholar in America." In Donald Fleming and Bernard Bailyn, eds. *The Intellectual Migration*. Cambridge: Harvard University Press.

Adorno, Theodor W., Else Frenkel-Brunswik, Daniel Levinson, and Nevitt Sanford. 1950. *The Authoritarian Personality*. New York: Harper.

Allport, Floyd. 1924. *Social Psychology*. Boston: Houghton Mifflin.

Allport, Gordon W., and Hadley Cantril. 1934. "Judging Personality from Voice." *Journal of Social Psychology* 5:37–55.

Allswang, John M., and Patrick Bova, eds. 1964. *NORC Social Research 1941– 1961: An Inventory of Studies and Publications in Social Research*. Chicago: University of Chicago National Opinion Research Center.

Almond, Gabriel. 1950. *The American People and Foreign Policy*. 1st ed. New York: Harcourt Brace.

Anderson, Odin W., and Jacob J. Feldman. 1956. *Family Medical Costs and Voluntary Health Insurance: A Nationwide Survey*. New York: McGraw-Hill, Blakiston Division.

Anderson, Odin W., Patricia Collette, and Jacob J. Feldman. 1963. *Changes in Family Medical Care Expenditures and Voluntary Health Insurance: A Five-year Resurvey*. Cambridge: Harvard University Press.

Anderson, Theodore W. 1954. "Probability Models for Analyzing Time Changes in Attitudes." In P. F. Lazarsfeld, ed. *Mathematical Thinking in the Social Sciences*. Glencoe, IL: Free Press.

This list of references was compiled after Herbert Hyman's death, from his notes, and although we tried to achieve completeness and accuracy, we may not always have succeeded. [Eds.]

223

Ansbacher, Heinz. 1950. "The Problem of Interpreting Attitude Survey Data; A Case Study of the Attitude of Russian Workers in Wartime Germany." *Public Opinion Quarterly* 14:126–138.

Arnheim, Rudolf. 1944. "The World of the Daytime Serial." In P. F. Lazarsfeld and F. N. Stanton, eds. *Radio Research 1942–43*. New York: Duell, Sloan and Pearce.

Bailyn, Bernard. 1979. "Recollections of PFL." In Robert K. Merton, James S. Coleman, and Peter H. Rossi, eds. *Qualitative and Quantitative Social Research: Papers in Honor of Paul F. Lazarsfeld*. New York: The Free Press.

Barton, Allen H. 1963. *Social Organization Under Stress: A Sociological Review of Disaster Studies*. Washington: National Academy of Sciences—National Research Council. Hard-cover edition, *Communities in Disaster*. New York: Doubleday, 1969.

Barton, Allen H. 1982. "Paul Lazarsfeld and the Invention of the University Institute for Applied Social Research." In Burkart Holtzner and Jeri Nehnevajsa, eds. *Organizing for Social Research*. Cambridge, MA: Schenkman, pp. 17–83.

Barton, Judith, ed. 1984. *Guide to the Bureau of Applied Social Research*. New York: Clearwater.

Berelson, Bernard, Paul F. Lazarsfeld, and William N. McPhee. 1954. *Voting: A Study of Opinion Formation in a Presidential Campaign*. Chicago: University of Chicago Press.

Beville, Hugh M., Jr. 1939. *Social Stratification of the Radio Audience*. Studies in the Social Psychology of Radio, No. 1. Columbia University Bureau of Applied Social Research, mimeo.

Beville, Hugh M., Jr. 1940. "The ABCD's of Radio Audiences." *Public Opinion Quarterly* 4:195–206.

Bower, Robert. 1973. *Television and the Public*. New York: Holt, Rinehart & Winston.

Bower, Robert. 1985. *The Changing Television Audience in America*. New York: Columbia University Press.

Boyd, Richard, and Herbert H. Hyman. 1975. "Survey Research." In Fred Greenstein and Nelson Polsby, eds. *Handbook of Political Science*. Vol. 7. Reading, MA: Addison-Wesley, pp. 265–350.

Bruner, Jerome S. 1944. *Mandate from the People*. New York: Duell, Sloan and Pearce.

Bucher, Rue. 1954. "Blame in Disasters: A Study of a Problematic Situation." Unpublished master's thesis, Department of Sociology, University of Chicago.

Bucher, Rue. 1957. "Blame and Hostility in Disaster." *American Journal of Sociology* 62:467–475.

Bucher, Rue, Charles E. Fritz, and E. L. Quarantelli. 1956a. "Tape-Recorded Interviews in Social Research." *American Sociological Review* 21:359–364.

Bucher, Rue, Charles E. Fritz, and E. L. Quarantelli. 1956b. "Tape-Recorded Research: Some Field and Data Processing Problems." *Public Opinion Quarterly* 20:427–439.

Cahalan, Don. 1948. "Opinion Research Training at the University of Denver." *International Journal of Opinion and Attitude Research* 2:341–348.

Cahalan, Don, Patricia Collette, and Norman Hillmar. 1957. "Career Interests and Expectations of O.S. Medical Students." *Journal of Medical Education* 32:557–563.

Cahalan, Don, and N. C. Meier. 1939. "The Validity of Mail-ballot Polls." *Psychological Record* 3:3–11.

Cahalan, Don, Valerie Tamulonis, and Helen Verner. 1947. "Interviewer Bias Involved in Certain Types of Opinion Survey Questions." *International Journal of Opinion and Attitude Research* 1:63–77.

Campbell, Angus. 1947. "Factors Associated with Attitudes toward Jews." In T. M. Newcomb and E. L. Hartley, eds. *Readings in Social Psychology.* New York: Henry Holt.

Cantril, Hadley. 1934. "The Social Psychology of Everyday Life." *Psychological Bulletin* 31:297–330.

Cantril, Hadley. 1967. *The Human Dimension: Experiences in Policy Research.* New Brunswick, NJ: Rutgers University Press.

Cantril, Hadley, and Associates. 1944. *Gauging Public Opinion.* Princeton, NJ: Princeton University Press.

Cantril, Hadley, and Gordon W. Allport. 1933. "Recent Applications of the Study of Values." *Journal of Abnormal and Social Psychology* 28:259–273.

Cantril, Hadley, and Gordon W. Allport 1935. *The Psychology of Radio.* New York: Harper.

Cantril, Hadley, and Hazel Gaudet. 1939. "Familiarity as a Factor in Determining the Selection and Enjoyment of Radio Programs." *Journal of Applied Psychology* 23:85–94.

Cantril, Hadley, with Hazel Gaudet and Herta Herzog. 1940. *The Invasion from Mars.* Princeton, NJ: Princeton University Press.

Cantril, Hadley, and Daniel Katz. 1937. "Public Opinion Polls." *Sociometry* 1:155–179.

Cartwright, Dorwin, 1949. "Some Principles of Mass Persuasion: Selected Findings of Research in the Sale of the United States War Bonds." *Human Relations* 2:253–267.

Cartwright, Dorwin, 1950. "Survey Research: Psychological Economics." In James G. Miller, ed. *Experiments in Social Process: A Symposium on Social Psychology.* New York: McGraw-Hill.

Clausen, John. 1984. "The American Soldier and Social Psychology: Research on the American Soldier as a Career Contingency." *Social Psychology Quarterly* 47:207–213.

Coleman, James S. 1978. "Lazarsfeld, Paul F." In William H. Kruskal and Judith M. Tanur, eds. *International Encyclopedia of Statistics.* Vol. I. New York: Free Press, pp. 505–507.

Coleman, James S. 1980. "Paul F. Lazarsfeld: The Substance and Style of His Work." In Matilda W. Riley and Robert K. Merton, eds. *Sociological Traditions from Generation to Generation.* Norwood, NJ: Ablex.

Converse, Jean. 1984. "Strong Arguments and Weak Evidence: The Open/

Closed Questioning Controversy of the 1940s." *Public Opinion Quarterly* 48: 267–282.

Converse, Jean. 1987. *Survey Research in the United States: Roots and Emergence, 1890–1960.* Berkeley: University of California Press.

Converse, Philip E., Stephen J. Cutler, Norval D. Glenn, and Herbert H. Hyman. 1978. "The General Social Surveys: A Symposium." *Contemporary Sociology* 7:532–549.

Davis, James A., and Tom W. Smith, 1982. "Have We Learned Anything from the General Social Survey? *Social Indicators Newsletter* 17 (August): 1–2; 8–11.

Duncan, Joseph, and William Shelton. 1978. *Revolution in United States Government Statistics, 1926–1976.* Washington, DC: Department of Commerce, Office of Federal Statistical Policy and Standards.

Durkheim, Emile. 1897. *Suicide.* Paris: Alcan.

Elinson, Jack, and David Nurco. 1976. *Operational Definitions in Socio-behavioral Drug Use Research.* Research Monograph Series 2. Rockville, MD: National Institute on Drug Abuse.

Elinson, Jack, and Ray Trussell. 1957. "Some Factors Relating to Degree of Correspondence for Diagnostic Information Obtained by Household Interviews and Clinical Examinations." *American Journal of Public Health* 47: 311–321.

Ellson, Douglas. 1983. Personal communication, February 3.

Erskine, Hazel Gaudet. 1975. "In Memoriam." *Public Opinion Quarterly* 39: 571–579.

Feldman, Jacob J. 1966. *The Dissemination of Health Information: A Case Study in Adult Learning.* Chicago: Aldine.

Feldman, Jacob J., Herbert H. Hyman, and Clyde Hart. 1951. "A Field Study of Interviewer Effects on the Quality of Survey Data." *Public Opinion Quarterly* 15:734–761.

Fleiss, Marjorie. 1940. "The Panel as an Aid in Measuring the Effects of Advertising." *Journal of Applied Psychology* 24:685–695.

Foster, H. Schuyler. 1983. *Activism Replaces Isolationism: U.S. Public Attitudes, 1940–1975.* Washington, DC: Foxhall.

Frankel, Lester, and J. Stevens Stock. 1942. "On the Sample Survey of Unemployment." *Journal of the American Statistical Association* 37:77–80.

Gallup, George. 1940. *The Pulse of Democracy.* New York: Simon & Schuster.

Gallup, George. 1947. "The Quintamensional Plan of Question Design." *Public Opinion Quarterly* 11:385–393.

Gaudet, Hazel. 1939. "The Favorite Radio Program." *Journal of Applied Psychology* 23:115–126.

Gaudet, Hazel. 1955. "A Model for Assessing Changes in Voting Intention." In Paul F. Lazarsfeld and Morris Rosenberg, eds. *The Language of Social Research.* Glencoe, IL: The Free Press.

Gaudet, Hazel. 1978. *See* Erskine, Hazel Gaudet.

Gaudet, Hazel, and Elmo Wilson. 1940. "Who Escapes the Personal Investigation?" *Journal of Applied Psychology* 24:773–777.

Glock, Charles Y. 1951. "Some Applications of the Panel Method to the Study of Social Change." In American Society for Testing Materials, "Symposium on Measurement of Consumer Wants." *Special Technical Publication No. 117.* Reprinted in Paul F. Lazarsfeld and Morris Rosenberg, eds. 1955. *The Language of Social Research.* Glencoe, IL: The Free Press.

Glock, Charles Y. 1967. "Survey Design and Analysis in Sociology." In Charles Y. Glock, ed. *Survey Research in the Social Sciences.* New York: Russell Sage Foundation.

Glock, Charles Y. 1979. "Organizational Innovation for Social Science Research and Training." In Robert K. Merton, James S. Coleman, and Peter H. Rossi, eds. *Qualitative and Quantitative Social Research: Papers in Honor of Paul F. Lazarsfeld.* New York: Free Press.

Goldsen, Rose Kohn. 1957. Paper Commemorating the Twentieth Anniversary of the Bureau of Applied Social Research. Cited in Paul Neurath. 1983. "Paul F. Lazarsfeld and the Institutionalization of Empirical Social Research." In Robert B. Smith, ed. *An Introduction to Social Research.* Cambridge, MA: Ballinger, p. 374.

Gosnell, Harold F., and Joyce C. David. 1949. "Public Opinion Research in Government." *The American Political Science Review* 43:564–572.

Greenblum, Joseph, and Leonard I. Pearlin. 1953. "Vertical Mobility and Prejudice: A Socio-Psychological Analysis" in R. Bendix and S. M. Lipset, eds. *Class, Status and Power.* Glencoe, IL: Free Press.

Hart, Clyde, and E. B. Reuter. 1933. *Introduction to Sociology.* New York: McGraw-Hill.

Henry, Jules. 1946. "Initial Reactions to the Americans in Japan." *Journal of Social Issues* 2:19–25.

Hero, Alfred O., Jr. 1965. *The Southerner and World Affairs.* Baton Rouge: Louisiana State University Press.

Herzog, Herta. 1933. Stimme und Persönlichkeit. *Zeitschrift für Psychologie:* 130.

Hodge, Robert W., Paul M. Siegel, and Peter Rossi. 1964. *Occupational Prestige in the United States: 1925–1963.* Chicago: University of Chicago Press.

Hollonquist, Tore, and Edward A. Suchman. 1944. "Listening to the Listener: Experiences with the Lazarsfeld-Stanton Program Analyzer." In Paul F. Lazarsfeld and Frank N. Stanton, eds. *Radio Research 1942–1943.* New York: Duell, Sloan and Pearce.

Hovland, Carl I., Arthur A. Lumsdaine, and Fred D. Sheffield. 1949. *Experiments on Mass Communication.* Studies in Social Psychology in World War II, Vol. III. Princeton University.

Hughes, Helen M. 1947. "The Compleat Antivivisectionist." *Scientific Monthly* 65:6.

Hyman, Herbert H. 1942. "The Psychology of Status." Unpublished doctoral dissertation, Columbia University.

Hyman, Herbert H. 1944–45. "Do They Tell the Truth?" *Public Opinion Quarterly* 8:557–559.

228   References

Hyman, Herbert H. 1945. "Community Background in Public Opinion Research." *Journal of Abnormal and Social Psychology* 40:411–413.
Hyman, Herbert H. 1953. "The Value System of Different Classes." In Reinhard Bendix and S. M. Lipset, eds. *Class, Status, and Power*, 1st ed. Glencoe, IL: Free Press.
Hyman, Herbert H. 1955. *Survey Design and Analysis.* Glencoe, IL: Free Press.
Hyman, Herbert H. 1959. *Political Socialization.* Glencoe, IL: Free Press.
Hyman, Herbert H. 1972. *Secondary Analysis of Sample Surveys.* New York: Wiley [1987: Harper & Row].
Hyman, Herbert H. 1980. "Samuel A. Stouffer." In *Dictionary of American Biography, Supplement Six, 1956–60.* New York: Scribner.
Hyman, Herbert H., William J. Cobb, Jacob J. Feldman, Clyde W. Hart, and Charles H. Stember. 1954. *Interviewing in Social Research.* Chicago: University of Chicago Press.
Hyman, Herbert H., and John S. Reed. 1969. "Black Matriarchy Reconsidered: Evidence from Secondary Analysis of Sample Surveys." *Public Opinion Quarterly* 33:346–354.
Hyman, Herbert H., and Paul B. Sheatsley. 1947. "Some Reasons Why Information Campaigns Fail." *Public Opinion Quarterly* 11:412–423.
Hyman, Herbert H., and Paul B. Sheatsley. 1950. "The Current Status of American Public Opinion." In J. C. Payne, ed. *The Teaching of Contemporary Affairs.* Twenty-first Yearbook of the National Council of Social Studies, pp. 11–34.
Hyman, Herbert H., and Paul B. Sheatsley. 1953. "Trends in Public Opinion on Civil Liberties." *Journal of Social Issues* 9(3):6–16.
Hyman, Herbert H., and Paul B. Sheatsley. 1956. "Attitudes Toward Desegregation." *Scientific American* 195 (6):35–39.
Hyman, Herbert H., and Paul B. Sheatsley. 1964. "Attitudes Toward Desegregation." *Scientific American* 211 (1):16–23.
Hyman, Herbert H., and Charles R. Wright. 1967. "Evaluating Social Programs." In Paul F. Lazarsfeld, William H. Sewell, and Harold L. Wilensky, eds. *The Uses of Sociology.* New York: Basic Books.
Hyman, Herbert H., and Charles R. Wright. 1979. *Education's Lasting Influence on Values.* Chicago: University of Chicago Press.
Hyman, Herbert H., Charles R. Wright, and Terence K. Hopkins. 1962. *Applications of Methods of Evaluation.* Berkeley: University of California Press.
Hyman, Herbert H., Charles R. Wright, and John S. Reed. 1975. *The Enduring Effects of Education.* Chicago: University of Chicago Press.
Ikle, Fred C. 1958. *The Social Impact of Bomb Destruction.* Norman: University of Oklahoma Press.
Jahoda, Marie. 1979. "PFL: Hedgehog or Fox?" In Robert K. Merton, James S. Coleman, and Peter H. Rossi, eds. *Qualitative and Quantitative Social Research: Papers in Honor of Paul F. Lazarsfeld.* New York: Free Press.
Jahoda, Marie, Morton Deutsch, and Stuart W. Cook, eds. 1951. *Research Methods in Social Relations.* New York: Dryden.
Jahoda, Marie, Paul F. Lazarsfeld, and Hans Zeisel. 1933. *The Unemployed of*

Marienthal. German ed., Leipzig: S. Hirzel. American ed., 1971. *Marienthal: The Sociography of an Unemployed Community*. Chicago: Aldine-Atherton.

Jessen, Raymond J., Oscar Kempthorne, Joseph F. Daly, and W. Edwards Deming. 1949. "Observations on the 1946 Elections in Greece." *American Sociological Review* 14: 11–16.

Janis, Irving L. 1951. *Air War and Emotional Stress: Psychological Studies of Bombing and Civil Defense*. New York: McGraw-Hill.

Katz, Daniel. 1941. "The Public Opinion Polls and the 1940 Election." *Public Opinion Quarterly* 5:52–78.

Katz, Daniel. 1942. "Do Interviewers Bias Poll Results?" *Public Opinion Quarterly* 6:248–268.

Katz, Daniel. 1944. "The Polls and the 1944 Election." *Public Opinion Quarterly* 8:468–482.

Katz, Daniel. 1946. "The Surveys Division of OWI." In Albert B. Blankenship, ed. *How to Conduct Consumer and Opinion Research*. New York: Harper.

Katz, Daniel. 1950. "Survey Techniques in the Evaluation of Morale." In James G. Miller, ed. *Experiments in Social Process: A Symposium on Social Psychology*. New York: McGraw-Hill.

Katz, Daniel. 1951. "Review of *American Soldier*." *Psychological Bulletin* 48: 512–519.

Katz, Daniel, and Kenneth Braly. 1933. "Racial Stereotypes of One Hundred College Students." *Journal of Abnormal and Social Psychology* 28:280–290.

Katz, Daniel, Dorwin Cartwright, Samuel Eldersveld, and Alfred McClung Lee, eds. 1954. *Public Opinion and Propaganda*. New York: Holt, Rinehart & Winston.

Katz, Daniel, and Herbert H. Hyman. 1947. "Industrial Morale and Public Opinion Methods." *International Journal of Opinion and Attitude Research* 1(3): 13–30.

Katz, Elihu, and Paul F. Lazarsfeld. 1955. *Personal Influence*. Glencoe, IL: Free Press.

Kendall, Patricia L. 1954. *Conflict and Mood: Factors Affecting Stability of Response*. New York: Free Press.

Kendall, Patricia L., and Paul F. Lazarsfeld. 1950. "Problems of Survey Analysis." In Robert K. Merton and Paul F. Lazarsfeld, eds. *Continuities in Social Research: Studies in the Scope and Method of "The American Soldier."* New York: Free Press.

Kendall, Patricia L., and Katherine W. Wolf. 1949. "The Analysis of Deviant Cases in Communications Research." In P. F. Lazarsfeld and F. N. Stanton, eds. *Communications Research 1948–1949*. New York: Harper.

Klineberg, Otto. 1935. *Negro Intelligence and Selective Migration*. New York: Columbia University Press.

Komarovsky, Mirra. 1940. *The Unemployed Man and His Family*. New York: Dryden. [1971: New York: Octagon].

Komarovsky, Mirra, ed. 1957. *Common Frontiers of the Social Sciences*. Glencoe, IL: Free Press.

Kornhauser, William. 1959. *The Politics of Mass Society.* New York: Free Press.

Krauss, Irving. 1955. "Individual and Group Behavior in a Disaster." Master's thesis, University of Chicago.

Krech, David, and Egerton Ballachey. 1948. "A Case Study of a Social Survey: Japanese Survey, United States Bombing Survey." University of California Press, mimeo.

Krech, David, and Richard Crutchfield. 1947. *Social Psychology.* New York: McGraw-Hill.

Kriesberg, Louis, and Beatrice R. Treiman. 1960. "Socio-Economic Status and the Utilization of Dentists' Services." *Journal of the American College of Dentists* 27:147–165.

Kriesberg, Louis, and Beatrice R. Treiman. 1962. "Preventive Utilization of Dentists' Services Among Teenagers." *Journal of the American College of Dentists* 29:28–45.

Lazarsfeld, Paul F. 1935. "The Art of Asking Why." *National Marketing Review* 1:32–43. Reprinted in Paul F. Lazarsfeld. 1972. *Qualitative Analysis.* Boston: Allyn & Bacon, pp. 183–202.

Lazarsfeld, Paul F. 1940a. "Panel Studies." *Public Opinion Quarterly* 4:122–188.

Lazarsfeld, Paul. 1940b. *Radio and the Printed Page.* New York: Duell, Sloan and Pearce.

Lazarsfeld, Paul F. 1944. "The Controversy Over Detailed Interviews—An Offer for Negotiation." *Public Opinion Quarterly* 8:38–60.

Lazarsfeld, Paul F. 1948. "The Use of Panels in Social Research." *Proceedings of the American Philosophical Society* 92:405–410.

Lazarsfeld, Paul F., ed. 1954. *Mathematical Thinking in the Social Sciences.* Glencoe, IL: Free Press.

Lazarsfeld, Paul F. 1962. "Introduction." In Samuel A. Stouffer. *Social Research to Test Ideas.* New York: Free Press.

Lazarsfeld, Paul F. 1968. "An Episode in the History of Social Research: A Memoir." In Donald Fleming and Bernard Bailyn, eds. *The Intellectual Migration: Europe and America 1930–1960.* Cambridge: Harvard University Press.

Lazarsfeld, Paul F. 1975. "Working with Merton." In Lewis A. Coser, ed. *The Idea of Social Structure: Papers in Honor of Robert K. Merton.* New York: Harcourt Brace Jovanovich.

Lazarsfeld, Paul F., Bernard Berelson, and Hazel Gaudet. 1944. *The People's Choice.* New York: Duell, Sloan and Pearce.

Lazarsfeld, Paul F., Bernard Berelson, and William N. McPhee. 1954. *Voting: A Study of Opinion Formation in a Presidential Campaign.* Chicago: University of Chicago Press.

Lazarsfeld, Paul F., and Ruth Durant. 1942. "National Morale, Social Cleavage and Political Allegiance." *Journalism Quarterly* 19:150–158.

Lazarsfeld, Paul F., and Harry Field. 1946. *The People Look at Radio.* Chapel Hill: University of North Carolina Press.

Lazarsfeld, Paul F., and Marjorie Fiske. 1938. "The 'Panel' as a New Tool for Measuring Opinion." *Public Opinion Quarterly* 2:596–612.

Lazarsfeld, Paul F., and Neil W. Henry. 1968. *Latent Structure Analysis*. Boston: Houghton Mifflin.

Lazarsfeld, Paul F., and Patricia L. Kendall. 1948. *Radio Listening in America: The People Look at Radio—Again*. New York: Prentice-Hall.

Lazarsfeld, Paul F., and Arthur W. Kornhauser. 1935. *The Techniques of Market Research From the Standpoint of a Psychologist*. New York: American Management Association.

Lazarsfeld, Paul F., and Robert K. Merton. 1972. "A Professional School for Training in Social Research." In Paul F. Lazarsfeld, ed. *Qualitative Analysis*. Boston: Allyn & Bacon.

Lazarsfeld, Paul F., and Morris Rosenberg, eds. 1955. *The Language of Social Research*. Glencoe, IL: Free Press.

Lazarsfeld, Paul F., and Frank N. Stanton, eds. 1941. *Radio Research 1941*. New York: Duell, Sloan and Pearce.

Lazarsfeld, Paul F., and Frank N. Stanton, eds. 1944. *Radio Research 1942–1943*. New York: Duell, Sloan and Pearce.

Lazarsfeld, Paul F., and Frank N. Stanton, eds. 1949. *Communications Research 1948–1949*. New York: Duell, Sloan and Pearce.

Lazarsfeld, Paul F., and Wagner Thielens. 1958. *The Academic Mind*. Glencoe, IL: Free Press.

Lebergott, Stanley. 1968. "Labor Force and Employment Trends." In E. G. Sheldon and W. E. Moore, eds. *Indicators of Social Change*. New York: Russell Sage Foundation.

Levenson, Bernard. 1968. "Panel Studies." *International Encyclopedia of the Social Sciences* 11:371–379.

Likert, Rensis. 1932. "A Technique for the Measurement Attitudes." Unpublished doctoral dissertation, Columbia University.

Likert, Rensis. 1947. "The Sample Interview Survey: A Fundamental Research Tool of the Social Sciences." In Wayne Dennis, ed. *Current Trends in Psychology*. Pittsburgh: University of Pittsburgh Press.

Likert, Rensis, and Sydney Roslow. 1934–35. "Eddie Cantor and the Chase and Sanborn Radio Program." *Market Research* 3 (5):3–4.

Link, Henry C. 1932. *The New Psychology of Advertising and Selling*. New York: Macmillan.

Link, Henry C. 1943. "An Experiment in Depth Interviewing on the Issue of Internationalism vs. Isolationism." *Public Opinion Quarterly* 7: 267–279.

Lipset, Seymour M. 1963. *Political Man*. New York: Doubleday, Anchor Books.

Longstaff, H. P. 1939. "A Method for Determining the Entertainment Value of Radio Programs." *Journal of Applied Psychology* 23:46–54.

Lowenthal, Leo. 1944. "Biographies in Popular Magazines." In Paul F. Lazarsfeld and Frank N. Stanton, eds. *Radio Research 1942–1943*. New York: Duell, Sloan and Pearce.

Lynd, Robert S., and Helen M. Lynd. 1929. *Middletown*. New York: Harcourt, Brace & World.

Lynd, Robert S., and Helen M. Lynd. 1937. *Middletown in Transition*. New York: Harcourt, Brace & World.

Maccoby, Eleanor, Theodore M. Newcomb, and Eugene L. Hartley, eds. 1958. *Readings in Social Psychology.* New York: Holt.

MacIsaac, David. 1976. *Strategic Bombing in World War II: The Story of the United States Bombing Survey.* New York: Garland.

Marks, E. S., and Charles Fritz. 1954. "Human Reactions in Disaster Situations." Unpublished report, National Opinion Research Center, University of Chicago.

Merton, Robert K. 1949. "Patterns of Influence." In Paul F. Lazarsfeld and Frank N. Stanton, eds. *Communications Research 1948–1949.* New York: Duell, Sloan and Pearce.

Merton, Robert K. 1949. *Social Theory and Social Structure.* Glencoe, IL: Free Press [1957: Revised and enlarged edition] [1968: Enlarged edition].

Merton, Robert K., with Marjorie Fiske and Alberta Curtis. 1946. *Mass Persuasion.* New York: Harper.

Merton, Robert K. 1979. "Remembering Paul Lazarsfeld." In Robert K. Merton, James S. Coleman, and Peter H. Rossi, eds. *Qualitative and Quantitative Sociological Research: Papers in Honor of Paul F. Lazarsfeld.* New York: Free Press.

Merton, Robert K., and Alice S. Kitt. 1950. "Contributions to the Theory of Reference Group Behavior." In Robert K. Merton and Paul F. Lazarsfeld, eds. *Continuities in Social Research: Studies in the Scope and Method of "The American Soldier."* New York: Free Press.

Merton, Robert K., and Paul F. Lazarsfeld, eds. 1950. *Continuities in Social Research: Studies in the Scope and Method of "The American Soldier."* New York: Free Press.

Morrison, David. 1978a. "The Beginning of Modern Mass Communication Research." *Archives Européenes de Sociologie.* 19:347–359.

Morrison, David. 1978b. "Kultur and Culture: The Case of Theodor W. Adorno and Paul F. Lazarsfeld." *Social Research* 45:331–355.

Mosteller, Frederick, Herbert Hyman, Philip McCarthy, E. S. Marks, and David Truman. 1949. *The Pre-election Polls of 1948.* New York: Social Science Research Council.

Murphy, Gardner, Lois Barclay Murphy, and Theodore M. Newcomb. 1937. *Experimental Social Psychology.* New York: Harper.

Neurath, Paul. 1979. "The Writings of Paul F. Lazarsfeld: A Topical Bibliography." In Robert K. Merton, James S. Coleman, and Peter H. Rossi, eds. *Qualitative and Quantitative Social Research: Papers in Honor of Paul F. Lazarsfeld.* New York: Free Press.

Neurath, Paul. 1983. "Paul F. Lazarsfeld and the Institutionalization of Empirical Social Research." In Robert B. Smith, ed. *An Introduction to Social Research.* Cambridge, MA: Ballinger.

Ogburn, William F., ed. 1933. *Recent Social Trends in the United States.* New York: McGraw-Hill.

Parry, Hugh and Helen M. Crossley. 1950. "Validity of Responses to Survey Questionnaires." *Public Opinion Quarterly* 14:61–80.

Peak, Helen. 1945. "Observations on the Characteristics and Distribution of German Nazis." *Psychological Monographs* no. 276.

Peak, Helen. 1946. "Some Psychological Problems in the Re-education of Germany." *Journal of Social Issues* 2:2–14.

Presser, Stanley. 1984. "Is Inaccuracy on Factual Survey Items Item-Specific or Respondent-Specific?" *Public Opinion Quarterly* 48:344–345.

Quarantelli, E. L. 1953. "A Study of Panic: Its Nature, Types, and Conditions." Master's thesis, University of Chicago.

Quarantelli, E. L. 1954. "Nature and Conditions of Panic." *American Journal of Sociology* 60:267–275.

Quarantelli, E. L. 1957. "The Behavior of Panic Participants." *Sociology and Sociology Research* 41:187–194.

Quarantelli, E. L. and Russell R. Dynes. 1976. "Community Conflict: Its Absence and its Presence in Natural Disasters." *Mass Emergencies* 1: 139–152.

Rice, Stuart. 1928. *Quantitative Methods in Politics.* New York: Knopf.

Roper, Elmo. 1941. *Roper Counts Customers.* New York: Columbia Broadcasting System.

Roper, Elmo. 1957. *You and Your Leaders.* New York: Morrow.

Rose, Arnold. 1964. *The Negro in America; The Condensed Version of Gunnar Myrdal's "An American Dilemma."* With a foreword by Gunnar Myrdal. New York: Harper & Row.

Rosenberg, Morris W., Wagner Thielens, and Paul F. Lazarsfeld. 1951. "The Panel Study." In Marie Jahoda, Morton Deutsch, and Stuart W. Cook, eds. *Research Methods in Social Relations.* Vol. II. New York: Dryden.

Rosenberg, Morris W. 1968. *The Logic of Survey Analysis.* New York: Basic Books.

Roshwalb, Irving. 1959. "The Voting Studies and Consumer Decisions." In Eugene Burdick and Arthur J. Brodbeck, eds. *American Voting Behavior.* Glencoe, IL: Free Press.

Roslow, Sydney, and Albert B. Blankenship. 1939. "Phrasing the Question in Consumer Research." *Journal of Applied Psychology* 23:612–622.

Roslow, Sydney, Wallace H. Wulfeck, and Philip G. Corby. 1940. "Consumer and Opinion Research: Experimental Studies on the Form of the Question." *Journal of Applied Psychology* 24:334–346.

Rossi, Peter. 1980. "The Presidential Address: The Challenge and Opportunities of Applied Social Research." *American Sociological Review* 45:889–900.

Schatzman, Leonard. 1960. "A Sequence Pattern of Disaster and Its Consequences for Community." Unpublished doctoral dissertation, Indiana University.

Schatzman, Leonard, and Anselm Strauss. 1955. "Social Class and Modes of Communication." *American Journal of Sociology* 60:329–338.

Schramm, Wilbur L., and Donald F. Roberts, eds. 1971. *The Process and Effects of Mass Communication.* Rev. ed. Urbana: University of Illinois.

Schuman, Howard, and Stanley Presser. 1981. *Questions and Answers in Attitude Surveys.* New York: Academic Press.

Scott, William A., and Stephen Withey. 1958. *The United States and the United Nations: The Public View. 1945–1955.* New York: Manhattan.

Selltiz, Claire, Marie Jahoda, Morton Deutsch, and Stuart W. Cook, eds.

1959. *Research Methods in Social Relations.* Rev. ed. New York: Holt, Rinehart & Winston.

Shanas, Ethel. 1961. *Family Relationships of Older People.* New York: Health Information Foundation.

Sheatsley, Paul B. 1944. "Area Control Experiment Tried on Survey T-32." Memorandum, April 21.

Sheatsley, Paul B. 1982. "NORC: The First Forty Years." In *NORC Report, 1981–82.* Chicago: NORC, pp. 5–21.

Sheridan, Phyllis. 1978. "The Research Bureau in a University Context: Case History of a Marginal Institution." Unpublished doctoral dissertation, Teachers College, Columbia University.

Sibley, Eldridge. 1963. *The Education of Sociologists in the United States.* New York: Russell Sage Foundation.

Sills, David L. 1961. "Three 'Climate of Opinion' Studies." *Public Opinion Quarterly* 25:571–573.

Sills, David L. 1979a. "Paul F. Lazarsfeld." In David L. Sills, ed. *Biographical Supplement, International Encyclopedia of the Social Sciences.* Vol. 18. New York: Free Press.

Sills, David L. 1979b. "Publications about Paul F. Lazarsfeld: A Selected Bibliography." In Robert K. Merton, James S. Coleman, and Peter H. Rossi, eds. *Qualitative and Quantitative Social Research: Papers in Honor of Paul F. Lazarsfeld.* New York: Free Press.

Sills, David L. 1981. "Bernard Berelson: Behavioral Scientist." *Journal of the History of the Behavioral Sciences* 17:305–311.

Sills, David L. 1987. "Paul F. Lazarsfeld 1901–1976: A Biographical Memoir." In *Biographical Memoirs.* Vol. 56. Washington, DC: National Academy Press, pp. 251–282.

Silvey, Robert J. E. 1944. "Radio Audience Research in Great Britain." In Paul F. Lazarsfeld and Frank Stanton, eds. *Radio Research 1942–1943.* New York: Duell, Sloan and Pearce.

Smith, M. Brewster. 1968. "Samuel A. Stouffer." In David Sills, ed. *International Encyclopedia of the Social Sciences.* New York: Macmillan.

Smith, M. Brewster. 1983. "The Shaping of American Social Psychology: A Personal Perspective from the Periphery." *Personality and Social Psychology Bulletin* 9:165–180.

Star, Shirley A., and Helen M. Hughes. 1950. "Report on an Educational Plan: The Cincinnati Plan for the United Nations." *American Journal of Sociology* 55:389–400.

Steiner, Gary Albert. 1963. *The People Look at Television.* New York: Knopf.

Stember, Charles Herbert. 1955. "The Effect of Field Procedures on Public Opinion Data." Unpublished doctoral dissertation, Columbia University.

Stember, Charles Herbert. 1961. *Education and Attitude Change.* New York: Institute of Human Relations.

Stember, Charles Herbert. 1966. *Jews in the Mind of America.* New York: Basic Books.

Stephan, Frederick F., and Philip J. McCarthy. 1958. *Sampling Opinions: An Analysis of Survey Procedure.* New York: Wiley.

Stern, James. 1947. *The Hidden Damage.* New York: Harcourt, Brace.

Stouffer, Samuel A. 1930. "Experimental Comparison of Statistical and Case History Methods of Attitude Research." Unpublished doctoral dissertation, University of Chicago.

Stouffer, Samuel A. 1949–50. *The American Soldier; Studies in Social Psychology in World War II.* Princeton: Princeton University Press. Vol. I: *Adjustment During Army Life.* Samuel A. Stouffer, Edward A. Suchman, Leland C. DeVinney, Shirley A. Star, and Robin M. Williams, Jr. Vol. II: *Combat and Its Aftermath.* Samuel A. Stouffer, Arthur A. Lumsdaine, Marion Harper Lumsdaine, Robin M. Williams, Jr., M. Brewster Smith, Irving L. Janis, Shirley A. Star, and Leonard S. Cottrell, Jr. 1950. Vol. III: *Experiments in Mass Communication.* Carl I. Hovland, Arthur A. Lumsdaine, and Fred D. Sheffield. Vol. IV: *Measurement and Prediction.* Samuel A. Stouffer, Louis Guttman, Edward A. Suchman, Paul F. Lazarsfeld, Shirley A. Star, and John A. Clausen.

Stouffer, Samuel A. 1950. "Some Afterthoughts of a Contributor to 'The American Soldier.' " In Robert K. Merton and Paul F. Lazarsfeld, eds. *Continuities in Social Research: Studies in the Scope and Method of "The American Soldier."* Glencoe, IL: Free Press.

Stouffer, Samuel A. 1955. *Communism, Conformity, and Civil Liberties: A Cross-Section of the Nation Speaks Its Mind.* Gloucester, MA: Peter Smith.

Stouffer, Samuel A. 1962. *Social Research to Test Ideas.* New York: Free Press.

Stouffer, Samuel A., and Paul F. Lazarsfeld, with Abram J. Jaffe. 1937. *Research Memorandum on the Family in the Depression.* New York: Social Science Research Council, Bulletin 29 [Reprinted 1972. New York: Arno.]

Strauss, Anselm, and Leonard Schatzman. 1958. "Cross-Class Interviewing: An Analysis of Interaction and Communicative Styles." *Human Organization* 14 (2):28–31.

Sturmthal, Adolf, and Alberta Curtis, 1944. "Program Analyzer Tests of Two Educational Films." In Paul F. Lazarsfeld and Frank N. Stanton, eds. *Radio Research 1942–1943.* New York: Duell, Sloan and Pearce.

Sudman, Seymour. 1967. *Reducing the Cost of Surveys.* Chicago: Aldine.

Swanson, Guy, Theodore M. Newcomb, and E. L. Hartley, eds. 1952. *Readings in Social Psychology.* New York: Holt.

Thurstone, L. L. 1928. "Attitudes Can Be Measured." *American Journal of Sociology* 33:529–554.

Thurstone, L. L. 1952. Untitled essay in E. G. Boring, H. S. Langfeld, H. Werner, and R. M. Yerkes, eds. *A History of Psychology in Autobiography.* Vol. IV. Worcester, MA: Clark University.

Tingsten, H. 1937. *Political Behavior: Studies in Election Statistics.* Stockholm Economic Studies, No. 7. London: P. S. King.

Toby, Jackson, 1980. "Samuel A. Stouffer, Social Research as a Calling." In Robert K. Merton and Matilda White Riley, eds. *Social Traditions from Generation to Generation: Glimpses of the American Experience.* Norwood, NJ: Ablex.

Trussell, Ray E., Jack Elinson, and Morton L. Levin. 1956. "Comparison of Various Methods of Estimating the Prevalence of Chronic Disease in a

Community—The Hunterdon County Study." *American Journal of Public Health* 46 (173).

U.S. Strategic Bombing Survey, Morale Division. 1945. *The Cross-Sectional Interviewing Study.* Interim report, August 27.

U.S. Strategic Bombing Survey, Morale Division. 1946–47. *The Effects of Strategic Bombing on German Morale.* 2 vols. Washington, DC: U.S. Government Printing Office.

U.S. Strategic Bombing Survey, Morale Division. 1947. *The Effects of Strategic Bombing on Japanese Morale.* Washington, DC: U.S. Government Printing Office.

Wallace, Henry A., and James L. McCamy. 1940. "Straw Polls and Public Administration." *Public Opinion Quarterly* 4:221–223.

Welch, Susan, and John Comer, eds. 1975. *Public Opinion.* Palo Alto, CA: Mayfield.

Wilensky, Harold L. 1967. *Organizational Intelligence: Knowledge and Policy in Government and Industry.* New York: Basic Books.

Williams, Robin M. 1984. "The American Soldier and Social Psychology: Field Observations and Surveys in Combat Zones." *Social Psychology Quarterly* 47:186–192.

Williams, Robert J., and Charles R. Wright. 1955. "Opinion Organization in a Heterogeneous Adult Population." *Journal of Abnormal and Social Psychology* 5:559–564.

Wolfe, Katherine, and Marjorie Fiske. 1949. "Why They Read Comics." In Paul F. Lazarsfeld and Frank N. Stanton, eds. *Communication Research 1948–49.* New York: Duell, Sloan and Pearce.

Woodward, Julian. 1944. "Making Government Opinion Research Bear upon Operations." *American Sociological Review* 9:670–677.

Wright, Charles R., and Herbert H. Hyman. 1964. "The Evaluators." In Phillip Hammond, ed. *Sociologists at Work.* New York: Basic Books.

Zeisel, Hans. 1947. *Say It with Figures.* New York: Harper.

Zeisel, Hans. 1968. "L'école viennoise des récherches de motivation." *Revue Française de Sociologie* 9:3–12.

Zeisel, Hans. 1979. "The Vienna Years." In Robert K. Merton, James S. Coleman, and Peter H. Rossi, eds. *Qualitative and Quantitative Social Research: Papers in Honor of Paul F. Lazarsfeld.* New York: Free Press.

Index

Boldface numbers refer to tables.

A

Absenteeism, xxii, 49, 52, 62*n*, 97; causes for, 49–52; of industrial workers in Germany, 120–121; punishments for, 51–52; study of, 51, 55; surveys of, 50–51

The Academic Mind (P. Lazarsfeld and W. Thielens), 210, 219*n*

Acheson-Lilienthal Report on Atomic Energy, 153

Activism Replaces Isolationism: U.S. Public Attitudes, 1940–1974 (S. Foster), 175*n*

Adams, Donald, 122

Adorno, Theodor, 195, 220*n*

AGCT scores, 65

Agencies: federal research, xviii; government, 4, 10; procedures used by, 6–7. *See also* specific agencies

Aggression, theories of, 75

Agricultural Marketing Service, Marketing Research Division of, 19

Agriculture, 6

Aircraft companies, 49

Air Forces, 91, 99, 109, 131*n*

Alameda County, California, 177*n*

Alaska, 66

Alexander, Henry C., 91

Allies, 111, 119, 132*n*; hatred for, 115, 119; view of, by Nazis, 103

Allport, Floyd, 15, 56–57

Allport, Gordon, 57, 87, 141, 174*n*, 190, 219*n*

Allswang, John M., 171, 177*n*

Almond, Gabriel, 97, 175*n*

Alpert, Harry, 175*n*

Amalgam survey, 155

American Association for Public Opinion Research (AAPOR), 146

The American Civilian, 14

American Institute of Public Opinion, 20*n*

American Jewish Committee, 164, 168; Division of Scientific Research of, 163

The American People and Foreign Policy (G. Almond), 175*n*

American Society for Testing Materials, 175*n*

American Sociological Association, 176*n*, 221*n*

The American Soldier (S. Stouffer), 64, 70, 81, 82, 88*n*, 89*n*, 92–93, 180, 212, 219*n*; attitude measurement reported in, 83; authors of, 79; beginning of, 67–68; conception of, 85; findings in, 14, 74, 75, 76, 77, 86; personnel listed in, 73